FASCIST ITALY AT WAR
1939–1943

THOMAS X. FERENCZI

FONTHILL

Fonthill Media Language Policy

Fonthill Media publishes in the international English language market. One language edition is published worldwide. As there are minor differences in spelling and presentation, especially with regard to American English and British English, a policy is necessary to define which form of English to use. The Fonthill Policy is to use the form of English native to the author. Thomas X. Ferenczi was born and educated in Canada; therefore Canadian English has been adopted in this publication.

Fonthill Media Limited
Fonthill Media LLC
www.fonthill.media
office@fonthillmedia.com

First published in the United Kingdom and the United States of America 2024

British Library Cataloguing in Publication Data:
A catalogue record for this book is available from the British Library

ISBN 978-1-78155-915-4

Typeset in 10.5 pt on13pt Sabon
Printed and bound in England

Contents

Introduction

Like his German counterpart across the Alps, Benito Mussolini—Italian prime minister and Duce (leader) of Fascism—had aggressive expansionist aims. Fascist ideology advocated the principle of *Spazio vitale* (vital space) for Italians, an expansionist doctrine comparable to the National Socialist theory of *Lebensraum* (living space) for Germans. In accordance with Fascism's revolutionary nature, *Spazio vitale* would be obtained by Italian force of arms. Mussolini justified this rationale by underscoring the fecundity of the Italian people: 'We have a right to empire as a fertile nation which has the pride and will to propagate its race over the face of the Earth, a virile people in the strict sense of the word.'[1]

Mussolini sought to dominate the Mediterranean–Balkan area as had the ancient Romans two millennia ago. This included the conquest of Albania and the expansion of 'Imperial Italy' into Yugoslavia and Greece. It was also intended to subordinate four Danubian nations to Italy as client states: Austria (until 1936, when Mussolini agreed to relinquish it into the German sphere), Hungary, Romania, and Bulgaria. In North Africa, a colonial policy was to be pursued, particularly in Libya and French Tunisia. Italian colonists had settled in both nations. And a high priority for many Italian nationalists was to reverse Italy's defeat by Ethiopia at Adowa (1896), which still rankled decades later.

Italian irredentists also wanted to reacquire specific territories in French possession containing a sizable number of ethnic Italians: Corsica, Nice, and Savoy. Other foreign territories included Ticino (Italian Switzerland) and Dalmatia (Croatian coastland). Fiume, a Yugoslav port city on the Adriatic coast, had been annexed by Italy early on per the Treaty of Rome (1924).

Mussolini planned to wrest control of the Mediterranean from Britain, which maintained powerful naval bases at Gibraltar, Malta, and Cyprus, plus controlled (together with France) the Suez Canal. For Mussolini, to achieve Italian supremacy in the Mediterranean Sea was of the greatest strategic importance, for the Mediterranean Sea afforded Italy access to two oceans: the Atlantic and the Indian. As early as September 1920, Mussolini had averred: 'Our imperialism which wishes to expand in the Mediterranean is not that of the violent Prussian, nor that of the hypocrite Englishman, instead it is that of the Roman.'[2] As the ancient Romans had done, Mussolini termed the Mediterranean Sea '*Mare Nostrum*' ('Our Sea'). And in 1926, Mussolini had stated to his generals: 'A nation which does not have free access to the sea cannot be considered a free country; a nation which does not have free access to the oceans cannot be considered a great power: Italy must become a great power.'[3]

Like many Italians, Mussolini was dissatisfied with the outcome of the Treaty of Versailles (1919). Mussolini felt that Italy had been dealt a bad hand, and this despite her costly sacrifices and contributions to the Allied cause in the Great War. Postwar concessions to Italy had been few (Trentino, Tyrol, Trieste, and Istria). Like the British, Mussolini believed, the Italians too deserved a large colonial empire, and the victorious nations at Versailles should have taken this into account when restructuring Europe into a hodgepodge of new nation-states.

Mussolini wanted power for himself and his movement, the *Partito Nazionale Fascista* (National Fascist Party). At a rally at Naples on 24 October 1922—just four days before the historic March on Rome by 30,000 Blackshirts—Mussolini proclaimed to a crowd of 60,000: 'Our program is simple: we want to rule Italy.'[4] Later, as head of government, Mussolini added: 'My objective is simple: I want to make Italy great, respected, and feared.'[5]

As far as Mussolini was concerned, the way to achieve greatness, command respect, and instill fear was through war and conquest.

By the late 1930s, Mussolini had severed ties with the British and French; partnered with a new redoubtable ally, Germany, to form the Axis; conquered Ethiopia and merged it with Eritrea and Italian Somaliland to establish Italian East Africa; and reached the peak of his popularity among the Italian people.

Two months after the Munich Conference, on 30 November 1938, Mussolini took his Fascist councillors into his confidence, divulging to them his secret aims:

> I announce to you the immediate goals of Fascist dynamism. As we have avenged Adowa, so we will avenge Valona. Albania will become Italian. I cannot yet—and I do not wish to—tell you how or when. But it will happen. Then, for the requirements of our security in this Mediterranean

> which still confines us, we need Tunisia and Corsica. The [Italo–French] frontier must be moved to the Var [River]. I do not aim at Savoy, because it is outside the circle of the Alps. But I have my eye on the Ticino, as Switzerland has lost her cohesive force and is destined one day, like many little countries, to be disrupted. All this is a programme. I cannot lay down fixed times. I merely indicate the lines on which we shall march. Anyone revealing what I have said, in whole or in part, will have to answer to a charge of treason.[6]

The next step for Mussolini—as Fascist Italy's warlord—was to put into reality his grandiose conception of a twentieth-century Roman Empire.

1

On the Precipice, 1939

No state is ever in ideal conditions to make war, when by this you mean to imply the mathematical assurance of victory...[1]

Mussolini to the Fascist Grand Council, 4 February 1939

... relations between states are relations of force and they are the determining element of their foreign policy.[2]

Mussolini to *Squadristi* in Rome, 26 March 1939

A key date in the annals of the 'Italian Fascist Era' was 4 February 1939. On this day, Mussolini presented a report—the importance of which cannot be overstated—to the Fascist Grand Council, 'the supreme body which controls all the activities of the regime'.[3] Mussolini's purpose was to instruct his highest *gerarchi* on the future course of Italian foreign policy. The report thoroughly and unambiguously synopsized Italy's war policy. A Fascist geopolitical manifesto, it was 'a sort of Mussolinian *Mein Kampf*'. It began:

> ... states are more or less independent according to their maritime position. In other words, states that possess coasts on the oceans or have free access to the oceans are independent. States that cannot communicate freely with the oceans and are enclosed in inland seas are semi-independent. States that are absolutely continental and have outlets neither on the oceans nor on [inland] seas are not independent.
>
> Italy belongs to the second category of states. It is bathed by a landlocked sea that communicates with the oceans through the Suez Canal,

> an artificial link easily blocked even by improvised methods, and through the Straits of Gibraltar,* dominated by the cannons of Great Britain.
>
> Italy therefore does not have free connection with the oceans. Italy is therefore in truth a prisoner of the Mediterranean, and the more populous and prosperous Italy becomes, the more its imprisonment will gall.
>
> The bars of this prison are Corsica, Tunisia, Malta, Cyprus. The sentinels of this prison are Gibraltar and Suez. Corsica is a pistol pointed at the heart of Italy; Tunisia at Sicily; while Malta and Cyprus constitute a threat to all our positions in the eastern and western Mediterranean. Greece, Turkey, and Egypt have been ready to form a chain with Great Britain and complete the politico-military encirclement of Italy. [Therefore] Greece, Turkey, and Egypt must be considered virtual enemies of Italy and of its expansion.

'From this situation,' Mussolini explained to his Fascist councillors, 'one can draw the following conclusions':

> 1. The task of Italian policy, which cannot have and does not have continental objectives of a European territorial nature except Albania, is to first of all break the bars of the prison.
> 2. Once the bars are broken, Italian policy can have only one watchword—to march to the ocean.
>
> Which ocean? The Indian Ocean, joining Libya with Ethiopia through the Sudan, or the Atlantic, through French North Africa.

But Italy would have to reckon with Allied interference. Therefore, from the Italian perspective, it was necessary to safeguard Italy's rear by entering into an alliance with Germany, Central Europe's strongest nation. Hence the Axis partnership: 'In either case [Mussolini reasoned], we will find ourselves confronted with Anglo–French opposition. To confront the solution to such a problem without having our backs protected on the Continent is absurd. The policy of the Rome–Berlin Axis therefore corresponds with a historical necessity of fundamental importance.'[4]

Mussolini also recognized that sooner or later there would be a reckoning with France due to conflicting Italian and French territorial interests in the Mediterranean and North Africa. Such a war would assume 'an air-sea character'. Mussolini judged the most suitable time for Fascist Italy's showdown with the Anglo–French democracies to be after the World Exhibition in late 1942 (celebrating the vicennial anniversary of

* Gibraltar: a promontory on the southernmost tip of Spain and a British colony. Maritime access into the Mediterranean from the Atlantic was gained via the narrow Gibraltar Strait.

the Fascist Era). Galeazzo Ciano, Italy's foreign minister (and Mussolini's son-in-law), who was present at the council session, noted that the Duce said of the report 'that it represents a password to future generations' and that he wished it to be titled 'The March to the Sea'.[5]

Five weeks earlier, on 11 January, Neville Chamberlain together with Lord Halifax arrived in Rome for a meeting with Mussolini. Prime Minister Chamberlain, 'the old man with the umbrella', was favourably received by the Italian masses, and the Duce was agreeable. But the talks accomplished little to nothing.

Mussolini outlined to Chamberlain the key points of Italian foreign policy. He stated that Italy would 'conduct a policy of peace not only for general reasons, but also ... to reap the benefits of her overseas possessions'. Mussolini assured Chamberlain that Italy would adhere strictly to the Anglo–Italian Agreements of 16 April 1938 (the Easter Accords). Most significantly, Italy would conduct its foreign policy on the basis of the Rome–Berlin Axis. But this did not preclude 'the possibility of wider and more permanent understandings between the four Western Powers'. Italo–French relations* were dictated by Italy's recent denunciation of the Rome Accords (1935), and Italy envisioned 'the liquidation of the Spanish question ... only in terms of a complete victory for General [Francisco] Franco'.[6] No British intercession in Italo–French affairs, however, was needed. Perhaps after the Spanish Civil War, Italo–French relations could be ameliorated. As regards Germany, Mussolini opined that Hitler intended to keep the peace and sought only the incorporation into the Reich of ethnic German elements abroad.

But these were all superficialities. Instead, the English statesmen should have taken a stronger line and made it crystal clear that the Allies were determined to put an end to German expansionism in Europe even if it necessitated military intervention. Like Hitler, Mussolini perceived that the British leaders were men of straw and that Chamberlain's principal concern was to keep the peace in Europe no matter what the cost. Mussolini thought little of Chamberlain and Halifax. To Ciano he said in private: 'These men are not made of the same stuff as the Francis Drakes and the other magnificent adventurers who created the [British] Empire. These, after all, are the tired sons of a long line of rich men and they will

* In December 1938, Italo–French relations had soured. Noting with envy Germany's recent territorial acquisitions, the Italians attempted to wrangle some for themselves. To the Chamber of Deputies on 30 November, Ciano spoke of the 'natural aspirations of the Italian people'. In response his audience, fuelled by intense nationalism, clamoured for 'Tunis! Corsica! Nice! Savoy!'[7] With the Duce's express approval, on 17 December Ciano denounced the Rome Accords (1935) and the ill-feeling between both nations intensified. Ciano recorded in his *Diary*: 'I ... sent a note to the French Ambassador affirming, with documentation, that the Mussolini–Laval Agreement of January 1935 is juridically, politically, and historically superceded.'[8]

lose their Empire.' As far as Ciano was concerned, 'the visit was a "big lemonade" [a farce], absolutely harmless'.[9]

Meanwhile, Italy's Teutonic ally, having occupied the chiefly ethnic German Sudetenland in early October 1938, began to turn to another victim: Poland. German–Polish relations had recently deteriorated over Danzig, a Baltic seaport city presently under the League of Nations' protection. The Versailles Treaty granted to Poland specific customs rights and privileges in the Free City.

On 5 January, Józef Beck, Poland's foreign minister, had met with Adolf Hitler at the Berghof. Hitler had tried to persuade Beck to permit the Reich to annex Danzig in exchange for a guarantee of Poland's present borders and a 'supplement' to the existing German–Polish Agreement (1934). Hitler had bluntly stated: 'Danzig is German, will always remain German, and will sooner or later become part of Germany.'[10] Next day Beck had conferred with Joachim von Ribbentrop in Munich, where the German foreign minister had (predictably) parroted his Führer's views. In Warsaw three weeks later, Ribbentrop tried once more to cajole Beck into making concessions to the Reich. But Beck would have none of it. The cession of Danzig was absolutely out of the question. For the Poles, Danzig was not just a port city in which economic factors played a critical role, but a symbol. Thereafter German–Polish relations were no longer 'one of the reassuring factors in the political life of Europe'.[11]

On 25 February, Ciano arrived in Warsaw for talks with Minister Beck. He found the Polish metropolis 'grey, flat, and very gloomy'. Contemplating the Polish nation and its people, Ciano reflected: 'Poland, in spite of all the efforts and the politics of Beck, is fundamentally and constitutionally anti-German. Its tradition, its instincts, and its interest make it opposed to Germany. It is a Catholic country with a large nuclei of Jews as well as strong German minorities. It inevitably contains all of the elements of opposition towards [German] imperialism.'[12]

In accordance with her foreign policy, Poland would strive to maintain amicable relations as necessary owing to her geographic position between a rock (Germany) and a hard place (Soviet Russia). In his *Diary*, Ciano described the contents of his discussion with Beck:

> With Russia, [Poland will maintain] nothing more than strictly necessary contacts. With France, a defensive alliance on which the Poles do not rely more than is necessary. With Germany, a good-neighbour policy, maintained with difficulty because of many spiritual and concrete elements of difference. It will be necessary [for the Polish Government] to arrive at a solution regarding Danzig, but Beck wants this solution to emerge from free diplomatic relations, avoiding any useless and damaging pressure by

> public opinion.... Beck frequently emphasizes with satisfaction, though without conviction, the assurances given him by Hitler.[13]

Ciano restricted himself to a general overview during which he emphasized to his interlocutor the unshakable bonds of Italo–German solidarity. The Axis relationship was the bedrock of Italian foreign policy. In his opinion, although Poland was certainly not in the Axis camp, it could not truly be considered an enemy either: 'Summarizing my impressions in terms of our own interests, it would be foolish to conclude that Poland has been won over to the Axis or to the triangle [Germany, Italy, Japan], but it would be too pessimistic to describe it as altogether hostile.'[14] Ciano returned to Rome on 3 March and reported to Mussolini the substance of his time in Poland. The Duce, whom Ciano credited as being able to assess the Polish situation more clearly than most, described Poland as 'an empty nut'.[15]

At six o'clock on the morning of 15 March, German forces broached the Czechoslovak frontier. Three hours later they entered Prague. As ordered by high brass, the formidable Czech Army did not resist the invaders. Within twenty-four hours, Czechoslovakia as a nation ceased to exist, and the Czech provinces of Bohemia and Moravia were incorporated into the 'Greater German Reich' as a protectorate. The previous day, the Slovaks, at the Germans' urging, had declared their independence. On 16 March, Jozef Tiso, the Slovak prime minister, sent Hitler a telegram requesting the Reich Government to 'take over' the protection of the new Slovak State. Meanwhile, Hungarian forces had invaded Carpathian Ruthenia and annexed it. Within three days, the Hungarian operation was complete. Czechoslovakia was no more. The Munich Agreement, concluded less than six months prior, lay on the scrap heap.

Mussolini was particularly displeased, for he had played an instrumental role at Munich. He had even been considered by some to be the preserver of European peace, a saviour of sorts. But it now appeared to all concerned—even the Italians—that the Germans were capable of any duplicitous, underhanded action. Ciano was perturbed, and rightfully so. He observed bitterly: 'Hitler had assured everyone [in September 1938] that he did not want to annex one single Czech.... What weight can be given in the future to those [German] declarations and promises which concern us more directly?'[16] And on 19 March, Ciano added: 'The events of the last few days have reversed my opinion of the Führer ... he, too, is unfaithful and treacherous and we cannot carry on any policy with him.'[17]

In the wake of Czechoslovakia's liquidation, alarming rumours began to circulate in the press. These concerned the possibility of imminent German intervention in Croatia. Mussolini was anxious that Croat politician Vladimir Maček, a leading figure, might 'proclaim [Croatian] independence and put himself under German protection'. The Duce indignantly stated to Ciano 'that a change of the Yugoslav *status quo* in Croatia could not be accepted by us without a total and fundamental re-examination of our political policy'.[18] (This was because Mussolini had imperialist designs in Croatia and he wished to establish an Italian kingdom there.)

To clarify the urgent matter, on 17 March Ciano summoned Ambassador Hans von Mackensen. He received the German diplomat at 7 p.m. Calmly but firmly Ciano underscored the fact that while Italy was disinterested in Czechoslovakia, the same could not be said for Yugoslavia. Preserving the *status quo* in Yugoslavia was 'a fundamental factor in the equilibrium of Central Europe'. Ciano reminded Mackensen of Hitler's repeated avowals of disinterest in the Mediterranean and especially in the Adriatic. In response Mackensen stated that the rumours in question were 'without foundation'.[19] After a further discussion with Mackensen on 20 March, Ciano recorded the following:

> 1. He [Mackensen] confirms that Germany has no aims in any area of the Mediterranean, which is considered by the Führer to be an Italian sea.
> 2. Germany denies any rumour of her interest in Croatian affairs. The problem does not in any way concern the German Government and people.
> 3. He takes note of the Italian statements that she cannot be disinterested in possible modifications in the *status quo* in Croatia. He adds that just as Italy was disinterested in the Czechoslovak question ... should the Croatian question arise, it will be Germany's turn to be completely disinterested in that problem and leave the solution of it to Italy.[20]

Four days later, Ciano received a message from Ribbentrop, who hastened to reassure his Italian colleague where Hitler stood: 'You are aware of the decision of the Führer that, in all questions affecting the Mediterranean, the policy of the Axis must be laid down by Rome ... Germany will never pursue in Mediterranean countries a policy independent of Italy. This decision by the Führer will always be an unalterable law governing our foreign policy. Just as the Duce did not intervene in Czechoslovakia, so we have no interest in the Croatian question ...'[21] Ciano replied with a letter of his own, noting 'with great satisfaction your [Ribbentrop's] statements on Mediterranean questions in general and the Croatian one in particular'.[22]

Before an assembly of *Squadristi* in Rome on 26 March, Mussolini reasserted his strong pro-Axis stance. The occasion was the twentieth anniversary of the *Fasci di Combattimento* (Fasci of Combat) which he had founded in Milan in 1919 at the age of thirty-five. The Duce proclaimed:

'The attempts to crack and break the Rome–Berlin Axis are childish. The Axis is not only a relationship between two States. It is a meeting between two revolutions which have shown themselves as opposed to all other conceptions of contemporary civilization.'[23] The previous day, Hitler had sent Mussolini a congratulatory letter, exalting the Fascist movement in glowing terms:

> You have lived to see the 20th anniversary of the day on which the foundation stone of Fascism was laid. Since 1920 the new history of your people and of your country, which found its crowning success in the rebuilding of the Roman Empire, is inseparably associated with your name and the name of your movement. But apart from that, I am aware of this: that from that day the evolution of Europe and, with it, the evolution of mankind, has been directed into a new channel.... The regeneration in the 20th century not only of Italy but also of Europe will be linked for ever [*sic*] with your name.[24]

After nearly three years of brutal internecine warfare, in late March 1939 the Spanish Civil War came to an end. On 28 March, General Franco's Nationalist forces (Rebels) took Madrid. The fall of the Spanish capital, Ciano noted, was 'a new formidable victory for Fascism, perhaps the greatest one so far'. There were demonstrations in the Piazza Venezia celebrating the event, and Ciano added: 'The Duce is overjoyed. On pointing to the atlas open at the page containing the map of Spain he said, "It has been open in this way for almost three years, and that is enough. But I know already that I must open it at another page."'[25] On 1 April, the last remnants of Spanish Republican forces (Loyalists) capitulated. Upwards of a half-million combatants and civilians had perished in the cruel and bloody conflict. Atrocities and executions, on both sides, had been the order of the day. Franco established a fascistic regime with himself as *Caudillo* (leader).

On the political front, Franco's Nationalist Government had already concluded with Portugal a ten-year friendship and non-aggression pact on 17 March, the Iberian Pact. It was intended to safeguard Spain and Portugal from foreign aggression and to keep both nations neutral should a general war break out in Europe. Francoist Spain joined the Anti-Comintern Pact on 27 March and left the League of Nations on 9 May. France was now in the unenviable position of being surrounded by three hostile fascist nations—Germany, Italy, and Spain.

Events began to accelerate. Chamberlain was greatly alarmed and angered over Germany's unlawful seizure of Bohemia–Moravia. In turn, he gave Poland a unilateral guarantee of British military assistance on 31

March, obviously directed against Germany. To the House of Commons, Chamberlain declared: '... in the event of any action which clearly threatened Polish independence, and which the Polish Government accordingly considered it vital to resist with their national forces, His Majesty's Government would feel themselves bound at once to lend the Polish Government all support in their power.'[26]

Mussolini took stock of the Reich's recent annexations of the Czech lands and the Memel District and began to perceive (not incorrectly) that he was fast becoming the junior Axis partner. In this frame of mind the Duce resolved to carry out a swift conquest of his own. He had long had his eyes on neighbouring Albania. This country, already a virtual satellite of Italy, would serve as a useful springboard for future Italian incursions into the Balkans. On 25 March, Mussolini gave the Albanian monarch, King Zog, an ultimatum for Albania's incorporation into the *Impero Italiano*. Italian troops were also to be permanently garrisoned in Albania. These terms, unacceptable to the Albanians, were rejected and behind the scenes the Italians began to prepare for the 'liquidation of the Albanian question'.

King Emmanuel III, however, was opposed to the imminent Italian action against Albania. On 27 March, Mussolini had an audience with the sovereign, who 'did not see the point of risking such a venture in order to "grab four rocks"'. To Ciano, Mussolini grumbled: 'If Hitler had had to deal with a nincompoop of a King he would never have been able to take Austria and Czechoslovakia.' The Duce added spitefully that the monarchy was opposed to the Fascist system 'because Fascism is a united party'. 'The Monarchy,' Mussolini fumed, 'desires that the country be divided into two or three factions, which could be played one against the other in such a way as to permit the Monarchy to control everybody without compromising itself.'[27] On top of everything else, the birth of Crown Prince Leka on 5 April gave King Zog an heir, a most unwelcome development for the Italians.

In the days leading up to the Albanian campaign, Mussolini was inwardly prepared and undeterred by the prospect of any negative foreign reaction. Ciano recorded: 'I saw the Duce several times. He is calm, frightfully calm, and more than ever convinced that no one will want to interfere in our affair with Albania. However, he has decided to march, and he will march even though all the world may be pitted against him.'[28]

On 7 April (Good Friday), Italy attacked. An expeditionary force commanded by General Alfredo Guzzoni landed along the Albanian coast and the Fascist invaders swiftly crushed all opposition. Tirana was captured on 8 April, but King Zog escaped to Greece. The official Italian *communiqué* offered the following explanation: 'During the past few days, while conversations were in progress between the Italian Government and

King Zog for the conclusion of a new and closer accord, at Tirana and elsewhere threatening demonstrations occurred, headed by armed bands, which seriously endangered the personal safety of Italians residing in Albania.'[29] On 12 April, the Albanian Parliament elected to remove Zog from the throne, appoint Shefqet Vërlaci (a conservative politician and wealthy landowner) to the post of prime minister, and accede to the Italian takeover of Albania.

But in spite of its success, the Albanian campaign had been wretchedly conducted. Fillipo Anfuso, Ciano's secretary, sardonically stated: '... if only the Albanians had possessed a well-armed fire-brigade, they could have driven us into the Adriatic.'[30] King Emmanuel III accepted the Albanian crown on 16 April, and the union of Italy and Albania became official thereby.* Ciano described the formal ceremony, held in Rome:

> The ceremony of offering the Albanian Crown to the King of Italy takes place at the Royal Palace. The Albanians, who seem to be lost in the great halls of the Quirinal, have a depressed air. Vërlaci especially appears depressed as he pronounces, with a tired air and without conviction, the words he has to say in offering the crown. The King answers in an uncertain and trembling voice; decidedly he is not an orator who makes any impression on an audience, and these Albanians who are a warrior mountain people look with amazement and timidity on the little man who is seated on a great gilt chair beside which stands a gigantic bronze statue of Mussolini. They cannot understand what this is all about.[32]

Former Minister to Albania Francesco Jacomoni was designated vice-regent as of 22 April. He governed in this capacity until March 1943; his rule was repressive, and he was hated. Albania would remain an Italian protectorate until September 1943. A month later, Hitler confirmed to Ciano in Berlin 'the fact that Mediterranean policy will be directed by Italy'. Ciano noted in his *Diary* that the Führer 'takes an interest in Albania and is enthusiastic about our [Italian] program for making of Albania a stronghold which will inexorably dominate the Balkans'.[33]

In light of Italy's rapid conquest of Albania, on 13 April additional Anglo–French guarantees of military assistance were given to Greece and Romania in case the Italians were contemplating further aggression in the Balkans. Both Mussolini and Hitler regarded these meddlesome Anglo–French assurances as hostile steps being taken to encircle the Axis.

---

* Per a treaty concluded in Rome on 3 June, the Italian Government 'assumed management of the foreign affairs of Albania and the representation of that country abroad'. And Italian Law No. 1,115, dated 13 July, provided for the 'fusion of the Albanian and Italian Armed Forces'.[31]

In mid-April, Ciano had two lengthy discussions with Luftwaffe chief Hermann Göring in Rome. One took place at the Ministry of the Armed Forces; the other at the Palazzo Venezia. During the first talk, held on 15 April, Göring pointed out to Ciano the benefits of Germany having annexed Bohemia–Moravia:

> The action taken by Germany in Czechoslovakia is to be viewed as an advantage for the Axis in case Poland should finally join the enemies of the Axis Powers. Germany could then attack this country from two flanks and would be within only 25 minutes flying distance from the new Polish industrial centre which had been moved further into the interior of the country, nearer to the other Polish industrial districts, because of its proximity to the border. Now by the turn of events it is located again in the proximity of the border.[34]

Ciano was disturbed by the belligerent tone Göring used while discussing German–Polish relations. To him it was disconcertingly reminiscent of the tone 'used at other times for Austria and for Czechoslovakia'.[35] But Ciano believed that if it came to war with Poland, the Germans would not 'make a triumphant entrance as they have done elsewhere [Vienna, Prague, Memel]'.[36] This time around the Poles, unlike the Czechs, would resist. Later a bit of comedy occurred when the Italians, wishing to convey the appearance of being prepared for war, staged an anti-aircraft simulation. But owing to a lack of anti-aircraft guns, artillery had to be transported into the capital to replicate the sound of air defence, in order to make the spectacle more convincing!

The time had now come for an Italo–Hungarian summit meeting. Accordingly, Hungarian Prime Minister Pál Teleki arrived in Rome on 18 April. Teleki had been in office for two months, since 16 February. He was accompanied by his foreign minister, Imre Czaky. The Hungarian party were received at the train station. Ciano observed: 'Teleki makes a good impression on the Duce; Czaky is what he appears to be: a small, presumptuous man and, most disturbing to note, apparently is a physical and spiritual weakling who wishes always to assume heroic airs.' The statesmen discussed European affairs over the course of the next three days. The first conference was held that afternoon. Czaky elaborated on the political situation 'in detail', placing great emphasis on Slovakia. It was his hope that the Reich would 'make a kind gift of it to Budapest'. Ciano did not bother to recapitulate what was said because he deemed it 'not important'.[37]

On 19 April, the 'more or less useless conversations' resumed. According to Ciano, Czaky's arguments became 'more and more prolix and futile'.

The Hungarian foreign minister, Ciano felt, had a tedious penchant for 'saying the obvious ... as if it were a matter of great importance'.[38] On the afternoon of 20 April, the final meeting took place. Ciano noted that Teleki 'scarcely opened his mouth' to speak. Moreover, his opinion of Czaky continued to grow 'more and more negative'. To Ciano's astonishment, Czaky even went so far as to openly express the view that Hitler was 'crazy', basing his opinion 'on the look of the Führer's eyes'. Afterwards, Mussolini summed up the political situation in connection with the Axis nations and their neighbours:

> (1) Italy and Germany desire some years of peace and will carry on the policy of the Axis.
> (2) Hungary is carrying on and will carry on the policy of the Axis.
> (3) No one wants the dismemberment of Yugoslavia, but everyone is working towards the maintenance of the *status quo*. If, however, any dismemberment should come about, Italian interests in Croatia are paramount.
> (4) As to the Slovak problem, Hungary will adopt a watchful attitude and will do nothing contrary to German wishes.[39]

Grigore Gafencu, Romania's foreign minister, entrained to Rome for a discussion with Mussolini on 1 May. (He had previously been in Berlin where, on 19 April—on the eve of Hitler's fiftieth birthday—he had been received by the Führer at the Reich Chancellery.) Gafencu first had a preliminary conversation with Ciano in the latter's lavish office at the Palazzo Chigi. There they touched on Italo–French relations. Ciano then took Gafencu to see Mussolini, leading the Romanian minister 'across the slippery tiles of the Palazzo Venezia's reception room'. Gafencu met the Italian dictator, who was 'most amiable', 'halfway between the massive door and his table'. After the Second World War, Gafencu described his personal impressions of the charismatic Duce:

> Contrary to Hitler, Mussolini was not like his photographs. In private life his face was free of the striking expression he assumed to impress the crowd. The man was not without charm. His eyes, when they did not flash lightning, seemed benevolent. He spoke French correctly, using phrases with a tang made keener by his southern accent. Not once in the course of the conversation did he seem to strive for effect. He seemed to enjoy the role of the simple man at rest after scenes played on the famous balcony. Avoiding monologue, he encouraged conversation by asking questions and listening to the replies.[40]

Mussolini first spoke to Gafencu of Axis interests and policy. He hinted that an official pact was in the works, soon to be concluded between Fascist Italy and Nazi Germany. The words 'up to now' were the giveaway. He stated: 'The policy of the Axis is a living reality even though *up to now* it may not have been defined in writing, or by any formal engagement.' The Duce continued: 'The bond uniting us to the National Socialist Reich, though not yet material, is still so firm as to withstand every trial. Those who might be tempted to break it are cherishing dangerous illusions. There is between us an identity of conception of the world which is stronger than all conventional texts. We are united by the same aim and the same revolutionary ardour.'

Mussolini was critical of Romania for having recently accepted from Britain and France assurances of military assistance in the event of an encroachment of Romanian territory. He remonstrated:

> What meaning was there in the Anglo–French guarantees? How could France and Britain ever keep their engagements? Romania was a big country; it needed nobody's protection. For the rest, the Western Powers were meddling in what was no business of theirs. They were trying to split the Axis and oppose Italian interests to German interests. It was all labour lost. The Axis would never give way.

In turn, Gafencu defended his government's policy: 'If everyone guaranteed his neighbour's security,' he reasoned, 'it would be possible to speak of peace without giving offence to anyone.' Gafencu shared his opinion of the Axis alliance: 'Such agreements should neither be weakened nor destroyed, but on the contrary extended and multiplied.'

Regarding present Italo–French differences, Mussolini stated: 'The difficulties which exist between Italy and France are serious, but they are not grave.' Gafencu perceived that it was this viewpoint the Italian dictator wished him to convey to Georges Bonnet, the French foreign minister. Mussolini then clarified the nature of these issues of contention: 'These difficulties are of a colonial order—they are not of a territorial order. We shall not make war on account of this.' With this utterance the interview came to a close. Gafencu's parting impression was that Mussolini was not averse to an agreement with France and that he believed Italo–French reconciliation was not beyond the realm of possibility.[41]

On 6 May, Ciano met with Ribbentrop in Milan for 'a close examination ... of the present general political situation'.[42] Ciano informed him that Italy required a lengthy interval of peace; he specified a three-year period. In turn, Ribbentrop assured his colleague that 'this Italian attitude coincided with the German views also'.[43] This was absolutely untrue, for unbeknown to the Italians, on 3 April Hitler had added three brief directives to Case White, the secret Nazi plan for the conquest of Poland. The first of these stated: 'Preparations must be made in such a way that the operation can be carried out at any time from 1.9.39 onwards.'[44] Thus a German attack on Poland was projected to begin as soon as September, less than four months distant!

But to perpetuate the deception, Ribbentrop—who was capable of lying with the greatest of ease—informed Ciano that Hitler was 'determined to follow the path of conciliation' *vis-à-vis* Poland. That being said, the Führer absolutely would not renounce Danzig. The Reich would 'make no further offers to Poland'. Instead, the German Government intended 'to allow the matter to mature'. Should the Poles 'pass over to an offensive policy', the Germans would be prepared 'to react in the sharpest manner'.[45] And the Soviet Union, Ribbentrop insisted, must not be permitted to align itself with the Anglo–French democracies: '... any favourable occasion ... must be seized to prevent the adhesion of Russia to the anti-totalitarian bloc.' It was essential, therefore, to cultivate the recent *détente* between the Axis and the U.S.S.R.[46]

That evening, Ciano recounted to Mussolini the favourable progress of the talks. Enthused, the Duce unexpectedly ordered Ciano to request 'the immediate conclusion of a military alliance between Italy and the Reich'.[47] Mussolini's initiative was recklessly spontaneous; he consulted neither the Fascist Grand Council nor the Italian Foreign Ministry beforehand. (Another impetus for Mussolini was the recent French claim that the Milanese were anti-German.) Ciano was averse, for he considered an Italo–German military pact to be fraught with peril. Ribbentrop, too, was hesitant. He would have preferred a trilateral alliance which included the Japanese. But Hitler, notified by telephone, accepted at once the Italian proposition.

Ribbentrop advised that he would provide the Italians with a draft copy of the military pact for their perusal in the near future. 'The signing of the pact,' Ribbentrop urged, 'should take place in Berlin as soon as possible and in the most solemn manner.' Ribbentrop was also appreciative of Mussolini's suggestion to tailor the pact 'in such a way ... which would allow the adhesion of such States as intend to take part in it at a later date'.[48] Afterwards, a *communiqué* underscoring Axis solidarity proclaimed to the world: 'The perfect identity of views of the two Governments was once more established, and it was decided finally to define, in a formal manner, the relations between the two States of the Axis in a political and military pact. In this way, Italy and Germany intend efficaciously to contribute to and ensure the peace of Europe.'[49]

On 14 May, Mussolini delivered a fiery speech at Turin. To his Piedmontese comrades, he thundered: 'We will march with Germany.' The

German press was gratified by the Duce's proclamation and noted that it was Mussolini's 'first speech as Germany's pledged military ally'.[50]

Ciano reached Berlin on 21 May for the ceremonial signing of the Pact of Steel. He was received with great acclaim by thousands of ecstatic Berliners. The first order of business was a private discussion with Ribbentrop; the conversation with his opposite number was most satisfactory: 'Nothing has changed in regard to what was said and decided upon in Milan. He [Ribbentrop] repeats Germany's interest in and intention to ensure for itself a long period of peace—at least three years.'[51] Ciano apparently overlooked the fact that the so-called 'period of peace' had, in the space of a fortnight, been truncated; for during the preceding talks with Ribbentrop in Milan on 6–7 May, the latter had assured Ciano: 'Germany, too, is convinced of the necessity for a period of peace, which should not be less than four or five years.'[52]

On 22 May, with Hitler and his retinue looking on, Ciano and Ribbentrop affixed their signatures to the Pact of Steel. The ten-year pact was directed chiefly against Britain and France. It consisted of a lengthy, bombastic preamble and seven articles (see Appendix A for the full text). The third was by far the most crucial:

> Article III
>
> If it should happen, against the wishes and hopes of the Contracting Parties, that one of them becomes involved in military complications with another Power or other Powers, the other Contracting Party will immediately step to its side as an ally and will support it with all its military might on land, at sea, and in the air.

The fifth article added that neither party would conclude a separate armistice or peace without the express approval of the other. Also, a Secret Additional Protocol provided for Italo–German collaboration on 'military questions', 'questions of war economy', and 'matters of the press, the news service, and propaganda'.[53] This supplementary section was not publicized.

Ciano recognized that the pact could lead Italy to utter ruin. He knew that the Führer was wholly unpredictable. Hitler might provoke a general war in which Italy—now contractually obligated to participate—was ill-prepared. But Mussolini was untroubled by the prospect. The appeal of a military alliance with the redoubtable Germany overshadowed (for the moment) any personal doubts. The pact was originally titled *Patto di Sangue* (Pact of Blood), but Mussolini was advised that the Italian people would find objectionable such a sinister-sounding appellation. Therefore, *Patto d'Acciaio* (Pact of Steel)—which connoted hardness and strength—was selected instead. Several days later, King Emmanuel III shared his cynical opinion of German friendship in a telegram to Ciano: 'The Germans as long as they have need of us will be courteous, and even servile, but at the first opportunity they will reveal themselves as the great rascals they really are.'[54]

Unknown to the Italians, behind the scenes Hitler was finalizing his plans for war. On 23 May, at a top-secret meeting held in Berlin, Hitler divulged with startling candour his plans for the conquest of Poland. Danzig was not the issue at hand. On the contrary, it was a matter of acquiring *Lebensraum* for the German *Volk*: 'It is not Danzig that is at stake,' Hitler explained to his subalterns. 'For us it is a matter of expanding our living space in the East ...' He added: 'There is therefore no question of sparing Poland and we are left with the decision: *To attack Poland at the first suitable opportunity*.' For Germany, detaching Poland from the Western Powers would be the crucial factor: 'Our task is to isolate Poland. Success in isolating her will be decisive.' Hitler underscored the fact that Germany's chief antagonist was Britain, not Poland: '*England* is the motive force driving against Germany.' It was a matter of Germany's survival and as such draconian measures were called for, the cost notwithstanding: 'The idea of getting out cheaply is dangerous; there is no such possibility. We must then burn our boats and it will no longer be a question of right or wrong but of to be or not to be for 80,000,000 people.' Lastly, Hitler emphasized the need for absolute discretion, even from Germany's partners: '*Secrecy* is the decisive prerequisite for success. Our objects must be kept secret from both Italy and Japan.'[55]

Mussolini decided to set down on paper his views on the Pact of Steel and its possible ramifications. This detailed and crucial document, prepared on 30 May and known as the 'Cavallero Memorandum', was dispatched to Hitler. Mussolini wrote:

> I. The war between the plutocratic and therefore selfishly conservative nations and the densely populated and poor nations is inevitable....
> II. Because of the strategic positions attained in Bohemia [by Germany] and Albania [by Italy], the Axis Powers have in their hands, a basic factor for success.

Mussolini recognized that before the climactic showdown with the Allies, Fascist Italy required 'a preparatory period which may extend to the end of 1942'. The Axis nations required a duration of peace lasting a minimum of three years. 'Only after 1943,' Mussolini soberly reflected, 'can a war have the greatest prospects of success.' The Duce cited numerous reasons for the foregoing:

> a. For the military organization of Libya and Albania; also for the pacification of Ethiopia; from which latter region an army of half a million must be created.
> b. To complete the building and rebuilding of six capital ships already started.
> c. To rejuvenate completely our medium and larger calibre artillery.
> d. For further development of our autarkic plans by which any attempt at blockade by the satiated democracies must be foiled.
> e. To carry out the world exposition in 1942 by which not only the activity of the Fascist regime for 20 years will be documented, but also reserves of foreign exchange can be obtained.
> f. To complete the return of Italians from France, which poses a very serious military and *moral* question.
> g. To complete the shifting of many war industries from the Po Plains to Southern Italy, which has already been started.
> h. To deepen further the relationships not only of the governments of the Axis Powers but also of the two nations.

Italy had to be made economically self-sufficient. Since the Anglo–French democracies were 'practically safe' from an attack on land (especially England) it would be necessary instead to combat the Allies by air and by sea. Mussolini also noted that Britain and France were readying themselves for a 'war of exhaustion'—a war in which the enemy's will to fight is itself defeated:

> It is further to be expected that the triangle London–Paris–Moscow will try everything during peace times to harm the Axis Powers especially in economic and moral spheres. The response in the economic sphere will be to develop the autarkic plans to the utmost, and in the moral sphere by making a counter attack in any case....
>
> V. From a strategic point of view the Western Powers are 'walled-in', i.e., they are to be considered as practically safe against land forces. The war in the West would therefore take the character of a predominantly air and sea war....
>
> VII. The war which the great democracies are preparing is a *war of exhaustion*. One must therefore start with the worst assumption which contains 100 percent probability. *The Axis will get nothing more from the rest of the world....*

War strategy would consist of conquering the entire Danubian and Balkan sectors in the opening phase of the conflict and thereafter exploiting them:

> ... one must take the whole Danube and Balkan area immediately after the first hours of the war. One cannot be satisfied with declarations of neutrality but must occupy the territories and use them for procurement of necessary food and industrial war supplies. By this lightning-like operation which is to be carried out decisively, not only the 'guaranteed states', like Greece, Romania, and Turkey, would be out of the fight, but one would also protect one's back. In this game we count—like in a chess game—on two favourable 'pawns': Hungary and Bulgaria.

Lastly, Mussolini contrasted Italo–German contributions to the inevitable war in terms of personnel *versus* materiel:

> VIII. Italy can mobilize a comparatively greater number of men than Germany. This mass of men is offset by a lack of means. Therefore Italy—in the war plan—will deliver more people than means; Germany will deliver more means than people.[56]

Serrano Suñer, the Spanish interior minister and General Franco's son-in-law, arrived in Rome on 5 June for a week-long visit. He was accompanied by the duke of Aosta (Prince Amedeo, viceroy of Italian East Africa). The Spaniard expressed to Ciano his thanks for Italy's valuable contributions to Spain's nationalist cause. Suñer's bugbear was France, whom he considered 'the eternal enemy of Greater Spain'. However, Spain was averse to a war at present since her resources were thoroughly exhausted due to the Spanish Civil War. In fact, certain parts of Spain were suffering from famine. Thus, Spain required two to three years in order to 'reconstitute herself and complete her military preparations'. A military alliance with the Axis at this point, therefore, 'would be premature'. But at the proper time Spain would align herself with her totalitarian Italo–German comrades. A priority for Spain was to settle the Gibraltar issue, for she could not consider herself 'completely free and sovereign' so long as the Union Jack fluttered on the rock fortress. Spain also intended to settle the score with France. The bone of contention in this regard was Morocco. A religious man, Suñer was lukewarm towards Germany due her current 'anti-Catholic excesses'. On 10 June, Ciano communicated to the Duce the salient points of his conferences with Suñer, and in turn Mussolini expressed that he wished to see Suñer in charge of the Spanish Foreign Ministry.[57]

Dino Grandi, veteran Fascist and Italy's ambassador to London since July 1932, was unexpectedly recalled by Mussolini on 12 July; the British Government did not receive any advance notification of this measure. Grandi, who had previously served as foreign minister (1929–1932), was—like Ciano—against Italian participation in a European general war.

On 9 July, Ciano flew to Madrid to confer with General Franco. After voyaging throughout Spain for some days, 'passing through eight Spanish cities and traversing many hundreds of kilometres of countryside', the meeting took place on 19 July at the Basque city of San Sebastián. Ciano described the Spanish dictator in his diplomatic papers: 'To deal with, *Generalissimo* Franco is the same man as one has learned to know from his achievements, his words, and his very photographs. There are no surprises and no disappointments. A man, simple in his bearing and his thought, calm in his examination of questions and in his judgment…'

When the conversation turned towards the subject of foreign policy, Franco explained that for the time being he had to '*ménager*' France. Nevertheless, Franco 'confirmed his firm intention to follow more and more definitely the line of the Rome–Berlin Axis'. Meanwhile, he would wait until 'Spain's general condition and military preparations' were back up to par. Franco pointed out that Spain needed more than just two or three years to recover from the Spanish Civil War. In fact, Spain required 'a period of peace of at least five years'. Even a half-decade was perceived by some to be an 'optimistic' estimation. Meanwhile, Spain would accelerate armaments production. For the Spanish Navy, four new 35,000-ton battleships and a powerful armada to dominate the seas. Plus, the establishment of a new *Ejército del Aire* (Air Force) independent of the Army or Navy.

Ciano wrapped up his report:

> Franco is completely dominated by the personality of Mussolini and feels that he requires him to face the peace just as he did to win the war. His journey to Rome—which will be followed immediately by a journey to Berlin—will be an event of fundamental importance in the *Caudillo*'s political life. He expects from the Duce … instructions and directives. And he himself spoke to me of an even greater event … the Duce's journey to Madrid, whereby Spain would be definitely united to the destiny of the Roman Empire.[58]

By early August, German–Polish tensions over Danzig were near the boiling point. The Axis Governments therefore found it necessary for another consultation to touch base. On 10 August, the day before his scheduled meeting with Ribbentrop at Salzburg, Ciano received some parting instructions from Mussolini. The Duce told Ciano to convey unequivocally to the Germans that 'we must avoid a conflict with Poland, since it will be impossible to localize it, and a general war would be disastrous for everybody'. Ciano was in total agreement with Mussolini's outlook but was skeptical as to whether his admonitions would be heeded by the arrogant Germans.[59]

The ten-hour conversation between the two foreign ministers at Ribbentrop's Fuschl estate on 11 August was frosty and strained. Ribbentrop finally came clean and disclosed to Ciano that the Germans were intent on war. From his prison cell in Verona in December 1943, while awaiting execution, Ciano reflected back on how Ribbentrop had broken the news:

> It was at his residence at Fuschl that von Ribbentrop, while we were waiting to be seated at the dinner table, told me of the German decision to set a match to the European powder keg. This he told me in much the same tone that he would have used about an inconsequential administrative detail.
>
> 'Well, Ribbentrop,' I asked, 'what do you want? The Corridor or Danzig?' 'Not that any more,' he said, gazing at me with his cold expressionless eyes, 'we want war!'[60]

Ciano was ardently opposed to Italian involvement in a conflict that was almost certain to mushroom into a general war and he was mortified by the Germans' inflexibility: 'I am certain that even if the Germans were given more than they ask for they would attack just the same, because they are possessed by the demon of destruction.'[61] Ribbentrop tried to fob Ciano off with unconvincing assurances that the British would remain aloof from the German–Polish war. He ascribed this conviction, mistaken though it was, to his 'psychological knowledge' of the British.

On 12 August, Ciano journeyed to Berchtesgaden to confer with Hitler. There the Führer adumbrated four chief reasons for the forthcoming German attack on Poland:

1. The daily Polish provocations offending German honour;
2. The abuse of ethnic German minorities at the hands of the Poles;
3. The (alleged) intention of the Poles to occupy Danzig after 15 October and thereafter destroy it; and
4. The threat posed by Poland to Germany's rear during the inevitable clash with Britain and France.

Hitler also recommended that Italy take the first opportunity to occupy Croatia and Dalmatia, dismembering Yugoslavia and neutralizing the multi-ethnic Balkan nation thereby.[62] Ciano hoped he might talk Hitler out of it, but the German dictator was implacable:

> I realize immediately that there is no longer anything that can be done. He [Hitler] has decided to strike, and strike he will.... He continues to repeat that he will localize the conflict with Poland, but his affirmation that the great war must be fought while he and the Duce are still young leads me to believe once more that he is acting in bad faith.

The callous attitude of the Germans incensed Ciano:

> ... he [Hitler] listens with a faraway and impersonal interest to what I tell him about the bad effects a war would have on the Italian people. Actually I feel that as far as the Germans are concerned an alliance with us means only that the enemy will be obliged to keep a certain number of divisions facing us, thus easing up the situation on the German war fronts. They care for nothing more. The fate that might befall us does not interest them in the least.[63]

Next day Ciano again conferred with the Führer at Berchtesgaden: 'The second meeting with Hitler is briefer, and, I would say, more concise. Even in his gestures the man reveals more than yesterday his imminent will to action.'[64] Hitler touched on Allied intervention, which he considered 'absurd'. If Britain and France took action, he stated, this would indicate that 'they had now decided on the fight against the Axis and that, even without the attack on Poland, they would not have allowed those years of preparation to pass which Italy and Germany might find useful'. Hitler reiterated his determination to smash Poland; the operation would 'be rapid, decisive, implacable'. When Ciano inquired of Hitler when hostilities were to begin, he was informed that the attack was projected for the end of August at the latest. 'The German General Staff,' Hitler added, 'consider four to six weeks necessary to liquidate the Polish question militarily.'[65] Thus the conflagration was to begin in a little over a fortnight. Afterwards, Ciano recorded his disaffection with the Germans:

> I return to Rome completely disgusted with the Germans, with their leader, with their way of doing things. They have betrayed us and lied to us. Now they are dragging us into an adventure which we have not wanted and which might compromise the [Fascist] regime and the country as a whole. The Italian people will boil over with horror when they know about the aggression against Poland ... I don't know whether to wish Italy a victory or Germany a defeat.

Ciano never recovered from the disillusionment he experienced at Salzburg and for the rest of his life remained a staunch Germanophobe. Back at the Palazzo Venezia, he reported to Mussolini the content of his talks with Ribbentrop and Hitler. He also shared with the Duce his 'judgment of the situation'. Ciano recommended to Mussolini that they inform the Germans unequivocally 'that we have no intention of participating in a war which we have neither wanted nor provoked'. Mussolini, however, was conflicted. Initially he agreed with Ciano but after further consideration felt that honour—and the Pact of Steel—compelled him to march with his Axis ally. In other words, *pacta sunt servanda*. And in the end, the Italian dictator could not resist the welcome prospect of acquiring war booty in Croatia and Dalmatia.[66]

Eight days later, Ciano was still earnestly attempting to dissuade the Duce from joining the Germans in their premeditated war of conquest. To Mussolini, he emphasized German perfidy, argued strongly against Italian participation, and offered to renounce the Pact of Steel personally:

> You, Duce, cannot and must not do it. The loyalty with which I have served you in carrying out the policy of the Axis warrants my speaking clearly to you now. I went to Salzburg in order to adopt a common line of action. I found myself face to face with a *diktat*. The Germans, not ourselves, have betrayed the alliance in which we were to have been partners, and not servants. Tear up the pact. Throw it in Hitler's face and Europe will recognize in you the natural leader of the anti-German crusade. Do you want me to go to Salzburg? Very well, I shall go and speak to the Germans as they should be spoken to. Hitler will not have me put out my cigarette as he did with Schuschnigg [in Vienna on 12 February 1938].[67]

On the morning of 22 August, a war conference was held at the Reich Chancellery. In a lengthy exposition, Hitler analyzed the state of European political affairs and explained to his service chiefs his reasons for marching against Poland. The Führer explained that there were three 'personal factors' that were crucial. The first, naturally, was his own personality and existence. He elucidated: 'Essentially all depends on me, on my existence, because of my political talents. Furthermore, the fact that probably no one will ever again have the confidence of the whole German people as I have. There will probably never again in the future be a man with more authority than I have. My existence is therefore a factor of great value.' The other two 'personal factors' were Europe's other Fascist leaders—Mussolini and Franco:

> The second personal factor is the Duce. His existence is also decisive. If anything happens to him, Italy's loyalty to the alliance will no longer be certain. The Italian Court is fundamentally opposed to the Duce. Above all, the Court regards the expansion of the [Italian] Empire as an encumbrance. The Duce is the man with the strongest nerves in Italy.
>
> The third personal factor in our favour is Franco. We can ask only for benevolent neutrality from Spain. But this depends on Franco's personality. He guarantees a certain uniformity and stability in the present

> system in Spain. We must accept the fact that Spain does not as yet have a Fascist party with our internal unity.[68]

Hitler addressed his generals once more, this time in the afternoon, to emphasize the *Wehrmacht*'s task: 'The wholesale destruction of Poland is the military objective.' This was the top priority. Hitler exhorted his generals not to concern themselves with the political aspect: 'I shall give a propagandist reason for starting the war, no matter whether it is plausible or not. The victor will not be asked afterwards whether he told the truth or not. When starting and waging a war it is not right that matters, but victory.'[69] In other words, the ends would justify the means. Poland would cease to exist, and the Reich would be left free to deal the Western democracies a mortal blow. But first it was necessary to remove the danger of a two-front war by placating the hated Bolsheviks.

For some time now, Germany and the U.S.S.R. had been hammering out the details of a political alliance, one that would checkmate the Western Powers. In a letter to Hitler dated 21 August, Soviet dictator Joseph Stalin agreed to receive Germany's foreign minister two days later. Ribbentrop accordingly flew to Moscow invested with plenary powers to conclude with the Russians a non-aggression pact. The German delegation arrived at midday. Following a quick lunch at the German Embassy, Ribbentrop left for the Kremlin to consult with Stalin and Vyacheslav Molotov, the recently appointed commissar of Foreign Affairs (as of 3 May).

The proceedings began with a three-hour conference. The negotiations were unexpectedly congenial, the German and Russian parties had no difficulty coming to terms, and Ribbentrop and Molotov appended their signatures to the Nazi–Soviet Pact that same night. The first part of the pact, containing a preamble and seven points, was made public. It contained the non-aggression provisions and specified that neither side would attack the other nor assist a belligerent third party waging war against the other. Any differences between them would be settled by diplomacy. The second part contained a 'Secret Additional Protocol'. It remained 'strictly secret' and came to light only after the end of the Second World War. The protocol carved Eastern Europe into German and Soviet zones of interest respectively:

> 1. In the event of a territorial and political rearrangement in the areas belonging to the Baltic States (Finland, Estonia, Latvia, Lithuania), the northern boundary of Lithuania shall represent the boundary of the spheres of influence of Germany and the U.S.S.R. In this connection the interest of Lithuania in the Vilna area is recognized by each party.

> 2. In the event of a territorial and political rearrangement of the areas belonging to the Polish State the spheres of influence of Germany and the U.S.S.R. shall be bounded approximately by the line of the rivers Narew, Vistula, and San....
> 3. With regard to Southeastern Europe attention is called by the Soviet side to its interest in Bessarabia. The German side declares its complete political disinterestedness in these areas.[70]

News of the German–Russian Pact astounded the entire world. Overnight the balance of power had shifted overwhelmingly in favour of the totalitarian countries. The British and French, who had also been involved in talks with the Soviets, were understandably angry at having been cynically manipulated and deceived. Next day there was a lull; Hitler was waiting to see precisely what kind of effect the new pact would have on the Allies. Meanwhile, Mussolini continued to follow the rapidly changing course of European affairs with a close and apprehensive eye.

While Ribbentrop was away at Moscow, the German finance minister, Schwerin von Krosigk, had an important meeting with Ciano, who spoke of foreign policy. Schwerin von Krosigk duly reported the substance of the discussion to Ribbentrop in writing:

> After the usual words of salutation Count Ciano immediately talked about foreign policy and stressed the importance of your trip to Russia. Nevertheless, in case of Germany's intervention in Poland, England and France would, in his opinion, immediately participate in the war. The Ambassadors of both powers had just confirmed this to him expressly and very seriously. This created a very serious situation. For actually the Axis was not yet sufficiently prepared, above all, economically. Only in three to four years—Count Ciano corrected himself and said with strong emphasis 'in three years'—would it be ready for war. We would certainly have initial military successes; but the enemy would recover and would wage a war of attrition of long duration along economic lines. Upon my objection that the Führer was of a different opinion and did not believe in a war with England and France, Count Ciano replied that he was aware of that, but that he was afraid that the Führer would not be proved right this time. Upon my reply that it was completely intolerable for a great nation to look on passively any longer at the systematic [mis]treatment of Germans by Poles, and that therefore a solution of the Polish problem was absolutely necessary and that the whole German people was of one mind on that score, Count Ciano replied that a great deal would depend upon the attitude of the Axis peoples. For it would be necessary to fight with utmost tenacity, since in case of a defeat we would have to count on

> a peace which would practically mean the end of the Axis Powers. Count Ciano concluded the conversation by stating that despite the great diplomatic success of the Russian pact he considered the situation as very serious.[71]

On 25 August, Hitler wrote a confidential letter to Mussolini in which he belatedly sought to justify the German–Russian Pact to his Axis ally. After being telephoned in by Ribbentrop, the lengthy document was handed to Mussolini at 3:20 p.m. by Hans Georg von Mackensen, the German ambassador in Rome. At the start of the letter, Hitler gave three main reasons for the political deal with Soviet Russia and explained courteously but unconvincingly why he had heretofore kept Mussolini out of the loop:

> 1. The general situation of world politics in so far as this is decisive for the Axis Powers.
> 2. The constant procrastination of the Japanese Cabinet over taking a definite attitude … against England, and this, from the standpoint not only of Germany but also of Italy, would have been one of the decisive factors. Months ago the military party had asserted that it would be able to induce the Japanese Government in a short time to take up a definite attitude towards England … but this had not been realized in practice.
> 3. Germany's relations with Poland, through no fault of the Reich, but largely as a result of England's interference, have been unsatisfactory since the spring, and in recent weeks simply intolerable. The reports about the persecution of Germans in this area are not invented press reports but represent only a fraction of the terrible truth. Poland's throttling of Danzig by a Customs policy which for weeks past has led to a complete paralysis of all trade, will destroy the City if continued even for a short time.
>
> These reasons led me to hasten the conclusion of the German–Russian conversations. I have not yet informed you in detail, Duce, since I had no idea of the possible extent of these conversations, or any assurance of the possibility of their success.

Hitler described the Nazi–Soviet Pact as 'the most extensive non-aggression pact in existence'. It was 'unconditional' and included a clause stipulating 'the obligation for consultation on all questions affecting Russia and Germany'. In the event of any conflict, Russia's benevolence was guaranteed, the danger of Romanian interference was eliminated, and even the Turks might re-evaluate their pro-British position. As a result of the pact with the Soviets, Hitler professed, 'a completely new situation in world politics has been produced which must be regarded as the greatest possible gain for the Axis'.

Concerning the Polish affair, Hitler enumerated the 'unendurable' Polish provocations. These included but were not limited to Polish mobilization, atrocities against ethnic German minorities, multiple border violations, and a blockade of Danzig. Because of the foregoing, Hitler cautioned, anything could happen: 'In these circumstances no one can say what the next hour may bring. I can only assure you that there is a definite limit beyond which I can in no circumstances retreat.' Hitler ended his missive by affirming that if the shoe were on the other foot, he would back Italy unreservedly: 'In conclusion I can assure you, Duce, that in a similar situation I should have complete understanding for Italy and that in any such case you could be sure of my attitude from the outset.'[72]

Mussolini read the letter to himself, then reread it aloud, translating it from German to Italian for the benefit of Ciano, who was present. To Mackensen, Mussolini stated that although he was a staunch anti-Communist, 'he was in complete agreement with the Moscow Non-Aggression Pact'. 'The deterioration of German–Polish relations,' Mussolini added, was 'so acute that an armed conflict could no longer be avoided.' Finally, the Duce confirmed to the German ambassador that 'he stood beside us unconditionally and with all his resources'.[73]

Ciano convinced the Duce to send Hitler a non-committal reply. 'Concerning the agreement with Russia,' Mussolini wrote, 'I approve of it completely.' Under the circumstances the Duce also deemed it advantageous to avoid a rift with the Japanese, who naturally were not keen on bringing the Soviets into the fold. Mussolini noted with satisfaction that the German–Russian Pact 'blockades Romania'. Plus, if Turkey were to revise her stance, it would 'upset all the strategic plans of the French and English in the Eastern Mediterranean'. As regards Poland, Mussolini was sympathetic: 'I have complete understanding for the German position and for the fact that such a tense situation cannot continue indefinitely.' Thereupon Mussolini dispensed with the pleasantries and came to the point:

> As for the *practical* attitude of Italy, in case of a military action, my point of view is as follows:
>
> If Germany attacks Poland and the conflict remains localized, Italy will afford Germany every form of political and economic assistance which is requested of her.
>
> If Poland attacks and her allies [Britain and France] open a counter attack against Germany, I inform you in advance that it will be opportune for me not to take the *initiative* in military operations in view of the

> *present* state of Italian war preparations, of which we have repeatedly and in good time informed you, Führer, and Herr von Ribbentrop.
>
> Our intervention can, nevertheless, take place at once if Germany delivers to us immediately the military supplies and the raw materials to resist the attack which the French and English would predominantly direct against us.
>
> At our meetings, the war was envisaged for after 1942, and by that time I would have been ready on land, on sea, and in the air, according to the plans which had been concerted.
>
> I am furthermore of the opinion that the purely military measures which have already been taken, and other measures to be taken later, will immobilize, in Europe and Africa, considerable French and British forces.
>
> I consider it my bounden duty as a loyal friend to tell you the whole truth and inform you beforehand about the real situation. Not to do so might have unpleasant consequences for us all. This is my view, and since within a short time I must summon the highest governmental bodies, I beg of you to let me know yours.[74]

Mussolini's letter was telephoned in to the Italian Embassy in Berlin at approximately 5 p.m. At the Reich Chancellery, Hitler was on pins and needles, repeatedly demanding to know what the delay was. He was irritable because the invasion of Poland was set to begin at 4:30 a.m. the very next day, and the clock was ticking. Finally, at about 6 p.m., the Duce's eagerly awaited response was delivered to Hitler by Bernardo Attolico, the Italian ambassador to Germany.

Around the same time, Hitler learned that an 'Agreement of Mutual Assistance' between the British and the Poles had just been concluded at London. Signed by Halifax, the British foreign secretary, and Edward Raczynski, the Polish ambassador, its first article provided: 'Should one of the Contracting Parties become engaged in hostilities with a European Power in consequence of aggression by the latter against that Contracting Party, the other Contracting Party will at once give the Contracting Party engaged in hostilities all the support and assistance in its power.'[75] The Anglo–Polish Agreement came into effect upon signature and was fixed for a duration of five years. Its text was received in Germany by telegram.

Shaken by the unwelcome news of the Anglo–Polish pact of mutual assistance, the Führer advised Attolico that he would reply to Mussolini's letter forthwith and he abruptly dismissed the diplomat. As Attolico stepped out, General Wilhelm Keitel, chief of the *Wehrmacht* High Command, was hastening to see Hitler. After several minutes elapsed, Keitel left the room, agitated. He called out to his adjutant, informing him with great urgency that the German invasion order had to be postponed.

Both of these unexpected developments had thrown a heavy wrench into the Führer's invasion plans. Nevertheless, of the two, it was the Anglo–Polish Agreement that proved to be the decisive factor in compelling Hitler to defer his assault on Poland to 1 September.

Mackensen returned to the Palazzo Venezia at 9:30 p.m. This time he brought with him a short letter by Hitler who wanted to know specifically which weapons and raw materials Italy needed and by when in order to defend against an Anglo–French attack. Hitler also expressed his gratitude for Italy's 'military measures', which he found most satisfactory:

> You have informed me that you can enter a major European conflict only if Germany supplies you at once with implements of war and raw materials in order to resist the attack which the French and British would launch predominantly against you. I would ask you to inform me what implements of war and raw materials you require and within what time, so that I may be in a position to judge whether and to what extent I can fulfill your demands for implements of war and raw materials.
>
> Furthermore, I thank you heartily for Italy's military measures, of which I have been acquainted in the meantime and which I already regard as a great relief.[76]

On the morning of 26 August, after consulting with his military chiefs, Mussolini composed another letter to Hitler. Ciano telephoned it in to the Italian Embassy in Berlin at 12:10 p.m., and within the space of an hour, Hitler was perusing it avidly. The Führer must have been beside himself with incredulity, for Mussolini's list of demands for Italian participation in a general war at Germany's side were excessive to the extreme. In his *Diary*, Ciano wrote, not without humour: 'We go over the list. It's enough to kill a bull—if a bull could read it.'[77] But the kicker was when Attolico, without Mussolini's knowledge or consent, dropped on Hitler the following bombshell: 'All material,' Attolico insisted, 'must be in Italy *before* the beginning of hostilities.' The letter read:

> ... this is the minimum required by the Italian Armed Forces to sustain a war lasting *twelve months* apart from what we have already:
>
> Coal for gas and metallurgy—6 million tons; Steel—2 million tons; Petroleum—7 million tons; Timber—1 million tons; Copper—150,000 tons; Sodium Nitrate—220,000 tons; Potassium Salts—70,000 tons; Colophony—25,000 tons; Rubber—22,000 tons; Methylbenzol—18,000 tons; Turpentine—6,000 tons; Lead—10,000 tons; Tin—7,000 tons; Nickel—5,000 tons; Molybdenum—600 tons; Tungsten—600 tons; Zirconium—20 tons; Titanium—400 tons....

> Apart from all the raw materials which are mentioned above, you are aware that all our war industries are situated in the Turin–Genoa–Milan–Savona quadrilateral and along the shores of the Tyrrhenian Sea ... The immediate dispatch of 150 90 mm. batteries and the appropriate ammunition is necessary for the protection of these industrial plants, the destruction of which could literally paralyze our war effort....
>
> It is my duty to tell you that unless I am certain of receiving these supplies, the sacrifices I should call on the Italian people to make ... could well be in vain and could compromise your cause along with my own.[78]

In response, Hitler swiftly prepared a letter that was conveyed to Mussolini by Ambassador Mackensen shortly after five o'clock that afternoon. The Führer was forced to admit that the Reich could fulfill Italy's colossal requirements in part only, and he listed a detailed breakdown of the specifics. Hitler made it absolutely clear that he considered the 'immediate delivery of all the material before the outbreak of the war ... as impossible ... purely for reasons of organization and for technical reasons'. Hitler was sympathetic to Italy's awkward situation and merely requested of the Duce that in the meantime he hoodwink the Allies by diverting their forces with deceptive, intimidating displays of Italian military strength. Meanwhile, Hitler reasoned, the decisive checkmate against the Anglo–French democracies had already been achieved by the recent German–Russian Non-Aggression Pact and, in any event, the superiority of the *Wehrmacht* would be more than sufficient. Hitler was determined to proceed with his plans for *Lebensraum* in the East even if the Western Powers should interfere:

> In these circumstances, Duce, I understand your position, and would only ask you to try to achieve the pinning down of Anglo–French forces by active propaganda and suitable military demonstrations such as you have already proposed to me. As neither France nor Britain can achieve any decisive successes in the West, and as Germany, as a result of the Agreement with Russia, will have all her forces free in the East after the defeat of Poland, and as air supremacy is undoubtedly on our side, I do not shrink from solving the Eastern question even at the risk of complications in the West.[79]

At 6:42 p.m., Mussolini's latest message to Hitler was telephoned in by Ciano 'for immediate delivery to the Führer'. Mussolini began by redressing Attolico's 'mistake'. He hastily explained that with the exception of the 90-mm anti-aircraft batteries all the items he had insisted upon were to be provided over the course of a full year, not prior to the outbreak of war. Next, Mussolini advised that Italy's armaments had been substantially depleted on account of her involvement in the Ethiopian and Spanish conflicts. Consequently, wrote Mussolini, Italy lacked the means at present to adequately contribute in a general war against the Western democracies. But he assured Hitler that he would do his utmost to pin down Anglo–French forces in order to alleviate the burden on the Reich. Meanwhile, Italy would continue to speedily rearm until the day she could take up arms alongside Germany:

> I believe that the misunderstanding into which Attolico involuntarily fell was cleared up immediately, in accordance with my instructions. That which I asked of you, except for the anti-aircraft batteries, was to be delivered in the course of twelve months. But even though the misunderstanding has been cleared up, it is evident that it is impossible for you to assist me materially in filling the large gaps which the wars in Ethiopia and Spain have made in Italian armaments.
>
> I will therefore adopt the attitude which you advise, at least during the initial phase of the conflict, thereby immobilizing the maximum Franco–British forces, as is already happening, while I shall speed up military preparations to the utmost possible extent.

The Duce knew perfectly well that after all his bombastic rhetoric, after all his grandstanding and theatrical bellicosity, he was now coming across to his Axis ally not as an iron man but as a fair-weather friend; or even worse, as a peacemonger. In the penultimate paragraph of his letter, Mussolini's discomfiture is obvious. And in conclusion, the Duce made it known that he still preferred a political solution to war:

> I leave you to imagine my state of mind in finding myself compelled by forces beyond my control not to afford you real solidarity at the moment of action.
>
> And it is also for this reason that I venture to insist anew, and not at all from considerations of a pacifist character foreign to my nature, but by reason of the interests of our two peoples and our two regimes, on the opportunity for a political solution, which I regard as still possible and such a one as will give full moral and material satisfaction to Germany.[80]

In the evening, Hitler drafted yet another communication to Mussolini. The message was transmitted by telegram on 27 August at precisely 12:10 a.m. and delivered to Mussolini by Ambassador Mackensen at nine o'clock that morning. To Hitler, it was evident that the Italians had left him holding the bag and that he would have to prosecute the war independently. Mussolini's defection must have irked him but there was no blame or disapprobation. Instead, Hitler empathized with the Duce's position and his decision to stay out of the conflict. However, Hitler did ask Mussolini, if it all possible, to immobilize Anglo–French forces with propaganda and aggressive military demonstrations:

> I have received your communication on your final attitude. I respect the reasons and motives which led you to take this decision. In certain circumstances it can nevertheless work out well. In my opinion, however, the prerequisite is that, at least until the outbreak of the struggle, the world should have no idea of the attitude Italy intends to adopt. I therefore cordially request you to support my struggle psychologically with your press or by other means. I would also ask you, Duce, if you possibly can, by demonstrative military measures, at least to compel Britain and France to tie down certain of their forces, or at all events to leave them in uncertainty.[81]

Mussolini's reply to Hitler was telephoned in at half-past four that afternoon. He promised the Führer that the Allies would not find out about Italian non-intervention until after hostilities had begun. Moreover, in a counterfeit exhibition of Italian strength, multiple divisions had been assembled along the Italo–French frontier. Such a ruse would keep the Allies in the dark about Italian intentions and leave them facing a menacing concentration of forces equivalent to their own:

> The world does not and will not know before the outbreak of hostilities what the attitude of Italy is, and will learn instead that Italy has concentrated her forces towards the frontiers of the great democracies. On the French frontiers I have actually concentrated seventeen divisions, plus twenty-seven *Alpini* battalions, plus the frontier guards. Two new divisions are proceeding to Libya—a weak point in our strategic dispositions—and these will bring up the number of metropolitan divisions to six, plus four of Libyan Arabs. These measures are more than a demonstration; they will leave the French and British in a state of uncertainty, and will confront them with a disposition of forces at least equal to theirs.

Meanwhile, every measure available to the Fascist regime would be used to reinforce to the Western Powers the indivisible bond between the Axis nations: 'All that can be done from the psychological point of view to underline Italian–German solidarity will be intensified by press, radio, cinema, and through propaganda.' Mussolini also told Hitler that he was ready to make available to the Reich an ample supply of Italian labourers: 'I am prepared to send you the greatest possible number of workers for your industries and agriculture compatible with my present and prospective mobilization measures.' Lastly, Mussolini emphasized his wish 'to keep in closest contact ... in order to coordinate the action of our two countries'.[82] With this final message by the Duce, the flurry of communications between the Axis dictators ceased for the time being.

During the last few days of peace, Ciano's *Diary* records Mussolini's mercurial state of mind, which oscillated from the fervent desire to join the war at the side of the Germans to recognizing that Italian non-participation was the only realistic option at this point: 'The Duce is now quite calm, as he always is after he has made a decision. He does not want to utter the word "neutrality", but it is this frame of mind that he has definitely reached. He even begins to hope that the struggle will be hard, long, and bloody for others, for he sees in this a possibility of great advantage for us.'[83] In other words, Britain, France, and Germany would wear themselves out, leaving Italy strong and untouched by the ravages of war. Ciano also noted that Mussolini was put off by Hitler's aversion to a political solution of the Danzig affair: 'Hitler is acting in this fashion for fear that intervention on the part of the Duce will settle the crisis at the last moment, as was done last year at Munich. This would have the effect of raising his [Mussolini's] prestige, of which Hitler is jealous.'[84] But on 29 August, Mussolini was agitated: 'The Duce is restless. He would like to do something. Certain articles in the English Press, which speak of the necessity of Italian neutrality have had a bad effect on him. Meanwhile, he sets down a series of military and civilian measures of a warlike nature, which, in my opinion, need not be taken at this time.'[85] And on 30 August, Mussolini was certain that the German attack on Poland was imminent:

> The Duce is convinced 'that the invasion will take place tomorrow'. Naturally, the idea of a neutrality imposed on us weighs more and more upon him. Not being able to wage war, he makes all the necessary preparations so that in case of a peaceful solution he may be able to say that he would have waged it. Calls to arms, blackouts, requisitions, close of cafés and amusement places.... All this carries with it two grave dangers: one of an external character, since it would cause London and Paris to believe that we are preparing to attack, and hence induce them to take the initiative in moving against us; the other of a more internal character, because it will alarm the population, which is more and more openly anti-German and opposed to war.[86]

On the last day of peace, Ciano made two eleventh-hour attempts to avert a general war. With Mussolini's approval, Ciano telephoned Halifax from the Palazzo Venezia to inform him 'that the Duce can intervene with Hitler only if he brings a fat prize: Danzig. Empty-handed he can do nothing.' However, by this time—as evidenced by Hitler's war council of 23 May—it was not the recovery of Danzig that mattered but the acquisition of *Lebensraum* in the East. In any event, Halifax later replied that the Italian offer concerning Danzig 'cannot be adopted'.[87]

Ciano called on Mussolini once more, who proposed 'as a last resort' a conference to be held on 5 September in order to review those articles of the Versailles Treaty 'which disturb European life'. Ciano was strongly in favour of the proposal and Halifax undertook to bring it to Chamberlain's attention. But no further reply from the British was received that day, and at 8:20 p.m. word was received from the telephone central office 'that London has cut off its communications with Italy'.[88]

Concerned that his aggressive posturing over the past few days might be misinterpreted by the Allies and result in an attack on Italy, Mussolini instructed Ciano (contrary to his emphatic assurance to Hitler of 27 August) to advise Ambassador Loraine that in the event of war between Germany and the Anglo–French democracies, Italy would remain inactive.

On 1 September, at dawn, Hitler's armies attacked Poland in full force from the north, south, and west, advancing relentlessly towards Warsaw. Mussolini had for the present decided to remain 'non-belligerent' and as such his nerves were steady. Ciano observed: 'The Duce is calm. He has already decided not to intervene, and the struggle which has agitated his spirit during these last weeks has ceased.'[89] Nevertheless, Mussolini, not wishing to appear as a back-slider to either the German or Italian people, contacted Attolico by telephone to ask that Hitler provide him with a telegram formally discharging him from his military obligations. Hitler, satisfied that his great armies could speedily overwhelm Poland and keep the Allies at bay independent of Italian assistance, sent a short reply granting his Axis partner's request:

> I thank you most cordially for the diplomatic and political support which you have been giving recently to Germany and her just cause. I am convinced that we can carry out the task imposed upon us with the military forces of Germany. I do not therefore expect to need Italy's military support in these circumstances. I also thank you, Duce, for everything which you will do in future for the common cause of Fascism and National Socialism.[90]

Another communication was sent to the Italians at 12:45 p.m. Hitler truculently asserted that since the Poles had spurned his offers and had taken to arms, he would treat them in the same language: 'I have now decided to answer force with force.' Hitler concluded:

> I thank you, Duce, for all your efforts. I thank you in particular also for your offers of mediation. But from the start I was skeptical about these attempts, because the Polish Government, if they had had even the slightest intention of solving the matter amicably, could have done so at any time. But they refused.... For this reason, Duce, I did not want to expose you to the danger of assuming the role of mediator which, in view of the Polish Government's intransigent attitude, would in all probability have been in vain.[91]

Although Mussolini perceived well enough that Hitler would be indisposed to third-party intervention at this stage, even from his Axis ally, the prospect of a diplomatic solution still seemed to be worthwhile. The Duce therefore once again proposed a conference to save the peace, and at 10 a.m. on 2 September, Attolico delivered to State Secretary Ernst Weizsäcker the subsequent urgent message:

> For purposes of information, Italy wishes to make known, naturally leaving any decision to the Führer, that she still has the possibility of getting France, Britain, and Poland to agree to a conference on the following bases:
>
> 1. An armistice, which leaves the armies *where* they now are.
> 2. Convening of the conference within two or three days.
> 3. Settlement of the Polish–German dispute which, as matters stand today, would certainly be favourable to Germany.
>
> The idea, which originally emanated from the Duce, is now supported particularly by France.
>
> Danzig is already German, and Germany has already in her hands pledges which guarantee her the greater part of her claims. Moreover Germany has already had her 'moral satisfaction'. If she accepted the proposal for a conference she would achieve all her aims and at the same time avoid a war, which even now looks like becoming general and of extremely long duration.
>
> The Duce does not want to insist, but it is of the greatest moment to him that the above should be immediately brought to the notice of Herr von Ribbentrop and the Führer.[92]

Ribbentrop felt that the British and French notes threatening war if German forces were not recalled from Poland precluded the possibility of a peace conference as proposed by Mussolini. Nevertheless, Hitler did 'not reject the proposal absolutely'. After first summoning Ambassadors Coulondre and Loraine, at 2 p.m. Ciano personally telephoned Bonnet and Halifax to advise them of the recent Italian initiative. In lively tones Bonnet expressed his gratitude to Ciano for all he had done to preserve the peace. Halifax, however, advised Ciano that unless the Germans vacated Polish territory, the British Government would most likely reject Mussolini's proposal. Still, he promised to convey the Italian offer to the British Cabinet and notify Ciano of its verdict. Halifax returned Ciano's call at 7 p.m. to advise that the British Government would agree to a conference only if Hitler withdrew his armies to German soil. This Hitler had no intention of doing under any circumstances, and there the matter died.

It was clear to Mussolini and Ciano that at this point there was nothing further to be done on their part. Diplomacy had failed. Ciano's final step was to contact Berlin to regretfully state that unless the German Government advised them otherwise, the Italians would 'let the conversations lapse'.[93] Ribbentrop received Attolico at the Reich Chancellery at 8:50 p.m. where the latter told him 'that the British were not prepared to enter into negotiations on the basis of the Italian proposal of mediation. The British demanded, before starting negotiations, the immediate withdrawal of all German troops from the occupied Polish areas and Danzig.' To this, the arrogant Ribbentrop did not even deign to reply.[94] Ciano ruefully wrote: 'The last note of hope has died.' He described Mussolini's sentiments and those of the Italian masses, which were not at all in concert: 'The Duce is convinced of the necessity of remaining neutral, but he is not at all happy. Whenever he can he reverts to the possibility of action. The Italian people, however, are happy about the decisions taken.'[95]

On 3 September, the hammer fell. England declared war on Germany at 11:15 a.m. Chamberlain solemnly addressed the House of Commons:

> … we decided to send to our Ambassador in Berlin [Henderson] instructions which he was to hand at nine o'clock this morning to the German Foreign Secretary [Ribbentrop] and which read as follows:
>
> 'Sir … I have accordingly the honour to inform you that, unless not later than 11 a.m., British Summer Time, today 3rd September, satisfactory assurances to the above effect have been given by the German Government and have reached His Majesty's Government in London, a state of war will exist between the two countries as from that hour.'
>
> That was the final Note. No such undertaking was received by the time stipulated, and, consequently, this country is at war with Germany.[96]

France followed suit in the late afternoon. Prime Minister Édouard Daladier gravely proclaimed to the men and women of France:

> The responsibility for the blood that is being shed falls entirely upon the Hitler Government. The fate of peace was in Hitler's hands. He chose war. France and England have made countless efforts to safeguard peace. This very morning they made a further urgent intervention in Berlin in order to address to the German Government a last appeal to reason and request it to stop hostilities and to open peaceful negotiations. Germany met us with a refusal.... In rising against the most frightful of tyrannies, in honouring our word, we fight to defend our soil, our homes, our liberties.[97]

But in spite of the Western Powers' firm resolve, Ciano accurately perceived that there was precious little they could do to aid Poland militarily before she was completely overrun by the *Wehrmacht*: 'In what way can France and England bring help to Poland?' Mussolini believed that once Poland was liquidated, the Allies would make peace 'after a short struggle'. Ciano was certain, however, that the conflict would be 'long, uncertain, and relentless'. British intervention guaranteed it. There could be only one of two outcomes to the war: 'Hitler's elimination or the defeat of Britain.'[98]

At 8:51 p.m., Hitler sent a final message to Mussolini before setting off for the Eastern Front aboard his *Sonderzug* (special train). He thanked Mussolini for his latest offer to mediate among the major powers but explained that he had not accepted because of the attitude of the British, who were 'determined from the outset to let it come to war in any case'. He anticipated that the Polish Army would 'collapse in a very short time' and he described the struggle in which he found himself as one 'of life and death'. Nevertheless, his faith in success was 'as firm as a rock'. Then came a subtle warning in which Hitler asserted that the destinies of their two nations were intertwined: 'If National Socialist Germany were destroyed by the Western democracies, Fascist Italy would also face a hard future. I personally was always aware that the future of our two regimes were bound up, and I know that you, Duce, are of exactly the same opinion.' Hitler explained his strategy on the Western Front: 'In the West I shall remain on the defensive. France can shed her blood there first.' He ended the letter with an expression of gratitude: 'Please accept once more my thanks, Duce, for all the support you have given me in the past, and which I ask you not to refuse me in future either.'[99] This communication was brought to Mussolini by Mackensen at 9:30 a.m. on 4 September. Mussolini's feelings were, as usual, mixed. Ciano observed:

> The Duce expresses full solidarity with Germany, and this is what he really feels.... He is convinced that France does not want and cannot fight this war, that the French people are tired even before they begin to

> fight.... At times the Duce seems attracted to the idea of neutrality which would permit us to gather economic and military strength, so that we could intervene effectively at the proper moment. But immediately afterwards he abandons this idea. The idea of joining the Germans attracts him.

Ciano believed that it fell to him to do his utmost to dissuade Mussolini from joining the war, which for Italy would spell 'the ruin of the country, the ruin of Fascism, and the ruin of the Duce himself'.[100]

The idea that some easily acquired war booty might slip through his fingers galled Mussolini. The overwhelming potency of Hitler's *Wehrmacht* excited him but it also disconcerted him, for the Germans were brutal and unscrupulous. What if they should turn on him? Above all, the Duce was highly embarrassed at having to remain inactive while the Germans were engaged in successful operations. Neutrality was repugnant to him. As far as Mussolini was concerned, neutrality meant weakness and pacifism, which he scorned. For a long time, Mussolini had been trumpeting Italy's martial might, representing Italy as a Great Power on par with Britain, France, and Germany. The truth was something else altogether, and it was a bitter pill for the Duce to swallow.

2

Non-Belligerent, 1939–1940

In politics it is undeniable that I am more intelligent than Hitler. [1]

Mussolini to Ciano, 17 January 1940

England will be beaten. Inexorably beaten. This is the pure truth, that you should get into your head. [2]

Mussolini to Ciano, 7 March 1940

Italy cannot remain neutral *for the entire duration of the war without resigning from her role, without disqualifying herself, without reducing herself to the level of a Switzerland multiplied by ten.* [3]

Mussolini in a secret memorandum to King Emmanuel III, 31 March 1940

Until Fascist Italy entered the war in June 1940, Mussolini incessantly grumbled about being sidelined during a cataclysm that promised to eclipse the magnitude of even the Great War. The Italian masses, however, favoured non-intervention in the conflict, as evidenced by their positive reaction to the official announcement that Fascist Italy would not enter the war, and it was not long before the country began to reap the benefits of 'non-belligerence', as Mussolini termed it. In the opening days of the war Ciano recognized that Italy's neutral stance was 'beginning to bear fruit'. On 5 September, he observed that 'stock market quotations soar, the first orders to buy Italian industrial and financial stock come from France, boats resume their sailings at double the normal rates and are jam-packed'. As for Mussolini, he took 'an interest in all this, but not a great deal as yet'.[4]

Initially, Mussolini entertained the notion, however unlikely, that a rapid settlement between the Allies and Germany might yet be possible. Ciano noted on 6 September that Mussolini was calmer and that 'he still believes that the opportunity of entering the game as a mediator will shortly present itself. Thus he is glad of German successes in Poland, believing that they will shorten the conflict.'[5] Two days later, Mussolini learned that the Germans had reached Warsaw. This news exhilarated him, for he perceived that it might mean 'a rapid conclusion of the conflict'. But Ciano disagreed. He did not think that the British would be amenable to Hitler's 'proposals for agreement': 'I do not believe that Hitler can have the wisdom to be moderate in victory, and I believe even less that the English, now that they have taken up the sword, are disposed to sheath it to their dishonour.'[6]

On 14 September, Ciano replied to Lord Halifax's letter of 8 September to inform him that Mussolini was watching very closely the progress of the European conflict. Ciano promised that the Italian dictator would do all in his power to localize the war and put a halt to it once circumstances allowed, granting the European peoples a lengthy period of peace thereby:

> The Duce ... is following the development of the grave events which are disturbing Europe with that attention and in that spirit with which you are familiar. He, more than any other, sees with profound anxiety the possible consequences of this war in the social field, and recognizes in it a factor particularly favourable to a reawakening of all those forces which are destructive of European civilization....
>
> I consider it a fitting occasion to assure you that the Duce intends to do all he can, both now and in the future, not only to prevent any spread of the conflict, but also to limit it and bring it to an end as soon as those physical conditions exist which will enable the peoples of Europe ... to be assured of twenty years of peace.[7]

Next day Ciano recorded that Mussolini 'still believes it possible that the war ... can be stopped, a European conference called, and a collective-security pact concluded among the six great European Powers'. But once more, Ciano did not see eye to eye with the Duce. Ciano simply did not believe that a solution could be reached at the bargaining table, for Hitler was utterly incapable of restraint. On the contrary, Ciano predicted that England would prosecute the war to the bitter end: 'I anticipate a bitter, hard, long, very long conflict, which will end in victory for Great Britain.'[8]

On 17 September, the Red Army invaded Eastern Poland in accordance with the terms of the Nazi–Soviet Pact's 'Secret Additional Protocol'. German and Russian troops met at Brest Litovsk, site of the onerous peace treaty of March 1918 between Russia and the Central Powers. The Soviets captured Wilno (Vilnius) on 19 September, Lwów (Lviv) on 22 September, and Grodno on 24 September. Over 300,000 Polish combatants were taken prisoner, and in November, the Soviet Union annexed Eastern Poland, bringing over 13 million Poles under Soviet control. Commissar Molotov justified Soviet operations in Poland with a cynical explanation: 'The Polish State had disintegrated and no longer existed; therefore, all agreements concluded [by the U.S.S.R.] with Poland were void; third powers [i.e. Germany] might try to profit by the chaos which had arisen; the Soviet Government considered itself obligated to intervene to protect its Ukrainian and White Russian brothers and make it possible for these unfortunate people to work in peace.'[9]

Ciano diarized his own brief account of the episode: 'This evening the Russians entered Poland. On the pretext of avoiding disorders the Bolsheviks have crossed the frontiers. The Poles have put up some resistance, but what can they do at this hour?' And although the Anglo–French democracies were obliged to come to Poland's defence, the Duce did not believe that the Allies would declare war on the Soviet Union. Nor did Mussolini believe that Germany intended to invade Romania; rather, the Germans would be content 'to impose economic servitude on it'.[10]

Ernst Weizsäcker of the Foreign Office submitted to Ribbentrop the following memorandum on 23 September, advising that the Italians were continuing to advocate that the German Government extend a generous peace offer to the democratic powers:

> The Italian Ambassador [Attolico] called my attention today to the well-known recent article in [*Il*] *Popolo d'Italia*, which, although not written by Mussolini, is entirely in accordance with his views. It also presents the idea repeatedly brought forward here by Attolico that a peace effort should now still be made in order not to miss the political turning-point marked by the transition of the war from the East to the West. Attolico now spoke for the third time about ... our setting up a residual Poland.
>
> When I asked the Ambassador whether these ideas were really those of the Duce ... Attolico stated that the Duce and Ciano were somewhat wary after the various fruitless suggestions of the past weeks and did not wish to call forth any more refusals from us. It was clear, however, that time is pressing, that the French people were still receptive to peace proposals, and that the chance would be gone once the war really began in earnest in the West....
>
> It should also be added that Attolico recommends a generous offer even in case we could not count on a favourable response from the enemy governments. The psychological effect in France would in any case remain and continue to promote peace.

Weizsäcker ended his report by advising Ribbentrop that Attolico's recommendation, which was 'urged upon us so strongly by Italy, should not be disregarded'.[11]

Also that day, in Rome, Mussolini addressed members of the vaunted Tenth Legion. To his comrades from Bologna (and the European community), he pointed out that bloodshed between the major powers could still be averted at this incipient phase of the war by acknowledging the futility of attempting to restore Poland to her pre-September existence. Mussolini proclaimed: 'Europe is not yet actually at war. The masses of the armies have not yet clashed. The clash can be avoided by recognizing that it is a vain illusion to try to maintain or, worse still, to reconstitute positions which history and the natural dynamism of peoples have condemned.' Mussolini added a sharp jab against the Allies: 'It has been with wise intention not to enlarge the conflict that the governments of London and Paris have not done more to face the Russian *fait accompli*, but the consequence is that these governments have compromised their moral justification in taking action against the German *fait accompli*.'[12]

A week later, on 30 September, Ribbentrop contacted Ciano to propose a summit meeting between the Duce and the Führer. Alternatively, Ribbentrop suggested that Ciano travel to Berlin where Hitler would receive him. The Italians chose to accept the latter suggestion, and in view of their concerns over Hitler's secret dealings with the Soviets behind their backs, time was considered to be of the essence. Ciano accordingly departed for Berlin that evening at six o'clock, although he was uncertain of the Germans' agenda: 'I leave without any definite idea of what the Germans will propose to me, but I have the unshakable and deeply rooted determination to safeguard our freedom of action.' In any event, Ciano was determined to 'fight like a lion to preserve peace for the Italian people'.[13]

Next day Ciano had a brief conversation with Ribbentrop, who did not believe that the conflict between Germany and the Anglo–French democracies could be settled diplomatically. Resolution of the conflict, Ribbentrop hoped, 'would be entrusted to force'. After his preliminary talk with Ribbentrop, Ciano was received by the Führer that evening at the new Reich Chancellery. The German dictator was affable and afterwards Ciano took care to mention in his diplomatic papers that 'every time the Duce was mentioned [Hitler] took the occasion to repeat his expression of friendship and of personal sympathy for the Leader of Fascism'. Hitler opened the three-hour conversation with a long and extremely detailed statistical summary of German operations in Poland. Now that Hela had capitulated, Hitler asserted, the Polish campaign was 'definitely at an end'. On the Western Front, the efforts of the French had been utterly ineffectual. 'The French attacks,' Hitler scoffed, 'have been on a very small scale and have not had the effect of making even a single German outpost withdraw.' At sea, German submarines were successfully waging war, and in just several months, these warships would 'be so numerous as to hinder Anglo–French shipping effectively'. The Luftwaffe's superiority, Hitler averred, was 'evident', for both the number and quality of the Allied air forces were inferior to those of Germany and therefore did not 'represent a serious obstacle to mastery of the air'. An assault against France could be carried out straightaway; the Maginot Line was not impenetrable, and Hitler was confident that it could be bypassed.

In spite of the dissolution of Poland and the conclusion of the German–Soviet Treaty of Friendship, Cooperation and Demarcation of 28 September, Hitler had not yet determined precisely what 'status' he intended to grant the Polish territories conquered by Germany. He stated that he was prepared to permit the existence of a certain type of Polish State that would ensure 'the peaceful development of Polish national life'. But this would be subject to the following prerequisites: all ethnic Germans would have to return home to the Reich; the resultant Polish State must not under any circumstances 'become a centre of propaganda and intrigue against Germany', nor must it in any way impede 'Soviet–German collaboration'. When Ciano inquired whether Hitler intended to grant the new Polish State some degree of independence, Hitler replied: 'This State must never be a military power and it must recognize German political and economic interests to be predominant and protected as such.' In any event, the formation of a Polish State would not be permitted until after peace terms with the Anglo–French democracies were finalized. Hitler speculated that the new Polish State would contain perhaps 8–10 million Poles; the rest would reside 'within the German frontiers' save for those in the Soviet zone of influence.

Hitler also informed Ciano that he would soon address the *Reichstag*. It would be his 'last warning' to the Western Powers before he took the offensive against them. The exact date for the speech was not yet established since Hitler first wished to visit Warsaw. If his terms were rejected, then the blame for the prolongation of the war would rest with the Allies. In that case, he would deal with them by force of arms. Meanwhile, the Duce could assist him greatly by establishing and leading 'a bloc of neutral states' in order to offset anti-German propaganda by the Western Powers. Hitler then gave Ciano an ominous warning: 'Italy's absence from the struggle and the defeat of Germany represent for Italy the end of her great imperial aspirations in the Mediterranean.'

Thereupon it was Ciano's turn to speak, and to Hitler he clarified the chief reasons for 'Italy's present line of conduct'. One point in particular

Ciano wished to make crystal clear: 'We have never made a declaration of neutrality but confined ourselves to stating that we would not take the initiative in military operations where Germany herself had not taken it ... and did not intend to do so.' He added that a substantial portion of French forces were concentrated on Italy's frontiers, both on the Continent and in Africa. Moreover, Italy was presently engaged in 'very intensive military preparations ... with a view to developments in the conflict, and to the possibility that she may have to reconsider her attitude to it'.

Hitler interjected that Italy's non-belligerent position had been, thus far, of greater value to the Reich than her 'immediate intervention' would have been. Nevertheless, when the time was ripe, Italy would have to act to secure her hegemony. Hitler declared: 'Italy ... must become the absolute master of the Mediterranean with predominant interests in all those countries of the Balkan peninsula directly in contact with the Mediterranean and Adriatic.'

The subsequent dialogue between Ciano and Ribbentrop yielded 'nothing of particular importance'. In spite of his extreme views, Ribbentrop also favoured a peaceful settlement with the Allies, but was highly skeptical as to the likelihood of such a prospect. Meanwhile, Ciano and Ribbentrop agreed to the following:

1. No action by either side would taken prior to the Führer's *Reichstag* speech, which was projected for either 5 or 6 October.

2. The two foreign ministers would consult with one another to discuss the Allies' initial reactions to the Führer's speech.

3. When circumstances permitted it, another meeting would be scheduled. Ribbentrop recommended that next time both Axis dictators should meet at the Brenner Pass.[14]

Later Ciano jotted down an insightful description of the more personal aspects of the meeting:

> I found Hitler very serene. At Salzburg the inner struggle of this man, decided upon action but not yet sure of his means and of his calculations, was apparent. Now, on the other hand, he seems absolutely sure of himself. The test he has met has given him confidence for future tests. He was wearing a green-grey jacket with his usual black trousers. His face bore traces of recent fatigue, but this was not reflected in the alertness of his mind. Hitler spoke for almost two hours and cited figure after figure without referring to a single note. With respect to Italy, his attitude was the same as before. What is past is past. From now on he looks to the future and wants to have us with him. But I must say that all our suggestions as to military collaboration have been discussed quite openly. What most impressed me is his confidence in ultimate victory. Either he is

> under hallucinations, or he really is a genius. He outlines plans of action and cites dates with an assurance that does not admit of contradiction. Will he be proved right? In my opinion the game will not be so simple as he believes.[15]

When Churchill—then first lord of the Admiralty—delivered his first wartime radio broadcast from London on 1 October, summarizing the first month of the European conflict, the Soviet Union was uppermost on his mind: 'Russia,' said Churchill, 'has pursued a cold policy of self-interest.' By entering onto Polish territory and forming a defensive line, Churchill asserted, the Russians had established a new Eastern Front 'which Nazi Germany does not dare assail'. The purpose, Churchill speculated, was to put a halt to 'Nazi designs upon the Baltic States and upon the Ukraine'. But he could not be absolutely certain because Russia's motives were shrouded in secrecy:

> I cannot forecast to you the action of Russia. It is a riddle wrapped in a mystery inside an enigma; but perhaps there is a key. That key is Russian national interest. It cannot be in accordance with the interest or safety of Russia that Germany should plant itself upon the shores of the Black Sea, or that it should overrun the Balkan States and subjugate the Slavonic peoples of Southeastern Europe. That would be contrary to the historic life interests of Russia.[16]

Having returned to Italy, Ciano ruminated upon the Italian people's feelings towards their militant Nordic neighbours: 'All the Italians in Germany heartily hate the Germans, but they are firmly convinced, without exception, that Hitler will win the war.'[17] On 3 October, however, Mussolini thought otherwise. On the basis of data provided by his military advisers, he believed that the British and French would not yield to Nazi aggression. Ciano observed that, like the Italian masses, Mussolini was in a decidedly anti-German mood himself: 'He is somewhat bitter about Hitler's sudden rise to fame. He would be greatly pleased if Hitler were slowed down, and, hoping this, predicts that it will come about.'[18]

On 6 October, Hitler addressed the *Reichstag* in one of his lengthiest speeches thus far. To his compliant deputies, the Führer first spoke of the Polish campaign, now successfully concluded, and of the grim fate of the Polish nation: 'By the capitulation of the fortresses of Warsaw and Modlin and the surrender of Hela, the Polish campaign has come to an end.... The outcome of the war was the annihilation of all Polish armies, followed by the dissolution of the Polish State.' With the Polish question having been disposed of, Hitler then made his plea for peace to the British:

> … I believe even today that there can only be real peace in Europe and throughout the world if Germany and England come to an understanding.…
>
> Why should this war in the West be fought? For restoration of Poland? Poland of the Versailles Treaty will never rise again. This is guaranteed by two of the largest States in the world.…
>
> Neither force of arms nor lapse of time will conquer Germany. There will never be another November 1918 in German history. It is infantile to hope for the disintegration of our people. Mr. Churchill may be convinced that Great Britain will win. I do not doubt for a single moment that Germany will be victorious.[19]

Ciano diarized Mussolini's impressions of the Führer's *Reichstag* address: '… the Duce read Hitler's speech and commented on it very favourably. He judges it to be so useful and effective in arousing emotion as to bring about a change in the international situation. He indulges himself in such a strain of wishful thinking that in the evening he telephones me to say that to his way of thinking the war is now ended.' But Ciano did not agree with Mussolini's assessment. All Hitler had to offer, thought Ciano, were 'fair words' and he did not believe that Britain and France would 'fall into Hitler's trap'. In fact, Ciano was positively certain that the war would 'really start soon'.[20] And two days later, on 8 October, Ciano noted the British reaction to the Führer's peace speech: 'Only two voices were heard in England in favour of the conference proposed by Hitler: those of Lloyd George and Bernard Shaw.' Ciano dryly added: 'Which proves conclusively that the English consider Hitler's proposals absolutely unacceptable.'[21]

On 9 October, Mussolini was depressed, for he recognized that the war would continue yet he would perforce have to remain inactive:

> The Italians, after having heard my warlike propaganda for eighteen years, cannot understand how I can become the herald of peace, now that Europe is in flames. There is no other explanation except the military unpreparedness of the country, but even for this I am made responsible—me, mind you—who have always proclaimed the power of our armed forces.[22]

And not surprisingly Hitler's overtures—including a rather ambiguous proposal for an 'international security conference'—were not accepted by either the British or French Governments. On 10 October, Daladier made the following pronouncement over the radio: 'We have taken up arms against [German] aggression; we shall not lay them down until we have sure guarantees of security—a security which cannot be called in question every six months.' And two days later, Chamberlain delivered a solemn speech to the House of Commons. The scales had long since fallen from his eyes:

> The proposals in the German Chancellor's speech are vague and uncertain and contain no suggestion for righting the wrongs done to Czechoslovakia and to Poland.
>
> Even if Herr Hitler's proposals were more closely defined and contained suggestions to right these wrongs, it would still be necessary to ask by what practical means the German Government intend to convince the world that aggression will cease and that pledges will be kept. Past experience has shown that no reliance can be placed upon the promises of the present German Government. Accordingly, acts—not words alone—must be forthcoming before we, the British peoples, and France, our gallant and trusted ally, would be justified in ceasing to wage war to the utmost of our strength.[23]

Mussolini, once he had read the text of Chamberlain's speech—one which 'makes the hope of even the most obstinate pacifists sink'—recognized beyond a shadow of a doubt 'that every possibility for an understanding has now disappeared'.[24] The Duce now knew perfectly well that any hopes of Germany and the Western Powers coming to terms were purely illusory.

A fortnight later, Mussolini decided it was time to clean house, and on 31 October, he saw fit to discharge five senior officials—deemed to be overly pro-German—from their posts: Alberto Pariani, undersecretary of state for war; Giuseppe Valle, minister of aviation; Luigi Russo, chief of staff of the Fascist Militia; Achille Starace, party secretary; and Dino Alfieri, minister of people's culture.[25]

On the evening of 8 November, an assassination attempt was made on Hitler's life at the Bürgerbräukeller in Munich. The occasion was the sixteenth anniversary of the Beer Hall *Putsch*. On this date, it was customary for the Führer to address the *Alte Kämpfer*, early members of the National Socialist Party. A time-bomb had exploded, narrowly missing Hitler by thirteen minutes.* Ciano speculated on the incident:

* The culprit was Georg Elser, a thirty-six-year-old carpenter with Communist Party affiliations. Acting on his own initiative, Elser had planted an explosive device in a pillar next to the rostrum where Hitler would be speaking. The bomb had detonated at 9:20 p.m. But on this occasion the Führer had finished his speech early (at 9:07 p.m.) and instead of lingering to chat with old Party comrades, as was his usual practice, he had left shortly thereafter. The explosion had killed eight persons and wounded over sixty others, but Hitler and other high-ranking attendees had escaped unscathed. Elser was executed at Dachau on 9 April 1945, aged forty-two.

> Either it is a master plot on the part of the police, with the overdone purpose of creating anti-British sentiment in the German people who are quite indifferent, or, if the attempted murder is real, it is a family brawl of people belonging to the inner circle of the Nazi Party; perhaps a carry-over of what took place on the thirtieth of June [1934] which cannot have been forgotten in Munich.

Mussolini drafted a congratulatory telegram expressing his relief that the Führer had been unharmed, but he had some inner difficulty doing so, for 'no Italian feels any great joy over the fact that Hitler had escaped death—least of all the Duce'.[26]

'Rumours about an imminent German invasion of Belgium and Holland,' Ciano wrote in his *Diary* on 11 November, have 'now been coming from too many quarters not to be given serious consideration.' If this alarming news was true, however, Berlin had made no mention of it to him. On the contrary, Ciano reflected, the Führer and Ribbentrop had 'always specifically excluded an attack on the neutrals for moral and technical reasons'. But taking into account the Germans' utter lack of scruple, as proven time and again—in Austria, Czechoslovakia, and Poland—Ciano had to concede 'that anything is possible'. But the Duce was unconvinced: 'Mussolini does not believe that such an attack will be made, but he admits that, if it did take place, Germany's actions would be totally discredited and that in Italy there would be such a wave of hatred for Germany as to make anybody think twice.'[27]

Nine days later, it came to Mussolini's attention that 'a Bohemian crisis' might sabotage the Germans' Western campaign, and he directed his representative in Prague to fan the flames of Czech discontent in an attempt to engineer a German–Soviet rift:

> News from Prague leads us to believe that the situation is more difficult than is admitted in official reports. The Duce is satisfied especially because he thinks that a Bohemian crisis will retard or, perhaps, torpedo the projected offensive on the Western Front. For Mussolini, the idea of Hitler's waging war, and, worse still, winning it, is altogether unbearable. He gives instructions to our Consul at Prague to advise the Bohemians to side with the Communists. This will make German repression harder and will accentuate the causes for disagreement between Moscow and Berlin.[28]

In another secret talk with his senior generals on 23 November, Hitler stated that in regard to Italy, it was solely Mussolini and the Fascists—and not the Italian sovereign or his royal court—who were in favour of waging war against the Allies with Germany:

> Much depends on Italy, and above all on Mussolini, whose death can alter everything. Italy has great goals for the consolidation of her empire. Fascism and the Duce personally are exclusively the proponents of this idea. The Court is opposed to it. As long as the Duce lives, so long can it be calculated that Italy will seize every opportunity to reach her imperialistic goals. However, it is too much to ask of Italy that she should join in the battle before Germany has seized the offensive in the West ... Italy will not attack until Germany has taken the offensive against France.[29]

The world's attention was momentarily shifted to Northeastern Europe, when on 30 November the U.S.S.R. invaded Finland, beginning the 105-day Winter War. The pretext was that Leningrad, just 20 miles from the Finnish frontier, was vulnerable; thus, the Soviet Government demanded the cession of specific tracts of Finnish borderland. Naturally the Finns refused, and in response, some 450,000 Red Army troops traversed the Finnish frontier and the Soviet Air Force bombed Helsinki. A fortnight later, on 14 December, the League of Nations expelled the Soviet Union from its ranks. The reaction of the Italian population to the grossly unequal conflict was entirely pro-Finnish, and the Germans' alliance with the Soviets caused further Italo–German friction. The Italians' displeasure was exhibited by widespread anti-Russian demonstrations: 'The Italian people are growing ever more anti-German. Even their violent anti-Bolshevik demonstrations can be interpreted as anti-German manifestations. The fate of the Finns would be of much less concern to the Italians if the Russians were not from all practical points of view the allies of Germany.'[30]

On 7–8 December, the Fascist Grand Council held its first wartime session during which the councillors issued an order of the day confirming Italy's war policy of 'non-belligerency'.[31] Moreover, the council 'requested the Italian Foreign Minister to make an early statement on the international situation to the Chamber of Corporations'.[32] Eight days later, in an atmosphere of ever-increasing anti-German sentiment amongst the Italian masses, Ciano addressed the Chamber of Corporations. He began by recapitulating European history during the interwar period, making reference to the inequity of the Versailles Treaty and the ineffectuality of the League of Nations. The Duce, Ciano proclaimed, had long opposed the 'dangerous aberrations of reparations, military guarantees, and collective security'.[33] In 1937, Italy—joining Germany, Japan, and Spain—had acceded to the Anti-Comintern Pact. Its purpose was to counteract the Third International (1919–1943). This was in conformity with Fascist ideology, for Mussolini had been the first to combat Bolshevism.

Ciano then accused the Germans of perfidy in their recent dealings with Italy. He revealed to the chamber that at Milan on 6–7 May, Italy and Germany had been 'in full agreement as to the need for every effort to preserve peace in Europe for a long period, if only to assure to both countries the time necessary for finishing their construction programs and completing their armaments'. He added: 'The length of this period was estimated by us as three years, by the Germans as four or five.'[34]

Both parties had resolved that meanwhile neither the Italian nor the German Governments would undertake any action intended to provoke conflict. These were the bases on which the Pact of Steel had been concluded. In the spring, Danzig had become an issue of contention between the Germans and Poles, and at Salzburg and Berchtesgaden in mid-August, the Führer and Ribbentrop had informed him that they no longer sought a pacific solution but were now intent on war. Ciano acknowledged that the Führer had assured him of his intention to localize the war but that he (Ciano) had advised the Germans that the Italian Government preferred a diplomatic settlement of the Polish affair.

Ciano ended his disquisition by championing Italy's non-participatory stance: 'It is universally recognized that it is the realistic attitude of Italy which has hitherto prevented the extension of the war; and it is towards our country that the eyes of all states are turning, who wish to safeguard, together with their own interests, the peace of the world.' Italy would moreover look out for her own welfare and protect her assets: 'Fascist Italy will continue to follow events with vigilant interest, ready, if this is possible, once more to make her contribution towards the pacification of the world, but also firmly resolved inflexibly to safeguard her interests, her land, sea, and air communications, her prestige, and her future as a Great Power.'[35]

Very self-satisfied, Ciano reflected on the positive reception to his address by the Chamber of Corporations' *consiglieri nazionali* (national councillors): 'I spoke to the Chamber. My speech had great success, even if everybody did not discern the subtle anti-German poison which permeated it. The first impression seemed merely anti-Bolshevik, but in substance it was anti-German. They tell me that the German Ambassador [Mackensen] listened to it in silence, and at times was not able to conceal his disappointment. Good.'[36]

The speech's carefully camouflaged anti-German underpinnings were certainly not lost on the Reich Government, and Ribbentrop in particular was furious. He took the view that Ciano's disclosure of the Axis pledge to abstain from war—the Italians for three years, the Germans for four to five years—undermined the Axis cause. The Allies, Ribbentrop feared, might conclude that the grace period of several years meant Germany and Italy were not the dynamos they painted themselves to be. In a memorandum dated 21 December concerning his conversation with Massimo

Magistrati, the Italian *chargé d'affaires*, Weizsäcker documented the following:

> During his visit today on routine business, the Italian *Chargé d'Affaires* once more reverted to Ciano's speech and the impression it made in Germany. He wanted to make it clear to me at some length in what a pro-German manner Ciano had spoken and how excellent the speech had been. I let Magistrati talk himself out and then referred him to the French, British, and neutral expressions of opinion, which had interpreted Ciano's speech somewhat differently.[37]

But by the month's end, Ribbentrop's anger had dissipated. In a conversation with Ambassador Attolico on 28 December, he explained that after perusing the text of Ciano's address 'he had merely felt some apprehension that a few points might be exploited by France and by England for their purposes'. The two parts which he had found objectionable were 'the passages on the Berchtesgaden negotiations preceding the outbreak of the war ... from which England and France deduced proof of Germany's war guilt' and 'the mention of the target periods, three years for Italy and five for Germany, which the two countries needed to be prepared for war'. However, Ribbentrop laid the subject to rest once and for all by stating 'that he did not attach any further importance to the matter'.[38]

On 31 December, Ciano observed, to his dismay, that Mussolini was 'still suffering from the usual recurrent waves of pro-Germanism'. But Ciano was as anti-war as ever. That day, in a pensive mood, Ciano contemplated the prospect of waging war with Germany and against her. He was staunchly opposed to the former, and as for the latter, he was only in favour if it was warranted: 'The war at the side of Germany must not be undertaken and will never be undertaken. It would be a crime and the height of folly! As for war against Germany, I do not for the moment see any reason for it. In any case, if necessary I acquiesce in war against Germany but not in her company.' The Duce felt otherwise, however: 'Mussolini's point of view is exactly the opposite. He would never have war against Germany, and, when we are ready, he would fight on the side of Germany against the democracies ...' But in Ciano's opinion, the British and French at least were honourable; they were 'the only countries with which one can deal seriously and honestly'.[39]

But Mussolini's 'pro-Germanism' did not last, and early in the new year his feelings towards Germany swung to the opposite end of the pendulum. On 3 January 1940, he sent to Hitler a cautionary and critical letter concerning Germany's non-aggression pact with Soviet Russia which, in Italy, had been very ill-received. Mussolini's letter was unsparing in its candour and his antipathy towards the recent *rapprochement* between the Nazi and Soviet Governments was intense:

> No one knows better than I, who have now had forty years of political experience, that politics—even revolutionary politics—has its tactical exigencies. I recognized the Soviets in 1924; in 1934 I concluded with them a treaty of commerce and friendship. So I realize that since von Ribbentrop's efforts towards non-intervention by the French and the British were not realized, you have avoided a second front. Without striking a blow, Russia has, in Poland and the Baltic, profited from the war.
>
> But I, a born revolutionist who has not modified his way of thinking, tell you that you cannot permanently sacrifice the principles of your [National Socialist] Revolution to the tactical exigencies of a certain political moment. I feel that you cannot abandon the anti-Semitic and anti-Bolshevist banner which you have been flying for twenty years and for which so many of your comrades have died; you cannot renounce your gospel, in which the German people have blindly believed. It is my definite duty to add that a further step in your relations with Moscow would have catastrophic repercussions in Italy, where the anti-Bolshevik unanimity, especially among the Fascist masses, is absolute, solid as rock, and indivisible.

The Duce asserted that German living space was to be found solely in Russia due to the latter's vast tracts of thinly populated land. Furthermore, with her heterogeneous composition of Slavic and Oriental peoples, Russia was not truly European, but foreign. Thus the Reich's fundamental purpose was to protect civilized Europe from the barbaric Asiatic hordes:

> The solution of your *Lebensraum* problem is in Russia and nowhere else; in Russia, which has the immense area of twenty-one million square kilometres and nine inhabitants per square kilometre. Russia is alien to Europe. In spite of her extent and her population, Russia is not a power but a weakness. The mass of her population is Slavic and Asiatic.... Germany's task is this: to defend Europe from Asia.

Mussolini warned that the unnatural alliance between Germany and the hated Bolsheviks had alienated Fascists and, in all likelihood, many otherwise committed National Socialists as well. The eradication of the Bolshevist creed was a fundamental aim for both the Fascist and National Socialist movements:

> Until four months ago Russia was world enemy number one; she cannot have become, and is not, friend number one. This has profoundly

> disturbed the Fascists in Italy and perhaps also many National Socialists in Germany. The day when we shall have demolished Bolshevism we shall have kept faith with our two Revolutions.

Mussolini's harsh and uncompromising condemnation of recent German foreign policy could not have failed to make a strong impression on Hitler. But so as not to leave the Führer in any doubt of where he ultimately stood, the Duce lastly made reference to:

1. Italy's 'accelerating' military preparations;
2. The benefits to Germany of Italian non-belligerence ('... intervention [by Italy] in the war against Poland would have been entirely superfluous'); and
3. Italy's loyalty to the Axis per the Pact of Steel ('... the attitude of Italy is within, not outside, the framework of the Pact of Alliance').[40]

Johann von Plessen, an official of the German Embassy in Italy, shrewdly assessed the future course of Italian action in an insightful memorandum dated 3 January:

> 1. The Axis is not popular with the Italian people; its fate depends on Mussolini. Mussolini is guided in his policy by very sober considerations, which are concerned only with Italy's advantage.
>
> 2. Mussolini is convinced that there is at present no other way for Italy than to go together with Germany.
>
> 3. There is no need to fear that Mussolini will join the ranks of our enemies.
>
> 4. The question whether Mussolini intends to wage war actively on our side cannot be answered with a simple 'yes' or 'no'. Prior to the outbreak of war, Mussolini left us not the least in doubt about what he could and would do. His conduct was unequivocally honest. The alliance with us was concluded on the assumption that nothing should happen during the next 3 or 4 years. In spite of different opinions which one sometimes hears, I think Mussolini never intended at the outbreak of the war to take part in it at once. He is unhappy, however, that he was also unable to do so because of Italy's inadequate military preparations. At present he is doing all he can to be armed by next spring so that he can make his decisions freely. He wants to be able to participate in the spring if this appears to him to be the correct thing. It is impossible to foresee whether it will seem correct to him. If at the given time Mussolini thinks he can achieve his aims by peaceful means he will not take military measures.[41]

A fortnight later, Ciano noted that Mussolini's anti-German sentiments had not yet abated: 'Mussolini, in his present seesawing of feelings, is today somewhat hostile to the Germans. He says, "They should allow themselves to be guided by me if they do not want to pull unpardonable boners. In politics it is undeniable that I am more intelligent than Hitler."' Ciano added with a touch of humour: 'I must say that the Chancellor of the Reich has not given proofs of sharing this opinion.'[42] Next day Ciano spoke to Ambassador Loraine, who confided in Ciano 'his concern over the attitude of the Duce, whom he feels and knows to be fundamentally hostile'. Loraine cautioned: 'The Duce must know that the Britain of today is no longer the Britain of a year ago. She is now strong and prepared for anything.' Ciano sombrely reflected that it was 'hard for me to argue with him because I am of the same opinion and he [Loraine] knows it'.[43]

On 23 January, Mussolini addressed the *Consiglio dei Ministri* (Council of Ministers). He declared that although Italy's armed forces were insufficiently strong, 'even today we could undertake and sustain a ... parallel war ...' Such a war—as Mussolini saw it—would be analogous to the one conducted by the Germans, but with the purpose of fulfilling distinctly Italian aims.[44] Ciano, who was present during the session, noted:

> The Duce takes advantage of this occasion to speak of the international situation. All of his shafts are aimed against France and England, who 'can no longer win the war'. He repeats that we cannot indefinitely remain neutral. To preserve neutrality until the end of the war would make us play second fiddle among the European Powers. He foresees that our military possibilities will enable us to make a move during the second half of 1940, or perhaps during the early part of 1941. Every allusion to action is pointed towards the Allies. He speaks of terror bombings over France, of the control of the Mediterranean. His declaration greatly impressed the ministers...[45]

The Duce apparently felt that the Italian people were poor material to work with, and on 29 February, he disparaged them for their docility: 'The Italian race is a race of sheep. Eighteen years [of Fascism] are not enough to change them. It takes a hundred and eighty, and maybe a hundred and eighty centuries.'[46] Nine days later, Mussolini once more lambasted his countrymen for their weak, unsoldierly qualities: 'We must keep them disciplined and in uniform from morning till night. Beat them and beat them and beat them.' Ciano noted that Mussolini was 'bitter towards the people' and that the Duce felt it was beneficial for the Italians 'to be put to tests that cause them to shake off their century-old mental laziness'.[47]

On 25 February, Undersecretary of State Sumner Welles, travelling on a peace mission as President Roosevelt's special emissary, arrived in Rome. At ten o'clock the following morning, he called on Ciano at the Palazzo Chigi. On this occasion, the Italian foreign minister spoke of German–Italian relations 'at considerable length' and his attitude was strongly anti-German. Ciano nursed a 'hearty dislike' for Ribbentrop expressly, and he declared: 'If Hitler wants anything—and God knows he always wants enough—Ribbentrop always goes him one better.' Ciano was also greatly put off by the Führer's repeated failure to apprise the Italian Government of German policy in advance and his 'complete disregard' for the Pact of Steel. A case in point was the conclusion of the German–Russian Pact of August 1939, which rankled deeply. The Germans, Ciano indignantly claimed, had nonchalantly referred to it as 'a *petit jeu*' [a little game], and he grumbled: 'Can you conceive of our being asked to regard a military alliance between Germany and Communist Russia as being merely "a *petit jeu*"?' 'Do you further realize,' Ciano added, 'that Hitler called me on the telephone only on 21 August last to announce the conclusion of this alliance to me, and that before I even had time to get Mussolini on the telephone to break the news to him, this very radio in my own office here was carrying the report already broadcast to the whole world?' Germany's Polish campaign did not sit well with Ciano either: 'And with regard to Poland, the clear-cut terms of our understanding with Germany provide that if Germany undertakes any military adventures, Italy must be first afforded the opportunity of consultation. We did everything we could to prevent the invasion of Poland, but we were never given any real chance to exert any influence upon Hitler to prevent it.' At one point, the Italian minister even went so far as to candidly declare to his interlocutor: 'No country would want to have Germany as a neighbour. We now have her as a neighbour, and we must do the best we can to get on with her.'[48] Hardly a ringing endorsement of the Axis alliance!

Afterwards, Ciano escorted Welles to the Palazzo Venezia for Welles' 5 p.m. appointment with Mussolini. After a brief three-minute wait, Welles and Ciano were admitted to the Duce's immense office, the imposing *Sala Mappamondo* (World Map Room). Mussolini genially welcomed Welles at the door and accompanied him to his desk. Later Welles recorded his personal impressions of the head of the Italian Government, which to him contrasted sharply with those from the newsreels:

> I was profoundly shocked by the Duce's appearance. In the countless times I had seen him in moving pictures and in photographs, and in the many descriptions I had read of him, he had always seemed to me as an active, quick-moving, exceedingly animated personality. The man I

> saw before me seemed fifteen years older than his actual age of fifty-eight. He was ponderous and static, rather than vital. He moved with an elephantine motion. Every step appeared an effort. He is very heavy for his height, and his face in repose falls into rolls of flesh. His close-clipped hair is snow white. During our long and rapid interchange of views, he kept his eyes shut a considerable part of the time, opening them with his dynamic and oft-described wide-open stare only when he desired particularly to underline some remark. At his side was a large cup of tea which he sipped from time to time.
>
> Mussolini impressed me as a man labouring under some tremendous strain; physical unquestionably … but in my definite judgment, mental as well. One could almost sense a leaden oppression.[49]

Welles first presented to the Duce a personal letter from President Roosevelt dated 14 February. It was addressed to 'My dear Signor Mussolini'. Roosevelt had written:

> My old friend Mr. Sumner Welles, my Undersecretary of State, will give you this when he has the privilege of being received by you. You may be sure that whatever views you express to him will be transmitted by him solely to myself and to the Secretary of State. At this grave moment I deeply hope that this exchange of views between us may be of real value to Italy, to the United States, and to the future of the world.[50]

Welles next informed Mussolini that Roosevelt desired, if possible, to conclude an Italo–American trade agreement. The Duce was receptive to the proposal, particularly since the present war in Europe made 'commercial relations with other countries … more difficult'. Welles inquired if Mussolini would be willing to confer with the neutral nations 'in order to lay down the conditions for an economic peace'. Mussolini acknowledged that economic relations between the nations necessitated readjustment, but he pointed out: 'The order of things cannot be reversed … economic peace must follow, but cannot precede, political peace between the various States.'

Turning to the subject of the European conflict, Welles inquired of Mussolini if he saw 'any factor' that might make it possible for Europe's 'warring States' to come to terms. Mussolini answered that in Hitler's latest speech the Führer had spoken of 'two points of vital importance'. The first was Germany's 'right' to *Lebensraum* in Central Europe and the second was the return of Germany's former overseas colonies, of which she had been stripped at Versailles. As far as the Duce was concerned, the 'war aims' of the Western Powers were 'absurd' to the extreme:

> First and foremost, the re-establishment of an independent Austria, Austria being nothing more or less than an old province of the Reich. Czechoslovakia, too, in the form in which it had been invented by the democracies, represented an artificial structure intended to threaten Germany. As far as Poland was concerned, one must recognize that certain regions and cities are clearly German and must stay with Germany. The other part of Poland, on the other hand, can constitute a Polish national State, in a form to be subsequently defined. It is certain that, should it be wished to reconstruct Poland within its old frontiers, it would be necessary to make up one's mind to fight not only Germany but also Russia, who has occupied a very considerable and important part of Poland itself.

Welles asked the Duce if he thought whether 'a possible contact' between the warring nations was still feasible. 'It was not out of the question,' Mussolini answered, 'provided that the war remained in its present static state; but should battle be joined on a large scale on both sides the difficulties would certainly be insurmountable.' The Duce hastily added that if the Western Powers and Germany did manage to settle their differences, 'the Italian question would also be raised'. It galled Mussolini that the British dominated the Mediterranean and access therefrom (at Gibraltar and Suez): 'Italy is a prisoner in the Mediterranean and will be so until such time as it has free access to the [Atlantic and Indian] oceans.... There is no doubt that this state of imprisonment is becoming more and more awkward with the growth in Italy's stature and power.' He, the Duce, had thus far not brought up 'the Italian question' in order to avoid exacerbating the political tensions afflicting Europe. However, just because he had elected not to stir the waters just now, this did not mean that the issue was not an exigent one. Welles concluded by expressing his gratitude to Mussolini for his valuable input, and the Duce invited the American peacemaker to return to see him once more if, at the end of his travels, he had anything further to discuss.[51]

On 1 March, the British implemented a new war measure: 'The British Press announces that as of today German coal will be treated as an article of contraband, and, hence, seized.'[52] Mussolini was greatly antagonized by the coal blockade and the following day he deemed it necessary to transmit a 'harsh and threatening' message to the British Government protesting the new policy. The Duce personally 'dictated the concluding phrases of the note'.[53] On 5 March, 'The first ships were held up ...' and Ciano recorded on 6 March that Mussolini was infuriated 'at this display of [British] force more than by the practical consequences that might come'. Mussolini railed against the British in impotent rage: 'Within a short time the guns will loose off by themselves. It is not possible that of all people I should become the laughingstock of Europe. I have to stand for one humiliation after another. As soon as I am ready I shall make the English repent. My intervention in the war will bring about their defeat.'[54] Next day Mussolini, still in a foul mood, exasperatedly chastised Ciano: 'England will be beaten. Inexorably beaten. This is the pure truth, that you should get into your head.' Ciano's reaction was like that of a sulking schoolboy reprimanded by a stern teacher: 'During our seven years of daily contacts this is the *first* time he picks on me personally.'[55]

On 10 March, Ribbentrop arrived in Rome bearing a communication from Hitler, the rather belated reply to Mussolini's critical letter of 3 January. To the Italians, the Reich *Aussenminister* garrulously expounded on Hitler's ideas, the substance of which was that the Führer intended to deal with the Allies militarily and that Italy's rightful place was alongside Germany. The Duce listened attentively, and when Ribbentrop finished his spiel, he (Mussolini) undertook to give both Hitler's personal letter and Ribbentrop's supplemental input his utmost consideration, and assured Ribbentrop that he would advise him of his position the following afternoon. In closing, Mussolini asseverated 'that the place of Fascism is at the side of Nazism on the firing line'.[56] When the conversation resumed the next day at 5 p.m., Mussolini 'declared that, reserving his freedom to choose the date, he intends to intervene in the conflict and to fight a war parallel to that of Germany.... The principal reason for this is that he considers Italy imprisoned in the Mediterranean'. In turn, Ribbentrop suggested a conference between the Axis dictators in the near future at the Brenner Pass, to which Mussolini agreed at once. But Ciano was apprehensive, and he found Ribbentrop's proposal 'to be quite dangerous because of the immediate consequences it may have, and also because of its influence on the future. I shall try to talk it over with the Duce.'[57]

Wasting no time, just two days later Ribbentrop telephoned the Italians and requested to fix the date for the Brenner summit meeting for 18 March. Mussolini was infuriated at the Germans' presumptuous manner, and he raged: 'These Germans are unbearable; they don't give one time to breathe nor to think matters over.' But upon further reflection, Mussolini decided that under the circumstances it would be best for the meeting to be held immediately. Thus Ciano informed Ribbentrop that 18 March would, in fact, be satisfactory. Still, Ciano was sufficiently perceptive to discern Mussolini's anxiety: 'Until now he has lived under the illusion that a real war would not be waged. The prospect of an imminent clash in which he might remain an outsider disturbs him and, to use his words, humiliates him. He still hopes, but less than before, that he can influence Hitler and persuade him to desist from his intention to attack.'[58]

The Winter War between the Soviet Union and Finland concluded on 13 March after peace talks were initiated a fortnight earlier, on 29 February. Despite inflicting heavy losses upon the Red Army, whose performance was poor (and which convinced Hitler that his invasion against the U.S.S.R. in 1941 would be a success), the beleaguered Finns lost the war. Per the Moscow Peace Treaty, Finland was forced to relinquish portions of Karelia and Salla to the U.S.S.R., plus permit the establishment of a Soviet naval base on Finnish soil (on the Hanko Peninsula). The Finns were permitted to retain Petsamo (with the exception of the Rybachy Peninsula). Marshal Carl Mannerheim, commander-in-chief of the Finnish Defence Forces, issued an order of the day on 14 March to the soldiers of the Finnish Army in solemn recognition of their valiant sacrifices:

> Peace has been concluded between our country and the Soviet Union, an exacting peace which has ceded to Russia nearly every battlefield on which you have shed your blood on behalf of every thing we hold dear and sacred. You did not want war. You loved peace, work and progress; but you were forced into a struggle in which you have done great deeds, deeds that will shine for centuries in the pages of history.[59]

In Rome a second time on 16 March, Welles again paid Ciano a visit. Welles began by expressing his certainty that Ciano and Mussolini would do all in their power 'to further the re-establishment of peace'. He had discovered, Welles recounted, that in London and Paris both governments were steadfast in their commitment to prosecute the war to its conclusion 'unless they could obtain practical and positive guarantees of security'.

In turn, Ciano divulged to Welles that Ribbentrop had revealed to him three key items:

1. The Germans intended to attack the Western Powers shortly.
2. The only resolution they were prepared to consider was a total military victory.
3. Thereafter peace terms—a '*Diktat*'—would be forcibly imposed upon the Allies by the German conquerors.

'Ribbentrop seemed to be convinced,' Ciano continued, 'that the German Army could achieve such a military victory within five months, and that the German Government believed that France would crumble first and England shortly after.' Ciano informed Welles that he had remonstrated with Ribbentrop—as he had done previously in August 1939 at Salzburg—that Germany's 'reasonable objectives' could be achieved through diplomacy. Unfortunately, Ciano related, Ribbentrop had dismissed his objections outright and spoken aggressively of Germany's martial might. Ciano added that he personally was not convinced that Germany could defeat the Allies as Ribbentrop supposed. 'The present German regime,' Ciano speculated, 'might well be ... like a man suffering from tuberculosis who looked strong and healthy, but who had within him the germ of a fatal disease that might lay him low at the most unexpected moment.' The Germans, Ciano posited, could only vanquish the Allies if they succeeded in penetrating their defences. Conversely, the Anglo–French Powers could triumph in one of two ways: either by penetrating through the German defences or by repelling the German offensive against them.

Welles replied that during his time in Berlin, he had found the manner of both the Führer and Göring 'moderate'. Nevertheless, both leaders were convinced that Germany had no alternative other than to take up arms, otherwise she would be destroyed. Ciano interposed to point out that in his estimation Hitler was wholly under the 'malignant influence' of Ribbentrop, and that his own relations with Göring, formerly pleasant, had deteriorated because Göring blamed him (Ciano) for Italian non-intervention. Ciano wished to emphasize to Welles that the Duce was, however, 'pro-German'. But one crucial point Ciano felt he had to make absolutely clear: 'Mussolini would never endanger the position of Italy, nor would he in any way change the present policy of Italy so as to add to the complexities of the present European situation.' As regards Ribbentrop's recent arrival in Rome, Ciano assured Welles: 'No new agreements of any kind had been entered into, nor would Italy deviate one inch from the course she had set herself.'

Thereupon Ciano mentioned that he was aware of rumours circulating that Italy was stirring the pot in Croatia, and he wished to dispel these tall tales. 'With regard to the Balkans,' Ciano asserted, 'the policy of Italy remained ... the maintenance of the *status quo* ... and the maintenance of peace in that area.' Italy sought, with Yugoslavia, to maintain 'friendly relations'. Returning to the subject of 'security in Europe', Ciano stated that he was unaware of how this might be achieved, save through the establishment of a quadripartite pact between England, France, Italy, and Germany. Should any one of the Big Four run amok, the remaining three nations would join forces against the aggressor.

Welles felt, however, that such a scheme was excessive, and he countered with three proposals which he believed would be conducive to European security:

1. An agreement upon measures of real disarmament,
2. A satisfactory measure of international control of certain offensive types of aviation, and
3. The control and destruction of certain categories of other offensive armaments.

Ciano at once replied that he was in accord with these initiatives.

Towards the end of their conversation, Ciano confided to Welles that he and the Duce were presently 'in contact with Berlin', but declined to reveal the specifics. Ciano then inquired of Welles when the latter planned to leave Rome. Upon being informed that Welles intended to depart on 18 March, Ciano proposed that the American undersecretary stay an extra day. This would allow Ciano to relay to him 'the last word' following the scheduled Mussolini–Hitler conference. Welles thanked Ciano, and after agreeing to the Italian minister's suggestion, also requested that he 'communicate any information of real significance to Mr. [William] Phillips so that the Ambassador could transmit it in as safe a way as possible to Washington'.[60]

At 6 p.m., Welles met with Mussolini at the Palazzo Venezia in the presence of Ciano, who served as interpreter. In Welles' opinion, Mussolini appeared 'far better physically' than he had at their previous encounter. The Duce was affable and seemed to be less burdened this time.[61] Welles opened the discussion by stating that during his recent time in Paris (7–8 March) and London (10–12 March) he had discovered 'a spirit of moderation and great reasonableness, and people therefore well disposed towards the conclusion of a long and lasting peace'. Nevertheless, he cautioned that the British and French were prepared to prosecute the war 'to the bitter end' once the conflict escalated to a more intensive phase and if they did not receive from Germany 'those guarantees of security which are considered indispensable'. In his conversation with Hitler and other Nazi grandees at Berlin, he was able to glean that the upper echelons were certain that the Allies were intent on destroying Germany and its *Volk*. This was untrue, said Welles. On the contrary, the British and French Governments sought only 'to obtain conditions of security for the future'. Mussolini stated reproachfully that on numerous occasions the Western Powers had tried to sunder the ties between the German people and the National Socialist regime. This was not only folly but unachievable, for the Germans stood behind Hitler to the last man.

As Welles saw it, the Allied Governments might be amenable to a political resolution if the subsequent conditions were met: 'Reconstitution of an independent Polish State on a national basis, but the frontiers of which would still have to be discussed as well as the granting of free access to the sea; a broadening of the autonomy and independence conceded to Bohemia and Moravia and, finally, a plebiscite for Austria.' Mussolini knew full well that Hitler would reject these terms out of hand, for the Nazi dictator would never voluntarily surrender his hard-won gains to mollify London and Paris. Mussolini nonetheless inquired politely of Welles whether he might put the question to the Führer on their next encounter. Welles replied that in order to permit this he would first need to 'obtain authorization' from President Roosevelt. Welles then asked Mussolini to elaborate further on the subject of European security. He would like, he said, 'to have some idea of the Duce's conception of the security system which might be introduced in Europe'.

'It is no longer possible,' Mussolini replied, 'for Europe to return to the League of Nations.' The League of Nations was by now an obsolete and feckless body. The Americans, recognizing this all along, had themselves failed to back it. And in his opinion, it would be impossible to establish 'a Federation of all the European States'. Mussolini continued:

> Agreement between the principal European States could guarantee a period of at least twenty to twenty-five years of peace. If the French and Poles had not sabotaged the Four Power Pact,* Germany's inevitable drive would have been set along evolutionary lines.... Only an international body like that foreseen in the Four Power Pact could assure Europe of a period of peace during which reduction of armaments could be decided upon and the economic reconstruction of the world worked out.

Welles reiterated to the Duce that for the Anglo–French democracies 'a system of guarantees' was the prerequisite to reaching 'any agreement with Germany'. Mussolini countered that if the Allies allowed themselves to be distracted by the issue of which should come first, the system of guarantees or the agreement itself, this quibbling would be 'such as to make any attempt at negotiations fail'. Mussolini informed Welles that he would be consulting with the Führer in the near future and would keep him apprised of any changes. 'Should any new factors,' Ciano recorded the Duce as saying, 'emerge from the conversations on the Brenner, he will not fail to inform the interested parties and Mr. Sumner Welles himself with a view to subsequent action.' Mussolini concluded the interview by reaffirming his own 'political solidarity with Germany'.[62] Of the two conversations with Welles, Ciano noted: 'The most important result is this: in London and in Paris there does not exist any of the uncompromising attitude which their speeches and papers indicate. If they had certain guarantees of security they would be ready to give in more or less and to recognize the *fait accompli*.'[63]

* Seeking to ameliorate Italo–French relations, on 19 March 1933 Mussolini had proposed a quadripartite pact for the purpose of maintaining international security. Four months later, on 15 July, Mussolini and the French, British, and German ambassadors had signed the Four Power Pact—formally known as the Agreement of Understanding Between France, Germany, Great Britain, and Italy—at the Palazzo Venezia in Rome. In brief, the international agreement had confirmed the four nations' commitment to abide by the Covenant of the League of Nations (1919), the Locarno Treaties (1925), and the Kellogg–Briand Pact (1928).

The first wartime meeting between Mussolini and Hitler took place on the snowy Monday morning of 18 March. The Axis chiefs had not seen each other since the Munich Conference nearly eighteen months prior. Mussolini reached the Brenner first in his armoured special train, and he awaited his ally's arrival 'with anxious elation'. Ciano, who was present, perceived that the Duce had already succumbed to Hitler's influence: 'Recently he [Mussolini] has felt more and more the fascination of the Führer. His military successes—the only successes that Mussolini really values and desires—are the cause of this.'[64] After Hitler detrained, the dictators entered Mussolini's private coach where the two-hour and thirty-minute meeting took place. As was customary, Hitler regaled Mussolini with a comprehensive description of Germany's military strength and superiority over the Allies.

Hitler declared that 'after long meditation', he had opted for an alliance with the U.S.S.R. since the British were not amenable. With Stalin he had managed to fix 'a hard and fast land frontier between the two countries'. Both nations had 'no opposing interests'. In fact, they were 'economically complimentary in every field'. Thus he intended permanently to keep the peace with Russia in spite of their antithetical ideologies. 'Russia,' Hitler mused contemplatively, 'was undergoing a far-reaching evolution, and the path Stalin has taken seems to lead to a sort of Slav-Muscovite nationalism and to be a move away from Bolshevism of a Jewish-international character.'

Hitler earnestly stated to Mussolini that he, the Führer, 'had not come to ask anything of him'. On the contrary, he only wished 'to give a picture of the situation' and to share with the Duce his own perspective 'on the future course of the war'. And then Hitler made his pitch: if Italy was satisfied to play second fiddle to the British and French then she could by all means let events pass her by. If, however, Italy wished to be mistress of the Mediterranean then she would have to take action against the Anglo–French plutocracies who were intent on preventing Italy from attaining her rightful place in the sun. The Duce had to decide. But on one point Hitler was absolutely certain: 'The fates of Germany and Italy are indissolubly connected; victory for Germany would be victory for Italy and the defeat of Germany would also imply the end of the Italian Empire.' That being said, Hitler stated that he was 'a realist' and as such he did not want Mussolini to act 'contrary to the interests of the Italian people'. Unlike the British, he did not expect other countries to 'pull the chestnuts of out the fire for him'.

When it was finally Mussolini's turn to speak, he declared that he was positive the German–Polish war could not have been put off any longer. And even if it had been possible to do so, such a course of action 'would only have complicated matters'. If he—on 1 September—'had made a military demonstration', Italy would most definitely have been drawn into the war. Italy would then have been in a 'difficult situation'. But now circumstances had changed: 'The Fascist Government and the Party,' Mussolini asserted, 'feel that it is impossible to remain neutral until the end of the war.... Therefore Italy's entry into the war is inevitable. Italy intends to march alongside Germany.' Mussolini recognized that Germany did not require any military assistance from Italy; the Reich could hold her own. Rather, he intended to intervene for reasons of honour and Italian interests. It was only a matter of determining the precise moment of Italian intervention. Mussolini spoke next of Italy's 'ever growing [military] power ... and the excellent morale of the troops'. However, he pointed out that Italy's 'financial situation ... would not allow her to wage a war of long duration'.

Mussolini deemed the German–Soviet alliance to be strategically sound, for it prevented Germany from becoming embroiled in a two-front war. And so long as the Soviets kept out of the rest of Europe, the threat of a 'Bolshevik contagion' could be contained. Mussolini emphasized—as he had done in his letter to Hitler of 3 January—that he had been the first to officially recognize the Soviet Union (1924) and that he had even concluded a non-aggression pact with her (1933). He was careful to differentiate 'between politics and ideology'. But in the final analysis, he would never see eye to eye with the Soviet Union *vis-à-vis* Bolshevism. As regards Italo–German collaboration, he would not hesitate to step in once Germany had achieved in the West 'a favourable situation'. But should the German march westwards 'develop with a slower tempo', he would remain inactive until Italy's intervention 'could be of real use to Germany'. Thereupon Mussolini touched on his talks with Roosevelt's intermediary, Sumner Welles. He had spoken to Welles unequivocally of 'the absurdity of the Allied war aims as far as Eastern Europe is concerned'. If the Western Powers desired a peaceful resolution, they would have to 'accept accomplished facts'.

Hitler wrapped up the meeting with a final discourse on German military strategy. 'The Maginot Line,' he confidently asserted, 'does not today represent an insurmountable obstacle to the German Army.' Moreover, defensive measures to protect the Ruhr region, Germany's industrial heartland, against Allied aerial bombardment and artillery attack were already well underway. The *Wehrmacht* was prepared for the great struggle, now more so than ever. He and the German *Volk* were 'firmly convinced' that Germany would smash the Allies thoroughly and decisively. The meeting concluded at 12:45 p.m. and a bare quarter of an hour later the *Führersonderzug* was winding its way down the mountain towards the Tyrolean city of Innsbruck. No official *communiqué* was issued, leaving the Allies in a state of uncertainty as to the specific nature of the discussion.[65] Afterwards, Ciano diarized his account of the Brenner conference:

> The Hitler meeting is very cordial on both sides. The conference ... is more a monologue than anything else. Hitler talks all the time, but is less agitated than usual. He makes few gestures and speaks in a quiet tone. He looks physically fit. Mussolini listens to him with interest and with deference. He speaks little and confirms his intention to move with Germany. He reserves to himself only the choice of the right moment.... The meeting has not substantially altered our position.[66]

Ciano received Welles a third time on 19 March to clarify where Italy stood following the Brenner conference. To the American envoy, Ciano downplayed it as 'nothing else but an event in the house of the Axis which leaves things exactly as they were before'. Welles was relieved to learn that there was 'no threat of an immediate military clash'. This would give Roosevelt the opportunity to review his reports and possibly make a few peace initiatives. Welles also proposed a potential meeting between Mussolini and Roosevelt in the Azores Islands—in Ciano's view, 'a rather complicated project for results so uncertain'.

Reflecting upon his recent talk with Hitler, Mussolini was certain that the Germans were 'not preparing to launch the land offensive'. There was also one aspect about the meeting which irked him: the Führer's monopolization of the conversation. Ciano wrote: 'Mussolini resented the fact that Hitler did all the talking; he had in mind to tell him many things, and instead he had to keep quiet most of the time, a thing which, as dictator, or rather the dean of dictators, he's not in the habit of doing.'[67]

To the House of Commons, Chamberlain briefly alluded to the Italo–German summit meeting:

> When he [Welles] returned to Italy he found himself in the presence of a new event, the meeting of the two dictators on the Brenner Pass. That meeting has naturally given rise to many speculations as to its purpose. Some have thought that it was for the purpose of elaborating new peace proposals. I do not know whether that is true or not. For aught I know these two gentlemen may have spent their time in discussing the conditions under which an Italian ship was destroyed yesterday by a German mine with the loss of Italian lives. Whatever may be the outcome ... we are ready to meet it, and we are not likely to be diverted from the purpose for which we entered this war.[68]

After the Brenner conference, Ambassador François-Poncet was convinced that Mussolini had resolved to throw in his lot with the Germans. On 20 March, Ciano spoke with the Frenchman and he noted in his *Diary*: 'Poncet … has expressed himself regretfully about the meeting, and my words did little to convince him that there is nothing new.' A perceptive man, François-Poncet was well able to read between the lines, and he declared to Ciano: 'You are mistaken. You have bet, and in fact the Duce himself has put his money on the losing horse, and now he is doubling his bet. But the Franco–British horse, even if at the beginning of the race it may lag behind, will win in the last lap.'[69] A week later, François-Poncet again called on Ciano at the Palazzo Chigi. The French diplomat was preparing to confer with Prime Minister Reynaud, and he wished to know if the Italians were now bent on war, and Ciano could not convince him otherwise. 'Poncet tried again,' Ciano wrote, 'to put before us the possibility of negotiations for conditions more favourable to Italy, and he has gone so far as to talk about the cession of French Somaliland.' But Ciano rejected this conciliatory offer on the basis of the Duce's present 'state of mind', for at this time the Duce was 'not much inclined to negotiation'. When Ciano reported to Mussolini the substance of his latest talk with François-Poncet, the Duce scornfully retorted: 'French offers are always made in bad faith.'[70]

Mussolini was becoming ever more warlike and, as was inevitable for a charismatic dictator, his fiery utterances in favour of military action were starting to make a strong impression on his Fascist lieutenants:

> Mussolini … is growing every day more definitely pro-German. He now speaks openly of entering the war at the side of Germany and even defines our course of action: defensive in the Alps, defensive in Libya, offensive in Ethiopia against Djibouti and Kenya, aero-naval offensive in the Mediterranean. The Duce's attitude is beginning to influence many Fascist chiefs, who, either because they follow him, or out of personal conviction, are lining up in the ranks of the interventionists.

Those in favour of war: Ettore Muti, Renato Ricci, Thaon di Revel, and Arturo Riccardi. Those against: Dino Grandi and Giuseppe Bottai. According to Party Secretary Achille Starace, Mussolini even declared to the commander of the University Student Volunteers, General Enzo Galbiati: 'Hold yourself ready. Shortly we will march in the West.'[71]

In late March, Ciano received word from numerous sources that Mussolini intended to dismiss him from the Foreign Ministry. Ciano did not believe that the rumours were true, but even if they were, he would have no regrets:

> ... I would be delighted to leave this job in which I have served for almost four years—and what years!—carrying my head high. Everything that I have done was done for the sole purpose of serving my country and the Duce, and whenever I took a stand which seemed to conflict with that of the Duce I did so to defend the Duce's position against offence from abroad. This has been the true and inmost cause of my incurable resentment, a resentment which I have nourished and reaffirmed against the Germans since the days of Salzburg. But all this is of no account. The Duce will do whatever he wishes to do.[72]

Several days later, Ciano noted that Mussolini was again in a belligerent frame of mind: 'Violent turn of the wheel in the direction of war. Today Mussolini wants full steam ahead to open conflict if France and England really intend, as they announce, to tighten the blockade.' And to the Council of Ministers, the Duce also spoke of the gathering storm: 'He [Mussolini] foresees that war may begin at any moment ... he concludes that we shall move with the Germans to promote our own purpose. He speaks of a Mediterranean empire and of access to the ocean. He believes blindly in Germany victory and in the word of Hitler as concerns our share of the booty.' But Ciano was skeptical—not only in a German victory over the formidable Anglo–French democracies, but in Hitler's assurances—and rightfully so: 'Is it so certain that Hitler, who has never kept his word to anyone, will keep it to us?'[73]

That spring, in a little-known but crucial memorandum, Mussolini committed to paper his political-strategic plans. The document, dated 31 March, was disseminated at the highest levels only. The following received a copy: King Emmanuel III, Ciano, the chiefs of staff of the Army (Pietro Badoglio), Navy (Domenico Cavagnari), and Air Force (Francesco Pricolo), the governor-general of Italian Libya (Rodolfo Graziani), the minister of Italian Africa (Attilio Terruzi), and Mussolini's private secretariat (Oswaldo Sebastiani).

Under the heading 'Italy's Position', Mussolini made reference to 'a war parallel to Germany's to achieve our objectives summed up as follows: freedom on the seas, window on the ocean'. Such a war was necessary for Italy to achieve her imperialist aims in the Mediterranean and Africa. It would end quickly and be kept apart from the German–Allied conflict. Repeating the theme expressed in his report to the Fascist Grand Council of February 1939, Mussolini added: 'Italy cannot be a truly independent nation so long as Corsica, Bizerta, and Malta are the window bars of her prison and Suez and Gibraltar the walls.... Italy, if she wants to be a world power, must resolve the problem of her maritime frontiers: the very security of the [Italian] Empire is tied to the solution of this problem.' He elaborated on the subject of Italian entry into the war, which was a matter of precise timing:

> Italy cannot remain *neutral* for the entire duration of the war without resigning from her role, without disqualifying herself, without reducing herself to the level of a Switzerland multiplied by ten. The problem is not therefore to know whether we will or will not enter the war; it's only a question of knowing when and how; it is a question of delaying our entry as long as it is possible and consistent with our honour and dignity.[74]

Naturally, as dictator, Mussolini himself would decide the right moment.

A fortnight later, he instructed the *Comando Supremo*:

> To prepare for military intervention on the side of Germany including:
>
> 1.) air and naval offensive operations against Allied naval and maritime units in the Mediterranean
>
> 2.) maintain a defensive stance against France and in Libya and East Africa
>
> 3.) remain neutral towards but look for convenient offensive opportunities against Yugoslavia and Greece.

The specific date for Italian intervention was not yet determined, however. It would be contingent upon the progress of Germany's invasion of France, which was imminent. These orders appalled General Pricolo, for as recently as December, he had made clear to the Duce the full extent of the Italian Air Force's lack of readiness. Pricolo knew perfectly well that in its present condition it was utterly incapable of handling effectively so vast a theatre as the Mediterranean—over 2,300 miles long and nearly 1,000 miles wide.[75]

After midnight on 9 April, a secretary from the German Embassy arrived at Ciano's home residence with an urgent message from Ambassador Mackensen, requesting to be received at 7 a.m. A weary Mackensen turned up at half-past six and informed Ciano that Hitler had decided to occupy Denmark and invade Norway; and that the German operation, code-named *Weserübung* (Weser Exercise), was already underway. It was, from the German perspective, a pre-emptive measure against a planned joint Allied occupation of Norway (Plan R 4). In response, Ciano advised the German diplomat 'that the reaction of the neutrals, and especially of the Americans, would be violent'. Mackensen concurred 'wholeheartedly'. The pair then set off to see Mussolini, to whom Mackensen handed a note from Hitler, 'the usual letter, in the usual style, announcing what he had already done'. Mussolini declared: 'I approve Hitler's action wholeheartedly. It is a gesture that can have incalculable results, and this is the way to win wars. The democracies have lost the race. I shall give orders to the press and to the Italian people to applaud this German action without reservation.' Mackensen departed the Palazzo Venezia fairly walking on air.

No sooner had Mackensen gone than Mussolini started to discuss with Ciano the possibility of an Italian operation against Yugoslavia, one in which he believed the Anglo–French democracies would not interfere: 'When we were alone, the Duce talked about Croatia. His hands fairly itch. He intends to quicken the tempo, taking advantage of the disorder that reigns in Europe. But he didn't specify, except to say that he is convinced that an attack against Yugoslavia will not lead France and England to strike at us.'[76]

The Duce had an audience with King Emmanuel III on the morning of 11 April which he felt had been unsatisfactory, and consequently he was in a dour mood. The elderly Italian monarch continued to drag his feet, and Mussolini railed against him to Ciano: 'The King would like us to enter [the war] only to gather up the broken dishes. I hope that they will not break them over our heads before that. And then it is humiliating to remain with our hands folded while others write history. It matters little who wins. To make a people great it is necessary to send them to battle even if you have to kick them in the pants. This is what I shall do.'[77]

Later in the day, Mackensen came bearing a personal letter from Hitler dated 9 April detailing the successful German advance into Scandinavia thus far. Mussolini promptly replied with an optimistic and complimentary letter endorsing the German operation, and he informed Hitler that as of the very next day the Italian Navy would be prepared for war. Meanwhile, the state of readiness of the other branches of the Italian Armed Forces was being accelerated. Lastly, he mentioned that the *popolo Italiano* understood full well that Italy's entry into the war was ineluctable:

> … I entirely approve your action, which has forestalled a French–English landing in Norway, a landing which, as you rightly say, would have created a difficult situation for Germany.
>
> The Italian people have been unanimous in admiring the truly lightning rapidity of your action and have realized that it was inevitable.
>
> The increasing vexations of the blockade against Italian traffic have created a very strong anti-Allied *Stimmung* [mood] in the Italian people, and those in Paris and London who assert the contrary are showing once again that they confuse reality with their desires.
>
> I consider that the French–English counteraction on the coast of Norway will be powerless to undo what you have already accomplished, the far-reaching consequences of which can already be foreseen.…

> I assure you that from tomorrow, the 12th, the Italian Fleet will be entirely on a war footing while I am speeding up the 'tempo' of the other armed forces....
>
> As to the Italian people, although they desire a delay in order to be better prepared, they are now aware that they will not be able to avoid entering the field.[78]

Three more letters from Hitler, dated 20 April, 28 April, and 4 May respectively, followed. Each in turn described to Mussolini the favourable progress of German military operations in Norway. Ciano perceived that the boastful letters were 'of meagre importance, but Hitler is a good psychologist and he knows that these messages go straight to Mussolini's heart'.[79]

In a speech to the heads of the labour confederations on 21 April, Mussolini inveighed against the Anglo–French coal blockade, complaining that over the past eight months Italian steamers had been subject to the arbitrary control of Allied ships in the Mediterranean. The Duce spoke indignantly of 'Anglo–French maritime hegemony' which sought to despoil the Italian nation and its people of resources, and once again reiterated the motif—which he considered a 'law'—that a nation's independence was contingent upon the extent of its access to the ocean.

Next day Mussolini had an animated conversation with the king, to whom he stated: 'Italy today is in fact a British colony, and certain Italians would be disposed to make this a legal fact, that is, they would make of her a Malta multiplied by a million.' At the mention of this appalling prospect, the king visibly paled.[80]

Meanwhile, Premier Reynaud was growing alarmed at the increasingly 'aggressive tone' of the Italian press towards the Allies. Under these trying circumstances, on 22 April the French statesman opted to write a personal letter to Mussolini. The missive was hand-delivered to Ciano by François-Poncet, who had no knowledge of its contents (and was displeased about this fact, for he felt it put him at a disadvantage and it seemed—he perceived—to indicate a lack of confidence in him by the French Government), in a sealed envelope two days later:

> It is as vital for Italy as for France that a balance of power should be maintained in Europe. Without this, no peace, no prosperity can be lasting. What are the disagreements which have been able to arise between us during the last four years, beside this fundamental fact?
>
> It is not too late to try to bridge this broad ditch which seems at present to separate us. Your frankness and my own should try to link a traditional regime like ours and a new regime like yours; each would,

> thereby, be reinforced in the future by the dissipation of this distrust of its neighbour....
>
> It will not be possible to say that France and Italy came to blows on the battlefield without a thorough discussion and a meeting on the part of their leaders.
>
> A war between us, and our people would feel the same as we do, would be a sacrilege against our common heritage and against the sacrifice of those who lost their lives at Bligny. In these days when peace is so much more difficult than war, I offer you the more difficult.[81]

In the second half of April, Ambassador Attolico was abruptly dismissed from his post. For some time now, he had been an irritant to the Reich Government; Hitler had declared that Attolico was a *persona non grata* and he wanted the Italian diplomat removed. The chief reason was that Attolico—whom Ciano characterized favourably as 'an Italian and a gentleman'—had long been critical of Nazi Germany and continued to make every effort to discourage Mussolini from entering the war at Germany's side. The matter came to a head when on 24 April Mackensen broached with Ciano the Germans' dissatisfaction with Attolico. 'In Berlin,' Mackensen stated, 'they would now welcome his recall.' To succeed him, Hitler had two candidates in mind: either Roberto Farinacci or Dino Alfieri. Ciano favoured the latter, and he was certain that the Duce would 'meet the German desire'.[82] Next day Ciano discussed with the Duce the issue of Attolico's successor and Mussolini agreed to appoint Alfieri. Ciano escorted Alfieri to the Palazzo Venezia where Mussolini immediately gave the new ambassador 'instructions as to his approaching mission to Germany'. Mussolini reiterated his loyalty to the Pact of Steel, but in connection with war stated that 'he will enter it only when he has a quasi-mathematical certainty of winning it'. Alfieri departed the great *Mappamondo* hall convinced that in Berlin he would have to tread 'slowly and cautiously'.[83] Attolico was reassigned, and he wryly noted that his transfer from Berlin to the Holy See was like going 'from the devil to holy water'.

By 26 April, Mussolini's reply to Reynaud was ready. Ciano described it as 'cold, cutting, and contemptuous'. He attempted to soften it but was unsuccessful. Ciano felt that the communication might be misused by the French Government to Italy's detriment: 'It is clear that the Duce's letter can be used by Reynaud against the remaining pro-Italian Frenchmen as proof of our provocative radicalism.'[84] On 27 April, François-Poncet conveyed Mussolini's icy letter to Reynaud:

> I hasten to reply to your letter of 22 April, which was handed to me on the 24th through your Ambassador in Rome. First of all, may I term as

> unjustified the reason which inspired your message, namely the telegram in which I expressed a wish for a German victory. This should not come as a surprise to you, nor make you forget that Italy is and means to stay the political and military ally of German in adherence to the Treaty of May, 1939, a treaty which Italy, like all nations who cherish their honour, intends to respect.
>
> Your remarks on the relations between democracy and Fascism and the need for a European balance of power would require developing at length, and this is not the place to do so.
>
> You seem in one passage of your letter to allude to the possibility of a meeting between us. I must, to my deep regret, decline such an offer. You will have no difficulty in understanding the reason for this.[85]

On 29 April, at 6 p.m., a letter from Roosevelt advocating peace was dispatched by telegram to 'My Dear Signor Mussolini'. It was brought to the Duce personally by American Ambassador to Italy William Phillips on 1 May:

> The people of the United States ... have seen with the deepest satisfaction the policy of the Italian Government in exerting every effort to prevent war from spreading to southern and to southeastern Europe. I fully recognize the profound truth of the statement you made recently to my representative, Mr. Welles, that because of Italy's determination to limit, so far as might be possible, the spread of the conflict, more than 200,000,000 of people in the region of the Mediterranean are still at peace.
>
> A further extension of the area of hostilities, which would bring into the war still other nations which have been seeking to maintain their neutrality, would necessarily have far-reaching and unforeseeable consequences, not only in Europe, but also in the Near and the Far East, in Africa, and in the three Americas....
>
> By reason of its geographical position, this country has a panoramic view of the existing hostilities in Europe. Because of the many imponderables involved, I see no reason to anticipate that any one nation, or any one combination of nations, can successfully undertake to dominate either the continent of Europe or much less a greater part of the world.
>
> I earnestly hope that the powerful influence of Italy and of the United States—an influence which is very strong so long as they remain at peace—may yet be exercised, when the appropriate opportunity is presented in behalf of the negotiation of a just and stable peace which will permit of the reconstruction of a gravely stricken world.[86]

Mussolini drafted a response to Roosevelt at once. Ciano noted that it was 'cutting and hostile'. Mussolini pointed out to the U.S. president—who was naturally sympathetic to the Anglo–French democracies—'that if the Monroe Doctrine has force for Americans, it must also have force for Europeans'.[87] The Americans received it on 2 May, and it read:

> 1. If two nations, Denmark and Norway, have been involved in the war, the responsibility does not fall upon Germany, but upon the initiatives of the Allies.
> 2. Italy's non-belligerence has effectively ensured peace for two hundred millions of men, but notwithstanding, Italian merchant traffic is subjected to a constant surveillance that is vexatious and harmful.
> 3. As far as I know, Germany is opposed to a further extension of the conflict, and Italy likewise. We must learn whether this is also the Franco–British aim.
> 4. The only European nation that dominates a large part of the world and possesses a monopoly on many basic raw materials is Great Britain. Italy has no programs of that kind, but declares that no peace is possible without the fundamental problems of Italian liberty being settled.
> 5. As to the repercussions which an extension of the war fronts might have on the three Americas [North, Central, and South], I call attention to the fact that Italy has never concerned itself with the relations of the American Republics with each other and with the United States (thereby respecting the Monroe Doctrine), and might therefore ask for 'reciprocity' with regard to European affairs.
> 6. Whenever conditions permit, and always starting with the recognition of the actual and accomplished facts, Italy is ready to make her contribution to a better order of the world.[88]

Ambassador Loraine, who had recently returned to Rome, paid a formal visit to Ciano on 8 May. From Loraine's remarks, Ciano gathered that he had been tasked by the British Government to do his utmost to maintain positive relations between Italy and Britain, and to do so 'honourably and in good faith'. However, on the basis of Italian 'press campaigns', large segments of the British population considered that Italy was 'to be numbered among the enemies'. Nevertheless, Loraine was certain that the European conflict would ultimately end in a British victory. To assuage his interlocutor, Ciano took it upon himself to clarify his government's policy. He explained that Mussolini intended to adhere to the Pact of Steel (and remain an ally of Germany thereby), but he stressed this should not be interpreted to mean that Italy would necessarily take up arms. But in spite of Ciano's assurances, the British diplomat was disquieted, and although Loraine 'did not leave reassured ... he remained very calm and altogether certain about the English future'.[89]

On 9 May, Hitler finally broke the news to his Fascist ally that the long-awaited German offensive against France and the Low Countries would commence the following morning:

> When you receive this letter I shall already have crossed the Rubicon.... I have therefore decided today to give the order to attack on the Western Front at 5:35 a.m. tomorrow to ensure the neutrality of Belgium and Holland, above all by military measures.... I will keep you informed as to the operations and you will thus be in a position to consider in complete freedom the decisions for which you deem it advisable to assume responsibility in the interests of your people.[90]

The following morning, as planned, the Germans attacked in the West. The so-called 'Phoney War' (or *Sitzkrieg*, as the Germans termed it) was over. Several other noteworthy events took place on 10 May: Chamberlain resigned* and King George VI summoned Winston Churchill, then first lord of the Admiralty, to request that he take over as prime minister. Churchill at once formed a war cabinet. And from Rome, Mussolini sent Hitler an earnest reply to his previous day's note:

> I thank you for the message you sent at the moment when your troops were receiving the order to march to the west. As in the case of the campaign in Norway the press and action of the [Fascist] Party will guide the mind of the Italian people towards understanding the necessity with which you were faced.
>
> I feel that time is pressing for Italy too, and I am deeply grateful for your promise to keep me informed of developments in the operations in order to put me in a position to make my decisions.
>
> As for the Italian Armed Forces, the Navy is ready and by the end of May two army groups in the east and west and also the Air Force and the anti-aircraft formations will be ready.
>
> It is superfluous for me to tell you that I am following the progress of your troops with confidence and in a spirit of comradeship.[91]

* On 7 May, Leo Amery, a Conservative MP, had excoriated Chamberlain in the House of Commons during a debate: 'Depart I say, and let us have done with you. In the name of God, go!' These words were the same as those uttered by Oliver Cromwell while addressing the Rump Parliament on 20 April 1653.

Hitler sent Mussolini another letter on 13 May detailing the astonishing success of the German advance into enemy territory, and it only served to whet Mussolini's appetite for war even further. He said to Ciano:

> Some months ago I said that the Allies had lost the victory. Today I tell you that they have lost the war. We Italians are already sufficiently dishonoured. Any delay is inconceivable. We have no time to lose. Within a month I shall declare war. I shall attack France and England in the air and on the sea. I am no longer thinking of taking up arms against Yugoslavia because it would be a humiliating expedient.

Perturbed, Ciano—who was, as ever, strongly opposed to Italian entry into the war—glumly wrote: 'Unfortunately, I can do nothing now to hold the Duce back. He has decided to act, and act he will. He believes in German success and in the rapidity of this success. Only a new turn in military events can induce him to revise his decision, but for the time being things are going so badly for the Allies that there is no hope.'[92]

Three days after the start of Germany's Western campaign, Churchill addressed the House of Commons for the first time as prime minister. It was on this occasion that he uttered the historic words, 'I have nothing to offer but blood, toil, tears, and sweat.' England's new head of government ended his inspirational speech with these noble words:

> You ask, what is our policy? I will say: It is to wage war, by sea, land, and air, with all our might and with all the strength that God can give us: to wage war against a monstrous tyranny, never surpassed in the dark, lamentable catalogue of human crime. That is our policy. You ask, What is our aim? I can answer in one word: Victory—victory at all costs, victory in spite of all terror; victory, however long and hard the road may be; for without victory, there is no survival.[93]

On 14 May, Roosevelt saw fit to contact Mussolini once more. It had been brought to his attention, from various points of origin, that the Duce possibly intended to enter the conflict against the Allies in the near future. Disturbed by the prospect of an extension of the conflict in the Mediterranean region, Roosevelt sent Mussolini a sincere imploration not to resort to arms:

> I do not know what Your Excellency plans or proposes but reports reaching me from many sources, to the effect that you may be contemplating early entry into the war, have given me great concern.... You whom the great Italian people call their leader have it in your own hands

> to stay the spread of this war to another group of 200,000,000 human souls in the Mediterranean area.... Therefore, I make the simple plea that you, responsible for Italy, withhold your hand, stay wholly apart from any war and refrain from any threat of attack.[94]

Mussolini answered Roosevelt's entreaty four days later. He recognized that the American president was well-intentioned but pointed out the inescapable fact that Fascist Italy was a full military ally of Nazi Germany and that, under the circumstances, Italy could not stay idle while the future of Europe was being decided:

> I reply to the message which you sent me ... I understand perfectly the motives by which it was inspired and I consider it worthy of much respect and of the greatest consideration but there are two fundamental motives which cannot escape your spirit of political realism and those are that Italy is and intends to remain allied with Germany and that Italy cannot remain absent at a moment when the fate of Europe is at stake.[95]

Churchill too wished, if possible, to prevent destruction and death on a large scale between the Italian people and his own, and on 16 May, he dispatched a heartfelt personal message to Mussolini, written in his usual majestic style:

> Is it too late to stop a river of blood from flowing between the British and Italian peoples? We can, no doubt, inflict grievous injuries upon one another and maul each other cruelly, and darken the Mediterranean with our strife. If you so decree, it must be so; but I declare that I have never been the enemy of Italian greatness nor ever at heart the foe of the Italian lawgiver. It is idle to predict the course of the great battles now raging in Europe, but I am sure that whatever may happen on the Continent, England will go on to the end, even quite alone, as we have done before...[96]

Mussolini answered Churchill two days later:

> I reply to the message which you have sent me in order to tell you that you are certainly aware of grave reasons of an historical and contingent character which have ranged our two countries in opposite camps. Without going back very far in time I remind you of the initiative taken in 1935 by your Government to organize at Geneva sanctions against Italy.... If it was to honour your signature that your Government declared war on Germany, you will understand that the same sense of

> honour and of respect for engagements assumed in the Italian–German treaty guides Italian policy today and tomorrow in the face of any event whatsoever.[97]

On 18 and 25 May, Hitler dispatched to Mussolini personal letters which were, in effect, progress reports of the German offensive. In the first, Hitler gave a thorough 'picture of the situation': German forces had overwhelmed the neutrals (Belgium, Holland, and Luxembourg), penetrated the Maginot Line, and gained mastery of the air. In the second, Hitler continued in the same vein, lauding the superiority of the German Army and Luftwaffe, and towards the end added some denigratory comments concerning the Allies' 'degenerate' parliamentary governments. Grateful to the Führer for taking the opportunity to keep him appraised of the *Wehrmacht*'s successful thrust into Western Europe, Mussolini replied:

> I thank you for having found time during a pause in the tremendous victory battle to send me a communication on the progress of the operations. I repeat that these operations have been followed not only with interest but with enthusiasm by the Italian people who are now convinced that the period of non-belligerency cannot last much longer. I intend to give you important news on this subject in the next few days.
>
> I assume that your Foreign Minister has already informed you of the messages which were sent to me by Roosevelt and Churchill recently and of my replies; but all this is only of relative importance now.
>
> I send you my most comradely greetings.[98]

The *Wehrmacht*'s staggering victories in Scandinavia, the Low Countries, and France had convinced Mussolini that he had to take immediate action if he wished to play a significant role in the restructuring of Europe and receive a generous slice of the war booty. On 26 May, Mussolini accordingly broke the news to Chief of Staff Badoglio and Air Marshal Balbo that he could remain inactive no longer and that he intended to attack Britain: 'I wish to tell you that yesterday I sent a messenger to Hitler with my written declaration that I do not intend to stand idly by with my hands in my pockets, and that after 5 June I am ready to declare war on England.' Badoglio, once he had recovered from his shock, strongly protested. He remonstrated that the Italian Armed Forces were 'absolutely unprepared', then added: 'We have about twenty divisions with seventy percent of the necessary equipment and training; and about another twenty divisions with fifty percent. We have no tanks. The Air Force, as you know from General Pricolo's reports, is grounded.... In such a state of affairs how is it possible to declare war?' But his words were in vain. After a momentary pause, Mussolini fixed his piercing gaze upon Badoglio and cynically declared: 'I assure you the war will be over by September, and that I need a few thousand dead so as to be able to attend the peace conference as a belligerent.'[99]

Three days later, the *Comando Supremo* (Supreme Command) was established in Rome. Ciano described the occasion and Mussolini's elation upon attaining his long-term goal of becoming Fascist Italy's warlord: 'Today at eleven at the Palazzo Venezia the High Command was born! Rarely have I seen Mussolini so happy. He has realized his dream: that of becoming the military *Condottiero* [leader] of the country at war. Under him will be Badoglio, Graziani, Pricolo, and Cavagnari.' Ciano also noted that the Duce was about to determine the precise date for joining the war at the Germans' side. 'The decision is about to be taken; after the fifth of June any day may be good.'[100] Marshal Badoglio, however, was plagued with doubts. His primary concern was Italian Libya. There an attack by the French might succeed. Above all, the war had to be of brief duration. General Umberto Favagrossa, a staff officer, underscored heavily that it must not exceed two or three months on account of limited supplies. Metals, in particular, were scant.

On 30 May, the die was cast. Mussolini informed Hitler of his decision concerning Italian entry into the war—one which would eventually prove fatal to both Mussolini and the Fascist regime. The Duce also advised Hitler that he would take over the leadership of the Italian Armed Forces. And, as was characteristic of him, Mussolini recklessly boasted that he had seventy divisions (a grossly inflated figure) raring to go:

> I have delayed my reply to you for some days because I wanted to announce to you my decision to enter the war as of 5 June. Should you consider that I ought to wait a few days longer for the sake of better coordination with your plans, you will tell me so....
>
> During these 9 months [September to May inclusive] the efforts made in the field of military preparations have been significant. Today there are 70 divisions whose striking power is good; of these, 12 are overseas (220,000 men in Libya, 100,000 in Albania). Italian East Africa has 350,000 men available—Italians and natives—who are not included in the figures given.
>
> As I have told you earlier, the Navy and Air Force are already on a wartime footing.
>
> I shall assume supreme command of all the Armed Forces....
>
> From the political point of view I consider it necessary not to extend the conflict to the Danube Basin and the Balkans, from which Italy must draw those supplies which she will no longer be able to obtain from beyond Gibraltar.

> I think that a statement on these lines which I shall make at an appropriate moment will have a reassuring effect on those nations and will render them impervious to any possible moves by the Allies.
>
> Once this is established, our General Staffs will take the requisite steps for the development of the operations.[101]

In his speedy reply of 31 May, Hitler asked his Fascist partner to postpone Italian entry into the war by up to three days in order to give the Luftwaffe the opportunity to destroy the French Air Force.* But Hitler also felt that it was high time for the Duce to fulfill his end of the bargain and he advised Mussolini that Italian intervention was welcome regardless of the date.

After mulling over for several days Hitler's request for a deferred Italian entry into the war, Mussolini eventually settled on 10 June for the formal declaration of war against France and Britain and 11 June to begin the attack. At this time, he did not plan to engage militarily the Danubian or Balkan nations. Mussolini also offered a modest contribution of some elite Italian units to the German war effort:

> Regarding the date of Italy's entry into the war ... My program is as follows: On Monday, 10 June, declaration of war and on the morning of 11 June the commencement of hostilities. In the speech which I shall make a few hours after the declaration of war, I shall say that, true to her policy, Italy does not intend to extend her theatre of war, and I shall name the Danube and Balkan countries including Greece and Turkey. Now I will express to you my wish to see at least a representative contingent of the Italian Army fighting side by side with your soldiers, in order to demonstrate in the field the affinity of arms and the comradeship between our revolutions. If you accept my offer I will send you a few regiments of *Bersaglieri*.... Meanwhile I send you my most heartfelt greetings and best wishes for the success of our armed forces.[102]

During the Battle of France, the British Expeditionary Force incurred heavy losses totalling some 68,000 men. Nevertheless, the evacuation of Allied troops from the French coast at Dunkirk (Operation Dynamo) was, overall, a success. Over 330,000 were rescued and would live to fight another day. To the House of Commons on 4 June, the same day the Battle of Dunkirk concluded, Churchill delivered a stirring and defiant speech:

---

* On 3 June, the Germans initiated Operation Paula, their plan to eliminate the French Air Force. But the French received advance warning of the imminent aerial attack by British intelligence and consequently were able to take the necessary anticipatory action to thwart the German undertaking.

> Even though large tracts of Europe and many old and famous States have fallen or may fall into the grip of the Gestapo and all the odious apparatus of Nazi rule, we shall not flag or fail. We shall go on to the end. We shall fight in France, we shall fight in the seas and oceans, we shall fight with growing confidence and growing strength in the air; we shall defend our island, whatever the cost may be. We shall fight on the beaches, we shall fight on the landing-grounds, we shall fight in the fields and in the streets, we shall fight in the hills, we shall never surrender, and even if, which I do not for a moment believe, this island or a large part of it were subjugated and starving, then our Empire beyond the seas, armed and guarded by the British Fleet, would carry on the struggle...[103]

The Dunkirk evacuation had been a most welcome reprieve, but Churchill was quick to point out a hard but true fact: 'Wars are not won by evacuations.'[104] Next day Hitler triumphantly proclaimed (not without embellishment): 'Dunkirk has fallen! 40,000 French and English troops are all that remains of the formerly great armies.... The greatest battle in the history of the world has come to an end.'

By this phase of the war, the demoralized French armies were on the verge of collapse, and Mussolini wholeheartedly believed (erroneously) that Britain would come to terms once France was removed from the equation. He did not expect a protracted conflict. Hitler had convinced him that once without European allies, the British would have to face the hard reality of Axis supremacy on the continent and sue for peace. Greedily seeking his share of the spoils of victory and irresponsibly choosing to overlook the Italian Armed Forces' lack of readiness, Mussolini declared war on Britain and France on 10 June as planned.

The British and French ambassadors were summoned to the Palazzo Chigo that afternoon. Ciano received François-Poncet at 4:30 p.m. and relayed to him the formal declaration of war: 'His Majesty the King-Emperor declares that Italy considers herself in a state of war against France beginning tomorrow, 11 June.'[105] François-Poncet said ruefully: 'It is a dagger blow to a man who has already fallen. I thank you nonetheless for using the velvet glove.' Before leaving the room, however, the French diplomat gave Ciano an ominous warning: 'The Germans are hard masters. You, too, will learn this.'[106] (François-Poncet would be proven right in due time.) Fifteen minutes later, the same message was given to Loraine who, after a brief inquiry, remained calm and composed and did not utter a word.

The Duce's war speech was delivered from the balcony of the Palazzo Venezia at 6 p.m. Roman Fascists were strategically planted throughout the square below to fan the flames. Mussolini's declamation was calculated to appeal to the emotions of the Italian masses. It underscored the injustices perpetrated against Italy, urged the people to demonstrate their bravery and desire to win, and cautioned the nations adjoining Italy not to violate their neutrality:

> Fighters of land, sea and air, Blackshirts of the revolution and of the legions, men and women of Italy, of the Empire and of the Kingdom of Albania, listen!
>
> The hour destined by fate is sounding for us. The hour of irrevocable decision has come. A declaration of war already has been handed to the ambassadors of Great Britain and France.
>
> We take the field against the plutocratic and reactionary democracies who always, have blocked the march and frequently plotted against the existence of the Italian people.
>
> Several decades of recent history may be summarized in these words: Phrases, promises, threats of blackmail, and finally, crowning that ignoble edifice, the League of Nations of fifty-two nations.
>
> Our conscience is absolutely clear.
>
> With you, the entire world is witness that the Italy of Fascism has done everything humanly possible to avoid the tempest that envelopes Europe, but all in vain.
>
> It would have sufficed to revise treaties to adapt them to changing requirements vital to nations and not consider them untouchable for eternity.
>
> It would have sufficed not to begin the stupid policy of guarantees, which proved particularly deadly for those who accepted them.
>
> It would have sufficed not to reject the proposal the Führer made last 6 October after the campaign in Poland ended.
>
> Now all that belongs to the past.
>
> If today we have decided to take the risks and sacrifices of war, it is because the honour, interests and future firmly impose it since a great people is truly such if it considers its obligations sacred and does not avoid the supreme trials that determine the course of history.
>
> We are taking up arms, after having solved the problem of our continental frontiers, to solve our maritime frontiers. We want to break the territorial and military chains that confine us in our sea because a country of 45,000,000 souls is not truly free if it has not free access to the ocean.
>
> This gigantic conflict is only a phase of the logical development of our revolution. It is the conflict of poor, numerous peoples who labour against starvers who ferociously cling to a monopoly of all riches and all gold on earth.
>
> It is a conflict of fruitful, useful peoples against peoples who are in a decline. It is a conflict between two ages, two ideas.
>
> Now the die is cast and our will has burned our ships behind us. I solemnly declare that Italy does not intend to drag other peoples bordering on her by sea or land into the conflict. Switzerland, Yugoslavia, Greece,

> Turkey and Egypt, take note of these words of mine. It depends on them and only on them if these words are rigorously confirmed or not.

Mussolini took the opportunity to publicly re-emphasize his unshakable loyalty to his German ally:

> Italians, in a memorable mass meeting in Berlin, I said that according to the rules of Fascist morals when one has a friend one marches with him to the end. This we have done and will continue to do with Germany, her people, and her victorious armed forces.

Mussolini's peroration was bombastic, but forceful and effective:

> On this eve of an event of import for centuries, we turn our thoughts to His Majesty, the King and Emperor, who always has understood the thought of the country.
>
> Lastly, we salute the new Führer, the chief of great allied Germany.
>
> Proletarian, Fascist Italy has arisen for the third time, strong, proud, compact as never before.
>
> There is only one order. It is categorical and obligatory for every one. It already wings over and inflames hearts from the Alps to the Indian Ocean: Conquer!
>
> And we will conquer in order, finally, to give a new world of peace with justice to Italy, to Europe and to the universe.
>
> Italian people, rush to arms and show your tenacity, your courage, your valour.[107]

The Allies regarded this treacherous act with contempt. President Roosevelt was especially disgusted. In an earnest speech to the class of 1940 at the University of Virginia in Charlottesville on 10 June, Roosevelt condemned Italy's opportunism and perfidy:

> The Government of Italy has now chosen to preserve what it terms its 'freedom of action' and to fulfill what it states are its promises to Germany. In so doing it has manifested disregard for the rights and security of other nations, disregard for the lives of the peoples of those nations which are directly threatened by this spread of the war; and has evidenced its unwillingness to find the means through pacific negotiations for the satisfaction of what it believes are its legitimate aspirations.

Roosevelt then uttered one of his most memorable quotes. To the students assembled before him, he declared: 'On this tenth day of June 1940, the hand that held the dagger has struck it into the back of its neighbour.'[108] It was an apt description.

The Anglo–French democracies were now confronted by a second powerful adversary (at least on paper). In June 1940, the Italian Army consisted of over 1.6 million men, the Italian Air Force of some 2,300 planes (only three-fourths were operational), and the Italian Navy was one of the world's strongest. For France, however, it made little difference since by this point German victory was virtually certain. But the consequences in future would be grave. With Italy now in a state of war against France and England, the European conflict would be extended from Western Europe to the Mediterranean basin and the scorching deserts of North Africa. What the Duce did not (and could not) foresee was that by plunging Fascist Italy into war with the Allies, his regime's days were numbered. Ciano gloomily wrote in his *Diary*: 'Mussolini speaks from the balcony of the Palazzo Venezia. The news of the war does not surprise anyone and does not arouse very much enthusiasm. I am sad, very sad. The adventure begins. May God help Italy!'[109]

At 9:40 p.m., Hitler dispatched a warm telegram to Mussolini. He welcomed the prospect of Italian troops serving next to their German brothers-in-arms in a common cause, and lambasted British and French leaders for refusing his peace terms and for stifling Italy's 'vital national rights'. Hitler's reverent attitude towards Mussolini could not have failed to appeal to the Duce's vanity:

> The historic decision which you announced today has moved me most profoundly. The whole German people is thinking of you and your country at this moment. The German *Wehrmacht* is glad to be able to stand at the side of its Italian comrades in battle.
>
> Last September the rulers of Britain and France declared war on the German Reich without any reason. They turned down every offer of a peaceful settlement. Your proposal for mediation, Duce, was also received at the time with a brusque 'No'. While we have always been very closely linked together ideologically by our two revolutions and politically by treaties, the increasing disregard shown by the rulers in London and Paris for Italy's vital national rights has now finally brought us together in the great struggle for the freedom and future of our peoples.
>
> Duce of Fascist Italy, accept the assurance of the indestructible community of arms between the German and the Italian peoples.
>
> I myself send you as always in loyal comradeship my sincerest greetings.[110]

For Mussolini and for Fascism, it was the beginning of the end.

3

War, 1940

I entrust the command of the troops in action on all fronts to the Head of the Government, Duce of Fascism, First Marshal of the [Italian] Empire.[1]

King Emmanuel III's proclamation to the Italian Armed Forces, 11 June 1940

After long and patient waiting, we have torn the mask from a country guaranteed by Great Britain, a perfidious enemy, Greece.[2]

Mussolini to Fascist Party leaders in Rome, 18 November 1940

Throughout the Second World War, the Axis nations—unlike the British and Americans from 1942 onwards—did not, for the most part, coordinate their military operations. The Germans and Italians often did not even bother to notify each other of their respective planned campaigns until the last possible moment—if at all. Now that Fascist Italy had joined the war, Hitler was under the impression that Mussolini intended to launch an immediate attack against the Allies in the Mediterranean sector. It was only logical to presume that the *Comando Supremo* had devised a plan to strike against the French, either at Corsica or Tunisia, or perhaps against the British at Malta. Mussolini's fiery declaration of war had led Hitler to believe that the Italians would take the initiative at once. But to the Führer's disbelief, the unthinkable occurred: the Italians did not act!

On 11 June, King Emmanuel III turned over command of the Italian Armed Forces to Mussolini and appealed to the martial intrepidity of Italy's 'Fighting Men':

Fighting Men on land, sea, and in the air!

As Supreme Head of all the Forces on land, sea, and in the air, in accordance with my own feelings and the tradition of my House, I once more, as twenty-five years ago, come among you.

I entrust the command of the troops in action on all fronts to the Head of the Government, Duce of Fascism, First Marshal of the [Italian] Empire.

My first thought goes out to you, while, sharing with me the deep attachment and complete devotion to our immortal country, you are preparing, together with our ally Germany, to face fresh and difficult trials with an invincible faith in overcoming them.

Fighting Men on land, sea, and in the air!

United with you as never before, I am sure that your courage and the patriotism of the Italian people will once more find means to ensure the victory of our glorious forces.[3]

For France, the end was in sight. German troops entered Paris on 14 June; French leaders had fled four days prior in the wake of the relentless German advance. On 17 June, Marshal Henri Philippe Pétain (who had taken over as prime minister the previous day following Paul Reynaud's resignation) sent word from Bordeaux to Berlin that the French Government sought an armistice. In a radio broadcast to the nation, Pétain, the 'Lion of Verdun', ruefully addressed his countrymen: 'It is futile to continue the struggle against an enemy superior in numbers and in arms. It is with a heavy heart that I say we must cease the fight. I have applied to our opponent to ask him if he is ready to sign with us, as between soldiers after the fight and in honour, a means to put an end to hostilities.'[4] On 18 June, General Charles de Gaulle, having reached London the day before, broadcast over the B.B.C. his famous *L'Appel du 18 Juin* (Appeal of 18 June) urging his French compatriots to continue resisting the Nazi occupiers. Later he solemnly proclaimed: 'France has lost a battle, she has not lost the war.'[5]

In anticipation of the imminent Anglo–German clash, Churchill addressed the House of Commons. He gravely stated:

What General [Maxime] Weygand called the Battle of France is over. I expect that the Battle of Britain is about to begin. Upon this battle depends the survival of Christian civilization. Upon it depends our own British life, and the long continuity of our institutions and our Empire. The whole fury and might of the enemy must very soon be turned on us. Hitler knows that he will have to break us in this Island or lose the war. If we can stand up to him, all Europe may be free and the life of the world may move forward into broad, sunlit uplands. But if we fail,

> then the whole world, including the United States, including all that we have known and cared for, will sink into the abyss of a new Dark Age, made more sinister, and perhaps more protracted, by the lights of perverted science. Let us therefore brace ourselves to our duties, and so bear ourselves that, if the British Empire and its Commonwealth last for a thousand years, men will still say: 'This was their finest hour.'[6]

Meanwhile, Hitler wished to discuss with Mussolini their respective terms for the French armistice. A summit meeting at Munich was therefore hastily arranged, and on 17 June, the Duce and his entourage left for Germany by rail. Aboard the train, Ciano observed that Mussolini felt uneasy at the prospect of an early peace, for the Italians had yet to contribute militarily towards the defeat of France:

> I find Mussolini dissatisfied. This sudden peace disquiets him. During the trip we speak at length in order to clarify conditions under which the armistice is to be granted to the French. The Duce is an extremist. He would like to go so far as the total occupation of French territory and demands the surrender of the French Fleet. But he is aware that his opinion has only a consultative value. The war has been won by Hitler without any active military participation on the part of Italy, and it is Hitler who will have the last word. This, naturally, disturbs and saddens him.[7]

The conference took place at the Führerhaus on 18 June, where Mussolini learned that Hitler had decided to establish a collaborationist relationship with the vanquished French. A new pro-Nazi regime under Pétain would reign. The armistice provisions would perforce have to be relatively moderate (i.e., a partial occupation of France) since Hitler was worried about the possibility that the French Government, if fatally alienated, 'might reject the German proposals and flee abroad, to London, to continue the war from there'. Above all, it was imperative that the formidable French Fleet 'be prevented from falling into British hands'. If this happened, the obvious danger was that British maritime strength would be substantially augmented. 'In certain categories,' Hitler stated, 'the present strength of the English Fleet would thereby be practically doubled or trebled…' Under such circumstances, the British would be better able to protect their convoys, and this would naturally prolong the war. It would be best for the Axis, therefore, to 'neutralize' the French Fleet by confining it to an area where it would pose no threat, perhaps Spain or Portugal. If the French were to scuttle it themselves, this too would be a 'favourable solution'.

The 'neutralization' of the French Fleet met with Mussolini's full approval. He knew very well that British possession of the powerful French Fleet would have dire consequences for Italy. If the British acquired the French Fleet, Mussolini believed that they would not remove it from the Mediterranean, but 'employ it against Italy there'. Moreover, it would be easier for the British to fortify their naval bases at Gibraltar, Malta, and the Suez Canal.

It was now time for Mussolini to enunciate his own demands. He wanted an Italian occupation of France 'from the Italian frontier to the Rhône, including Toulon and Marseilles ...' and 'disarmament of Corsica and Tunisia'. Ciano, at Mussolini's side, quickly tossed in Djibouti (French Somaliland) as well. But Hitler brushed aside Mussolini's claims. After further talks, it was decided that Italy's interests would be assured by an article included in the Franco–German Armistice that it would not enter into force until the French had also come to terms with the Italians. But when Ciano suggested that the Germans and Italians conduct negotiations together opposite the French, Hitler's ambiguous reply was that 'he did not suppose Italy would wish to negotiate at the place where the German–French negotiations for an armistice would be held...' Nor did he specify the location.

The last piece of business was to agree on the text of a short *communiqué* which revealed nothing other than that the Axis chiefs saw eye to eye on the armistice question: 'At a discussion in Munich today the Führer and the Duce have agreed on the attitude of the two allied Governments to the French request for an armistice.'[8] But this was untrue. Mussolini, to his chagrin, felt that he was being marginalized. Ciano perceptively assessed the Duce's sentiments: 'He [Mussolini] feels that his role is secondary.... In truth, the Duce fears that the hour of peace is growing near and sees fading once again the unattainable dream of his life: glory on the field of battle.'[9]

Meanwhile, General Franco was closely following the progress of the war. Thus far he had kept his country out of the conflict. But with France all but defeated, on 13 June Spain's neutral status escalated to one of 'non-belligerence'. And on 19 June, a memorandum was transmitted from the Spanish Ambassador to Ernst Weizsäcker, State Secretary, 'concerning Spanish claims in Africa and Spain's possible participation in the war':

> Since the Spanish Government considers the further existence of the French Empire in North Africa, which was partly created by the efforts of Spanish workers, to be impossible, it demands the territory of Oran, the unification of Morocco under a Spanish Protectorate, the extension of Spanish territory in the Sahara to the 20th parallel, and the extension

> of Spain's coastal territories situated in the area on the coast between the mouth of the Niger and Cape Lopez.
>
> Should England continue the war after France has ceased fighting, Spain would be willing to enter the war after a short period of preparing the public. In this case she would need some support from Germany in the form of war materials, heavy artillery, aircraft for the attack on Gibraltar, and perhaps the cooperation of German submarines in the defence of the Canary Islands. Also supplies of some foodstuffs, ammunition, motor fuels and equipment, which will certainly be available from French war stocks.[10]

But by the end of the summer, Franco had changed his mind about joining the war. The chief reason was that the expected German victory over England had not been achieved. The Germans had not yet delivered to the Anglo–Saxons the *coup de grâce*. On the contrary, the British were still in the fight and as determined as ever. The bottom line was that Spain was not militarily ready, the Spanish Civil War had devastated the nation, and Spanish colonies abroad—the Canary Islands and Spanish Morocco—could not be adequately defended from the Allies.

A few days after their meeting at Munich, Mussolini advised Hitler in a private letter that after thinking it over, he had opted to limit Italian claims against France 'to a minimum' so as not to unduly antagonize the French:

> In order to facilitate the acceptance of the armistice by the French I have not included among the clauses the occupation of the left side of the Rhône, or of Corsica, Tunis, and Djibouti, as we had intended at Munich. I have limited myself to a minimum, that is, to the demand for a demilitarized zone 50 kilometres in width. I consider this to be an indispensable minimum, also in order to avoid incidents. For the rest I have used the clauses of the German Armistice.[11]

On 21 June, the Italian Army attacked France through the Alps, in a hurry lest the Germans defeat their Gallic foe before the Italians had the chance to score a victory of their own. The French Army put up stiff resistance and made the Fascist legions pay heavily for their gains, which were minimal. Some 300,000 invaders confronted 85,000 defenders. Yet in spite of the unequal contest on the Alpine Front—thirty-two Italian divisions *versus* six French divisions—the former managed to advance only several miles.

A secondary assault was made along the French Riviera, where the Italian capture of the town of Menton was the highlight. Unlike their German counterparts, the Italians did not occupy vast tracts of French territory. Mussolini was greatly displeased by the lack of progress made and in private he excoriated the Italian people for their unwarlike qualities: 'It is the material that I lack. Even Michaelangelo had need of marble to make statues. If he had had only clay he would have been nothing more than a potter. A people who for sixteen centuries have been an anvil cannot become a hammer within a few years.'[12]

The French signed an armistice with the Germans at Compiègne on 22 June. The terms were onerous and the Germans uncompromising. Hitler, who had flown to France for the occasion, sought to humiliate the French and repay them in kind for their heavy-handed treatment of the vanquished Germans in 1918. The French signed another armistice with the Italians at the Villa Incisa, 12 miles from Rome, on the evening of 24 June. Marshal Badoglio (for Italy) and General Charles Huntzinger (for France) duly affixed their names to the historic document. The first, second, and third articles of the Italo–French Armistice were paramount:

> Article 1.
>
> France will cease hostilities in metropolitan territory, in French North Africa, in the colonies, and in territories under French mandate. France will also cease hostilities in the air and on the sea.
>
> Article 2.
>
> When the armistice comes into force and for the duration of the armistice the Italian troops will stand on the advanced lines in all theatres of operations.
>
> Article 3.
>
> In French metropolitan territory, a zone situated between the lines referred to in Article 2 and a line drawn 50 kilometres [30 miles] as the crow flies beyond the Italian lines proper, shall be demilitarized for the duration of the armistice.
>
> In Tunis the militarized zone between the present Libyan–Tunisian frontier and the line drawn on the attached map shall be demilitarized for the duration of the armistice.
>
> In Algeria and in French African territories south of Algeria which border on Libya a zone 200 kilometres wide [about 120 miles] adjoining the Libyan frontier shall be demilitarized for the duration of the armistice.
>
> For the duration of hostilities between Italy and the British Empire and for the duration of the armistice the French Somaliland coast shall be entirely demilitarized.

The sixth article also stipulated 'that so long as hostilities continue between Italy and the British Empire, the maritime military fortified areas and naval bases of Toulon, Bizerta, Ajaccio, and Oran shall be demilitarized until the cessation of hostilities against the above-named Empire'.[13] The Italo–French Armistice came into force thirty-five minutes after midnight on 25 June. Its provisions were enforced by an Italian commission established at Turin.

On 26 June, Mussolini drafted a brief letter to Hitler reiterating his wish, now that one-half of the Allied coalition had been defeated, for Italian forces to take part in the forthcoming attack against England:

> Now that the problem is to conquer Great Britain, I remind you of what I said to you at Munich [on 18 June] about the direct participation of Italy in the assault on the island. I am ready to contribute ground forces and air forces, and you know how much I desire to do so. I ask you to answer me in such a way that it will be possible for me to pass to the phase of execution. In this expectation I send you the most comradely greetings.[14]

Air Marshal Italo Balbo, governor-general of Italian Libya, was accidentally killed on 28 June by his own countrymen. Ciano described the incident: 'Balbo is dead. A tragic mistake has brought his end. The anti-aircraft battery at Tobruk fired on his plane, mistaking it for an English plane, and brought it to the ground.'[15] All passengers aboard perished. Three days later, Balbo was succeeded by the brutal Marshal Rodolfo Graziani.

Mussolini was restlessly awaiting the next phase of the conflict—the war against the Anglo–Saxons. The big question remained: would Hitler come to terms with the British, or would he be forced to launch a Channel crossing and occupy the British Isles? In the meantime, while Hitler contemplated his options, Mussolini was compelled to stay his hand and impatiently await the Germans' chosen course of action.

Over the next week, Ciano noticed that Hitler did not reply to Mussolini in connection with the latter's express wish to contribute militarily to the operation against England. On 30 June, Ciano spoke with Ambassador Alfieri by telephone, who reported: 'Hitler is going through one of his periods of isolation, which, with him, precede the making of great decisions. Therefore, he has not yet answered the Duce's message, in which he [the Duce] offered the participation of our land and air forces in the attack on Great Britain.'[16] And on 2 July, Ciano added that 'he [Hitler] does not answer Mussolini's offer to send men and planes to participate in an attack on England.... Evidently he does not place much trust in us.'[17]

Two days later, Mussolini was fretting that the conquering Germans may have discovered various sensitive papers in French possession that could be damaging to Italo–German relations: 'Mussolini is worried over the possibility that the Germans may have got hold of certain documents among those that they captured from the French which might compromise us.'[18] Another worrisome prospect to the Duce was that of Franco–German collaboration. Such an alliance might result in Italy being bilked of her war plunder, and Mussolini mentioned it to Ciano on 5 July when he briefed him on specific points to convey to Hitler during their scheduled meeting of 7 July:

> The Duce gives me instructions for my trip to Germany. He wants definitely to participate in the attack on Great Britain, if it occurs, and he is concerned over the fact that France is trying to slip gradually into the anti-British camp. He fears that this may cause us to be defrauded of our booty [Italian claims on France]. He charges me also to tell Hitler that he intends to land on the Ionian Islands and to tell him about the necessity of splitting up Yugoslavia, a typical Versailles creation, functioning against us.[19]

Ciano was received by Hitler at the Reich Chancellery at 12:30 p.m. The Führer was affable, and the two-hour meeting opened with Hitler stating that he had been contemplating whether or not to extend to the British 'another gesture of psychological and propagandist importance' (in other words, another peace offer). Thus far he had not made up his mind, although such a gambit might be 'useful in principle'. As for the invasion of England, the problem was 'a very delicate and difficult one'. The operation would unquestionably result in an extension of the war 'to other fronts'. In any event, he was not yet prepared 'to say in what form the attack against England would develop' until his General Staff had finished their assessment. With respect to Mussolini's 'keen desire' to contribute Italian land and air forces to the attack (ten divisions and thirty squadrons respectively, Ciano specified), Hitler advised 'that he was not in a position to give an answer until the planning stage was over'.

In connection with France, Hitler expressed his pleasure at the 'favourable situation' stemming from Italy's 'moderate' claims. It was absolutely essential, however, to make no mistake: 'France still continues to be the enemy of Italy and Germany, continues to be the country which, if the opportunity arose, would attempt to damage to the utmost the two Axis Powers. Therefore France will have to pay, and pay dearly…' Ciano took note of these words 'with lively satisfaction'.

Thereupon Ciano briefly touched on the Italians' upcoming Egyptian campaign. He also mentioned to Hitler his apprehensions concerning Greece; namely, 'the possibility of England's occupying the Ionian Islands in order to convert them into anti-Italian bases…' Hitler replied that all matters involving the Mediterranean sector were entirely within Italy's purview, and that he had no intention of interfering with Italian decisions and operations there. Nevertheless, Hitler did advise Ciano to refrain from 'liquidating' the Yugoslav problem just then, for the 'distinctly hostile' Yugoslavs should be dealt with at a more opportune time. Hitler's chief worry was that precipitous Italian action against Yugoslavia might 'set the whole Balkan peninsula ablaze, provoke Russian intervention, and eventually even set up a community of interests between Russia and England'. His dire injunctions notwithstanding, Hitler was of the opinion that 'Italy should immediately intervene in Yugoslavia should an outbreak arise elsewhere in the Balkans…'[20]

Afterwards, Ciano noted his personal impressions of the talk: 'Conference with Hitler.... He is rather inclined to continue the struggle and to unleash a storm of wrath and of steel upon the English. But the final decision has not been reached.... As to his health—he is well. He is calm and reserved, very reserved for a German who has won.'[21] Four days later, Ciano reported to Mussolini the particulars of his discussion with the Führer. The Duce was 'satisfied with the results'.[22]

On 13 July, Hitler at last responded to Mussolini's letter of 26 June. He turned down Mussolini's offer of ground forces for logistical reasons but was willing to accept seacraft and airplanes:

> However much, Duce, I appreciated your offer—of making a substantial number of Italian divisions available for the attack on England—at the same time we must give consideration to everything that is likely to secure a successful outcome for this very bold decision. With my advisers I have also gone fully into your other offers, Duce, to provide ships or aircraft. Here it will probably be easier to find a possibility for cooperation between our units.

This rebuff displeased Mussolini, who had been eagerly expecting an affirmative reply. He was satisfied to learn, however, that on account of the German peace offers having been repeatedly spurned by the refractory British, the Führer had at last resolved to carry out an invasion: 'I have made to Britain [Hitler wrote] so many offers of agreement, even of cooperation, and have been treated so shabbily that I am even now convinced that any new appeal to reason would meet with a similar rejection. For in that country at present it is not reason that rules, but probably the smallest portion of wisdom in history.'[23]

Fed up with British intransigence, on 16 July Hitler issued to his service chiefs his notorious Directive No. 16, the secret Nazi plan for a cross-Channel invasion of England. The preamble stated:

> Directive No. 16 on the Preparation of a Landing Operation against England

> Since England, despite her militarily hopeless situation still shows no sign of willingness to come to terms, I have decided to prepare a landing operation against England, and if necessary to carry it out.
>
> The aim of this operation is to eliminate the English homeland as a base for the carrying on of the war against Germany, and if it should become necessary to occupy it completely....

As for the landing itself, Hitler instructed that it 'must be carried out in the form of a surprise crossing on a broad front approximately from Ramsgate to the area west of the Isle of Wight, in which Luftwaffe units will take the role of artillery, and units of the Navy the role of the engineers'. Above all, it was crucial that the Royal Air Force be subdued to the extent that it could no longer oppose the German crossing; in other words, the R.A.F. had to be neutralized. Hitler also specified to his commanders-in-chief: 'The preparations for the entire operation must be completed by *mid-August*.... The project will bear the code name *Seelöwe* [Sea Lion].'[24]

A fortnight earlier, in a secret document titled 'The Continuation of the War Against England', Hitler's *Wehrmacht* operations chief, General Alfred Jodl, wrote: 'Germany's final victory over England is only a question of time.' Elaborating on the subject of a German invasion of England, he added:

> A landing in England can only be contemplated after Germany has gained control of the air. A landing in England, therefore, should not have as its objective the military conquest of the island, an objective which can be obtained by the Luftwaffe and the German Navy. Its sole purpose should be to provide the *coup de grâce*, if it should still be necessary, to a country whose war economy is already paralyzed and whose air force is no longer capable of action.[25]

In spite of what he had written to Mussolini in his recent letter, Hitler did make one final attempt to make peace with Britain. On 19 July, Ciano learned during a conference with Ribbentrop in Berlin that Hitler's major *Reichstag* speech, scheduled for 7 p.m., would be 'a last appeal to Great Britain'. Ciano apprehended that the Germans were earnestly 'hoping and praying that this appeal will not be rejected'. Ciano, who attended the speech, described the ceremony as 'solemn and stagy. Hitler speaks simply, and, I should say also, in an unusually humane tone. I believe that his desire for peace is sincere.'[26]

In his peroration Hitler declared:

> Mr. Churchill ought perhaps, for once, to believe me when I prophesy that a great Empire will be destroyed—an Empire which it was never

> my intention to destroy or even to harm. I do, however, realize that this struggle, if it continues, can end only with the complete annihilation of one or the other of the two adversaries. Mr. Churchill may believe that this will be Germany. I know that it will be different.
>
> In this hour, I feel it to be my duty before my own conscience to appeal once more to reason and common sense in Great Britain as much as elsewhere. I consider myself in a position to make this appeal since I am not the vanquished, begging favours, but the victor speaking in the name of reason.
>
> I can see no reason why this war must go on.[27]

In his lengthy speech, Hitler did not specify Germany's terms for peace, nor did he elaborate on the fate of the tens of millions of conquered peoples now under Germany's control. In any event, the B.B.C. broadcast a categorical rejection in the space of an hour. Ciano recorded the sentiment of the Germans to the British decision: 'Late in the evening, when the first cold English reactions to the speech arrive, a sense of ill-concealed disappointment spreads among the Germans.'[28]

But Mussolini 'had been against Hitler's speaking'. The Duce found Hitler's *Reichstag* address to be 'much too cunning', and in his *Diary*, Ciano explained why this was so: 'He fears that the British may find in it a pretext to begin negotiations. That would be sad for Mussolini, because now more than ever he wants war.'[29] After the war, Churchill ironically noted that this was the very least of Mussolini's concerns: 'He [Mussolini] need not have fretted himself. He was not to be denied all the war he wanted.'[30]

Although the German masses had swallowed Hitler's crafty speech, the English people had most assuredly not, and on 22 July, Foreign Secretary Halifax broadcast the official British response:

> He [Hitler] says he has no desire to destroy the British Empire, but there was in his speech no suggestion that peace must be based on justice; no word of recognition for other nations in Europe, of any right to self-determination, a principle which he so often invokes for Germany.… Hitler has now made it plain that he is preparing to direct the whole of the German might against this country.… We never wanted war. Certainly no one here wants the war to go on for a day longer than is necessary, but we shall not cease fighting until freedom for ourselves and others is secured.[31]

The day after Hitler's *Reichstag* speech, Ciano was received by the Führer for a discussion. Hitler informed Ciano that due to the unsparingly negative reaction of the British press, he had decided 'to strike the military blow at England'. 'Germany's strategic position,' Hitler confidently stated, 'as well as her sphere of influence and of economic control, are such as to have already greatly weakened the possibilities of resistance by Great Britain, which will collapse under the first blows.' In fact, the German air war against England—*die Luftschlacht um England* (the Battle of Britain)—was already underway and was 'continually growing in intensity'. British anti-aircraft defences and fighters were, to date, 'not seriously hindering the German air attack'. And Operation Sea Lion, the great German offensive against the English motherland, was presently in the works.

On a separate topic, Hitler felt it was critical that the peace not be broken in the Danubian and Balkan sectors. It was the role of the Axis Powers, Hitler averred, 'to induce Hungary and Romania to negotiate directly, and to advise moderation and prudence to both parties'. He did not wish to take sides on the issue, but personally was of the opinion that Bulgaria's territorial claims on Romania were 'moderate and her demands easily acceptable'. Hitler then praised Fascist Italy's contributions to the war (which were in actuality all but nil), and Ciano noted that Hitler was 'very well informed on our [Italy's] combined sea and air operations'. To Hitler, it appeared that Italian forces had already inflicted upon the British 'a large number of heavy blows'. Hitler concluded the meeting by advising Ciano that once his plans for the subsequent phase of the war had been finalized, he would contact Mussolini in writing and, if feasible, propose a conference at the Brenner Pass.[32] Later Ciano reflected on his conversation with Hitler: 'He would like an understanding with Great Britain. He knows that war with the English will be hard and bloody, and knows also that people everywhere today are averse to bloodshed.'[33]

On 21 July, Mussolini dispatched a cordial telegram to Hitler in reference to the latter's recent *Reichstag* address: 'The words of your great *Reichstag* speech have gone directly to the hearts of the Italian people. I thank you and repeat that the Italian people, whatever may happen, will march together with your people until the end, that is to say, until victory.' Hitler sent a brief reply: 'I thank you, Duce, for your friendly telegram. United in our ideologies and in the force of our arms, Fascist Italy and National Socialist Germany will victoriously conquer liberty for our peoples.'[34]

Romania, situated at the nexus of Central and Southeastern Europe, fared badly in 1940. That summer she was compelled to yield considerable territory to no less than three of her neighbours. The first was the U.S.S.R. Two days after Molotov's ultimatum of 26 June, Soviet forces occupied

Bessarabia, Northern Bukovina, and Hertza. Italo–German pressure was instrumental in the Romanian Crown Council's decision to submit to Soviet terms. Nevertheless, six of twenty-seven council members had rejected the ultimatum. Further concessions were to follow—to Hungary and Bulgaria.

To discuss his government's fervent wish to preserve what was left of Romanian territory, Prime Minister Ion Gigurtu conferred with Mussolini at the Palazzo Venezia on 27 July. Gigurtu's 'main preoccupation' was the Soviet Union. After the recent annexations Russia appeared to be 'maintaining a calmer attitude towards Romania', but this could change at any time, for the Soviets were insatiable. He was concerned that the Soviets might interpret 'territorial concessions by Romania to Hungary and Bulgaria ... as a pretext for further claims on Bucharest'. Gigurtu emphasized that it was his government's wish 'to bring Romania's policy into line with ... a programme which is represented by complete adhesion to the policy of the Axis'.

Mussolini was critical of two of Romania's erstwhile policies: 'First error—faith in Geneva [i.e. the League of Nations]; second—acceptance of the English guarantees.'* Conversely, Mussolini approved of Romania's 'realistic policy' regarding Russia, for war with the Soviet colossus would inevitably end in a Romanian defeat. The Hungarians, Mussolini explained, were 'ready to make a compromise solution'. It was necessary for 'all States to make their political frontiers coincide with the ethnological ones'. If this resulted in a truncated Romania, at least it would have the benefit of making her 'more homogeneous'. As for the Bulgarians, their moderate claims would render a Romano–Bulgar understanding 'very easy to reach'. Once these territorial matters were resolved, Mussolini added, Romania would need to work out 'problems of an internal nature'. Among these included the necessity 'to eliminate the Jews from the life of the State and to restrict all their activities'. The Duce described Romania as 'an agricultural country', one with 'great productive capacities'. So long as she exercised 'a sound policy' Romania would remain 'the most thickly-populated and strongest State in the Danube Basin'.[35]

Gigurtu's efforts proved to be in vain. At a meeting in Vienna arbitrated by Ciano and Ribbentrop on 30 August, Northern Transylvania was awarded to Hungary. Gigurtu's foreign minister, Mihail Manoilescu, collapsed in a faint when he saw the map delineating Romania's new frontier. And on 7 September, Southern Dobruja was returned to Bulgaria per the Treaty of Craiova.

* Renounced by Bucharest on 1 July 1940.

Meanwhile, the negative reception of the British to his recent *Reichstag* peace speech had convinced Hitler to unleash the Luftwaffe against them. Operation Sea Lion would be launched once the R.A.F. had been eliminated from the skies. Hitler's Directive No. 17, issued to his service chiefs on 1 August, outlined the particulars for 'intensified' aerial and naval measures against Britain:

> Directive No. 17 for the Conduct of Air and Naval Warfare against England
>
> In order to establish the conditions necessary for the final conquest of England, I intend to continue the air and naval war against the English homeland more intensively than heretofore.
>
> To this end I issue the following orders:
>
> 1. The German air arm is to overcome the English Air Force with all means at its disposal and in the shortest possible time....
> 2. After gaining temporary or local air superiority, the air war is to be carried on against harbours, especially against establishments connected with food supply ...
> 4. The Luftwaffe ... is to stand by in force for Operation *Seelöwe* [Sea Lion].
> 5. I reserve for myself the decision on terror attacks as a means of reprisal.
> 6. The intensified air war may commence on or after 5 August....
>
> The Navy is authorized to begin the projected intensified naval warfare at the same time.[36]

On 13 August, *Reichsmarschall* Göring initiated Operation Eagle Attack, the Luftwaffe's air offensive aimed at knocking out the R.A.F. Göring believed, and had boastfully assured Hitler, that his vaunted Luftwaffe would succeed—independently of the other branches of the *Wehrmacht*—in defeating the British, thereby rendering the necessity for an invasion superfluous. The Luftwaffe conducted heavy bombing raids against British airfields and engaged the R.A.F. in fierce aerial combat over British airspace. Throughout the Battle of Britain both sides incurred heavy losses. Nevertheless, the British continued to valorously defend their Island and refused to give in. To the House of Commons on 20 August, Churchill extolled the heroism of R.A.F. airmen: 'Never in the field of human conflict was so much owed by so many to so few.'[37]

By mid-September, the Germans recognized that the prerequisite to invasion, the destruction of the R.A.F., had not been achieved. Owing to this failure, on 17 September Hitler called off Operation Sea Lion. (This decision, of course, was unknown to the British, who were still apprehensive.) The *German Naval War Diary* recorded: 'The enemy Air Force is still by no means defeated. On the contrary, it shows increasing activity. The weather situation as a whole does not permit us to expect a period of calm.... *The Führer therefore decides to postpone Sea Lion indefinitely*.'[38]

Mussolini had previously expressed to Hitler his wish for Italian fliers to participate in the air war against Britain. Thus, on 10 September 1940, the *Corpo Aereo Italiano* (Italian Air Corps) was established. In overall command was General Rino Corso Fougier, future chief of staff of the Italian Air Force. The C.A.I. consisted of some 200 planes headquartered on Belgian soil. Italian air raids commenced in late October. Harwich and Felixstowe were bombed on 24 October, Ramsgate and Deal on 29 October. A major clash with the R.A.F., albeit unsuccessful, took place on 11 November. A week later, Mussolini declared to provincial Fascist Party leaders:

> In order to consecrate the fraternity of arms of Italy and Germany, I asked for and obtained from the Führer permission for direct Italian participation in the battle against Britain with Italian planes and submarines. I may add that Germany has no need of our help. Notwithstanding this, the grateful Führer accepted my offer. Nothing can better make for lasting relations between people animated by common ideas than bloodshed in a common cause and sacrifices shared. I am sure the Italian airmen and submarine crews will bring honour to their flag.[39]

But the C.A.I.'s track record against technically superior British Spitfires and Hurricanes was mediocre. Beset by poor weather and substandard aircraft, Italian losses were high, both in terms of planes and airmen. In the final analysis, the Italian contribution to the Battle of Britain was negligible.

In accordance with Mussolini's conception of a 'parallel war', in early August a new, distant theatre of war opened in East Africa. The Somalian campaign pitted the Italians against their primary foe, the British, for the first time. It was one of the Italians' few military successes.

British Commander-in-Chief Middle East General Archibald Wavell had available in 1940 aggregate forces consisting of approximately 86,000 men.* His opposition in the East African sector consisted of 200,000 troops in Italian East Africa commanded by the duke of Aosta (Prince Amedeo). Wavell's forces were substantially outnumbered, and with France out of the picture, Mussolini's Fascist legions could now direct their entire focus upon the British.

---

* A partial breakdown of British forces under General Wavell: Egypt—36,000; Palestine—27,000; Sudan—9,000; Kenya—8,500; and British Somaliland—1,500. Small garrisons were also present at Aden and Cyprus—2,500 and 800 respectively.[41]

On 3 August, Italian forces—approximately 24,000 men—invaded British Somaliland, broaching the frontier in a three-pronged attack. Ciano noted in his *Diary* that 'the Duke of Aosta has begun his offensive against British Somaliland, with excellent prospects'.[40] On 5 August, the left formation (under Lieutenant-General Sisto Bertoldi) took Zeila, the central-primary formation (under Lieutenant-General Carlo De Simone) took Hargeisa, and on 6 August, the right formation (under Brigadier-General Arturo Bertello) took Odweina. By 10 August, the Italian invaders—*en route* to Berbera, the colonial capital—had reached British defences at Tug Argan. Next day they attacked.

On 14 August, an impatient Mussolini dispatched a telegram to Viceroy Aosta ordering him to throw in 'all available reserves ... to stimulate the operation'. Facing overwhelming odds and superior Italian firepower, the only viable option for the British defenders was to fall back. A withdrawal to Berbera was authorized on 15 August by General Henry Wilson, Wavell's fill-in. On 16 August, British evacuees began boarding Royal Navy ships at Berbera in haste, destination Aden. Some 7,000 escaped. Berbera was captured on 19 August, but the Somalian campaign ended, for the Italians, in a pyrrhic victory. Italian fatalities were 2,052; on the British side they were 260 (a ratio of nearly 8:1). But in spite of the high death toll, Fascist propaganda proclaimed a glorious triumph over the decadent British, and Mussolini was overjoyed. The protectorate was incorporated into Italian East Africa.*

Save for their operations in East Africa, that summer the Italian Armed Forces remained unengaged. Two major concerns weighed heavily on Mussolini at this time: first, that the British and German antagonists might reach an agreement, ending the war prematurely thereby; and second, that the war might conclude without Fascist Italy having made any territorial acquisitions or achieved any military victories whatsoever. Seeking, therefore, to further implement his theory of a 'parallel war', on 6 August Mussolini discussed with Ciano the prospect of launching an operation against Yugoslavia: 'Mussolini talks very much about an Italian attack on Yugoslavia during the second half of September.' But Ciano felt that the Führer would not countenance any disruptions in Southeastern Europe: 'As regards the attack on Yugoslavia, I do not believe that, unless something new comes up, Hitler will permit the *status quo* of the Balkans to be disturbed.'[42]

* British Somaliland was recaptured just seven months later, in March 1941 (Operation Appearance).

Several days later, on 10 August, Mussolini was still contemplating further aggression, this time against Greece: 'The Duce is considering an "act of force because since 1923 [the Corfu Incident] he has some accounts to settle, and the Greeks deceive themselves if they think that he has forgotten".'[43] And the following day, the Duce continued in the same vein: 'Mussolini speaks of the Greek question and wants particulars on Ciamuria.... He has had Jacomoni and Visconti Prasca come to Rome and intends to confer with them. He speaks of a surprise attack against Greece towards the end of September.'[44]

Ciano, Jacomoni, and Visconti Prasca were received at the Palazzo Venezia by Mussolini on 12 August to discuss the feasibility of initiating a Greek campaign:

> I [Ciano] accompany Jacomoni and Visconti Prasca to the Duce, who sets down the political and military lines for action against Greece. If Ciamuria and Corfu are yielded without striking a blow, we shall not ask for anything more. If, on the other hand, any resistance is attempted, we shall go to the limit. Jacomoni and Visconti Prasca consider the action possible, and even easy, provided, however, that it be undertaken at once. On the other hand, the Duce is still of the opinion, for general military reasons, that the action should be postponed until towards the end of September.[45]

But after being alerted to the Italians' aggressive intentions, Ribbentrop sent for Alfieri and reproachfully informed him that any Italian plans of conquest, either in Yugoslavia or Greece, had to be abandoned and were 'not at all welcome in Berlin'. On the contrary, he added, 'every effort must be concentrated against Great Britain ... there and there alone is "the question of life or death"'. Ciano was incredulous at the Germans' peremptory attitude: 'It is a complete order to halt all along the line.'[46]

Shortly thereafter, his tail between his legs, Alfieri met with Ribbentrop again and presented him with a document which affirmed that the Italians would toe the German line. The war against England would take the highest priority; no operations against Yugoslavia would be undertaken; Italo–Greek differences would be resolved by diplomacy; and Italian measures in Albania would be limited to buttressing Italian forces with several divisions:

> The Italian Government is in accord with the German Government in the conviction that the war against England is one of fundamental significance....
>
> No action of any sort is intended against Yugoslavia....
>
> The attempt is now being made to transfer the controversy with Greece to a diplomatic plane, and nothing more will be done than to reinforce the six divisions presently in Albania by an additional three divisions.[47]

Franco sent Mussolini a personal letter on 15 August to inform him of the Spanish Government's plan 'to make the greatest efforts in our preparations, in order to enter the foreign war at a favourable opportunity'. Ever since Italy had entered the war, Franco stated, Spain has 'had to take a clearer stand ... changing to one of non-belligerency'. Unfortunately for Spain, her new stance had resulted in 'great repercussions ... in the field of foreign affairs'. Punitive economic measures had been undertaken by both the British and Americans in the form of a blockade and ban on Spanish exports respectively.

On a positive note, however, Franco pointed out that 'the defeat of France liberated our frontiers, lessening the grave tension which we along with our Moroccans have been bearing since our Civil War'. It was now necessary for him to submit to the Duce 'the Spanish aspirations and claims traditionally maintained throughout our history'. For security reasons, it was necessary to strengthen Spain's border and safeguard Spanish 'communications with the Canary Island group'.* Franco concluded by requesting Italy's solidarity in the achievement of Spanish aspirations. He assured Mussolini of Spain's 'unconditional support' and expressed his 'greatest admiration' for the courageous Italian soldiers 'who are fighting so gloriously'.[48]

Ten days later, Mussolini replied to Franco's letter. He adjured Franco that it was absolutely critical for Spain to enter the war at the side of the Axis. Otherwise, Spain would be excluded from the New European Order and the Italo–German victors would disinterest themselves in any Spanish territorial claims in Africa. Mussolini understood full well that the Spanish Civil War had taken a severe toll on Spain and that having an ample amount of time to recover would, in a perfect world, be ideal. But this was not to be, for the exigencies of war ruled it out. Mussolini again touched upon Spanish expansionism is Africa—a subject which struck a deep chord with Franco—and urged the *Caudillo* not to let the chance slip to expand Spain's colonial empire. Mussolini repeated the refrain that following the fall of France, Britain would be crushed beneath the Axis boot. Lastly, he assured Franco of Italian unity with Spanish aims:

> Ever since the outbreak of the war I have been constantly of the opinion that 'your' Spain, the Spain of the Falange Revolution, could not remain neutral until the end of the war, but at the right moment would change to non-belligerency and finally to intervention.
>
> Should that not happen, Spain would alienate herself from European history, especially the history of the future, which the two victorious Axis Powers will determine....

* In the event the Axis—with Spanish participation or without—were to invade Gibraltar, the British intended in turn to seize the Spanish Canary Islands (an archipelago 60 miles off the Moroccan coast).

> It is clear to me that Spain, after three years of civil war, needed a long period of recuperation, but events will not permit it, and your domestic economic condition will not get worse when you change from non-belligerency to intervention.
>
> I should like to say to you, dear Franco, that I ... am sure that in your decisions you will proceed on the basis of the protection of the vital interests of your people and am just as certain that you will not let this opportunity go by of giving Spain her African *Lebensraum*.
>
> There is no doubt that after France, Great Britain will be defeated; the British regime exists only on one single element: the lie.
>
> I certainly do not need to tell you that you, in your aspirations, can count on the full solidarity of Fascist Italy.[49]

On 28 August Ciano, *en route* to Vienna to arbitrate a Hungarian–Romanian territorial dispute with Ribbentrop, detoured along the way to confer with Hitler at Berchtesgaden. There, the Führer informed Ciano that 'three stages of preparations' for Operation Sea Lion were necessary. These entailed: '(*a*) prepare large landing craft and transport; (*b*) site heavy artillery on [the] French coast; (*c*) destroy [the] British Air Force, and especially fighters.' The first two criteria had been achieved, and only the third remained. Hitler explained that thus far 'persistent bad weather had hindered the German Air Force'. What was needed was two weeks of clear weather to enable the Luftwaffe to gain supremacy in the air. It would then be possible 'to neutralize British naval superiority and carry out the landing'.

But Ciano was able to perceive that in spite of Hitler's unwavering certainty in ultimate victory, the Germans now expected the war against England to continue throughout the winter. Furthermore, Ciano was able to discern that both Hitler and Ribbentrop were extremely distrustful of the Soviet Union, 'whose present policy is to exploit to the maximum eventual complications, thrusting forward, with the complicity of Bulgaria and Yugoslavia, "as far as the Straits, the Aegean, and even the Adriatic"'. Next day Ciano cabled a brief summary of the meeting to the Duce.[50]

Back in early August, with the German invasion of Britain apparently in the offing, Mussolini had decided that the time was ripe to strike against the British in Egypt. He had therefore instructed Rodolfo Graziani, commander of Italian forces in Libya, to invade Egypt by 8 August. Marshal Graziani had strongly argued against a desert campaign which he believed was bound to fail. But the Duce sought battlefield glory and he had not been interested in Graziani's misgivings. Mussolini had therefore ordered Graziani to proceed or else he would be replaced, and Graziani had reluctantly 'answered that he will obey. The attack will begin tomorrow.' Nevertheless, Ciano observed, not without irony: 'Never has a military operation been conducted so much against the will of the commanders.'[51] Finally, after yet another delay, on 13 September Graziani's Tenth Army marched into Egypt (*Operazione E*). The Italians' ultimate objective was to capture the Suez Canal, then protected by a British garrison per the Anglo–Egyptian Treaty (1936). Enjoying initial success, Italian troops advanced 60 miles to the seaport town of Sidi Barrani. Ciano recorded the Duce's exultation: 'Mussolini is radiant with joy. He has taken the entire responsibility of the offensive on his shoulders, and he is proud that he was right.'[52] On 16 September, Graziani ordered a halt to construct defensive fortifications (camps) and await the completion of the *Via Della Vittoria* (Victory Road) before pushing on to Mersa Matruh 80 miles distant. The drive to Mersa Matruh was eventually set for the middle of December.

Ribbentrop arrived in Rome on 19 September to discuss with Mussolini 'the present stage of the war between Germany and Great Britain'. Owing to the importance of the subject matter, Ciano and Ambassadors Alfieri and Mackensen were also present. Ribbentrop explained that in the Führer's view, the reason for the 'impudent attitude' of the British, i.e. their continued refusal to submit under the relentless German bombing campaign (the 'Blitz', as the British Press termed it), was 'desperation, and also, in certain cases, by lack of comprehension, as well as the hope of double intervention in favour of Great Britain—by Russia and America'. Ribbentrop desired to 'now submit for the Duce's approval, the project for a tripartite alliance with Japan'. From the German standpoint, Ribbentrop explained, its purpose would be to intensify American isolationist sentiment. The other matter he wished to discuss with the Duce was the substance of his talk with Foreign Minister Suñer. Spain was prepared to enter the war on the side of the Axis in exchange for 'grain and raw materials, the dispatch of certain specialized weapons, as well as ... the coastal strip of Morocco from Oran to Cap Blanc' (the latter to be transferred to Spain after the ultimate victory had been achieved). 'Spain's entry into the war,' Ribbentrop continued, 'would have as its immediate object the occupation of Gibraltar.' The Mediterranean could then be sealed off at its western point of access.

The Duce was entirely in accord with Ribbentrop's propositions. He agreed that an Italo–German–Japanese alliance would 'have the effect of paralyzing American action'. As for Spain taking up arms with the Axis, it would be 'an event of great importance'. Should the Axis snatch Gibraltar from the English, the British Empire would be dealt 'a severe blow'. Furthermore, it would afford the Italian Navy 'free passage in the Straits'.

To his German interlocutor, Mussolini did not neglect to expatiate on 'the problem' of Greece. The Duce explained: 'The Greeks are to Italy what the Norwegians were to Germany before the April operation. For us, too, it is therefore necessary to take steps to liquidate Greece; all the more since, when our land forces have made further progress in Egypt, the English Fleet will no longer be able to remain in Alexandria and will attempt to make for Greek ports.' Nevertheless, Mussolini fully recognized that that the primary Italo–German objective was, above all, 'to defeat England'. Lastly, Mussolini inquired as to 'the attitude of Portugal'; Ribbentrop replied that the Portuguese were wary of 'being absorbed by Spain'. But once Spain had joined the war, it would then be opportune 'to attract Salazar* into the orbit of the Axis and its allies'.[53]

Five days later, after a night-time telephone conversation with Ambassador Mackensen concerning General de Gaulle and his unclear agenda, Ciano noticed 'that as time works against the possibility of a British collapse, solidarity between Free France and the French Colonial Empire appears more evident'. He discussed the matter with Mussolini, who was contemplating the occupation of Corsica. This was a move Ciano unreservedly agreed with: 'He [Mussolini] is right. If we don't get there the British will, and from Ghisonaccia the Royal Air Force will attack Italy.'[54]

On 27 September, the governments of Fascist Italy, Nazi Germany, and Imperial Japan concluded at Berlin the Tripartite Pact (see Appendix B for the full text). The signatories were Ciano, Ribbentrop, and the Japanese ambassador to Germany, Saburō Korusu. But unlike the Pact of Steel signed sixteen months earlier, the Tripartite Pact targeted not England and France, but America. The latter was perceived to be a rapidly growing threat, for American neutrality might not last. What the Tripartite Pact signified to the democratic Powers is that the three aggressor nations had combined forces to dominate the world and to implement an oppressive 'new order' within their respective spheres of influence—Europe and Greater East Asia. The first three articles stipulated:

> Article 1.
>
> Japan recognizes and respects the leadership of Germany and Italy in the establishment of a new order in Europe.
>
> Article 2.
>
> Germany and Italy recognize and respect the leadership of Japan in the establishment of a new order in Greater East Asia.
>
> Article 3.
>
> Germany, Italy, and Japan agree to cooperate in their efforts on the aforesaid basis. They further undertake to assist one another with all political, economic, and military means, if one of the three Contracting Parties is attacked by a Power at present not involved in the European war or in the Chinese–Japanese conflict.[55]

* Nationalist leader António de Oliveira Salazar, prime minister of Portugal from 1932–68.

'The pact is signed,' Ciano wrote contemplatively in his *Diary*. 'The signature takes place more or less like that of the Pact of Steel. But the atmosphere is cooler. Even the Berlin street crowd, a comparatively small one, composed mostly of school children, cheers with regularity but without conviction. Japan is far away. Its help is doubtful. One thing is certain: that the war will be long.'[56]

In spite of its propaganda value, the Tripartite Pact had a severe defect, as Ciano had observed. In practice, on account of the enormous distances separating both Italy and Germany from Japan, it was not feasible for the respective parties to render effective military aid to the other. And on top of everything else, Britain's powerful naval forces continued to dominate the seas worldwide.

Four days later, on 1 October, Suñer arrived in Rome for a discussion with Mussolini. To the Duce, Suñer declared that Spain was preparing to wage war against her age-old historic enemy, England. He pointed out that since the outbreak of war, Spain had 'always given the Axis Powers moral support'. However, at present, Spain was burdened with serious domestic problems. On the economic front there was a shortage of crops, and on the political front anti-Francoist elements were 'still strong and numerous'. On a positive note, he felt that for Spain, war would have the salutary effect of reunifying the nation into 'one group', for both Morocco and Gibraltar were sensitive issues that affected the Spanish people deeply, the youth especially. Thereupon Suñer related details of his recent activities and contacts *vis-à-vis* Germany, and listed Spain's numerous requirements for her early entry into the war: 'grain, fuel, special weapons, aircraft, etc.'.

Thereupon Mussolini replied to Suñer's points. From the outbreak of hostilities, he had known positively that Francoist Spain could not remain aloof from the final showdown with the Allies, the outcome of which would 'decide the fate of the nations [of Europe] for a long period to come'. Mussolini acknowledged that Spain had 'certain vital needs'; this was a fact the Axis Powers had 'always recognized'. 'It is precisely in the pursuit of these requirements,' Mussolini asserted, 'that the Spanish revolution will complete the process of natural unification.' In his letter of 25 August, he had outlined these precepts.

What now remained was to determine the exact moment for Francoist Spain to enter the war. In this connection, two possibilities existed: one, that the British would attack Spain, drawing first blood thereby; or two, that the Spanish, alternatively, would take the bull by the horns and strike first. Mussolini felt that since the British were far too preoccupied elsewhere by the Axis to initiate hostilities against the Spaniards, the second option was the only viable one. Accordingly, Mussolini believed that Spain—with Italo–German assistance—had to 'accelerate her military preparations'. It was necessary that Spanish intervention 'be decided on collectively' and that it occur precisely when it would burden Spain the least and benefit the Axis most. 'As far as the aid which Italy can give is concerned,' Mussolini stated, 'it is out of the question—in view of the scanty grain harvest—for us to help make up the large Spanish deficit.' As for what Italy could contribute, that could be negotiated at another time. Nevertheless, Italy could at once guarantee 'a concentration of air strength'. The entry of America into the war, added the Duce, was one factor 'which might precipitate Spanish intervention'. However, this did not seem likely for at least several months. Mussolini concluded 'by affirming his faith in the Spanish contribution to the victory of the Axis' and assured Suñer that he intended to give timely consideration to the question of Italian aid to Spain.[57]

On 4 October, Mussolini and Hitler discussed war strategy at the Brenner. The question of how to draw Spain into the war on the Axis side was examined. As was his wont, Hitler thoroughly monopolized the conversation. Mussolini had by then resolved to invade Greece, although he did not openly disclose this to Hitler. Nevertheless, he alluded to it by disparaging the Greek Government's 'treachery', i.e. their friendly relations and cooperation with England behind the scenes. Hitler, however, was opposed to any Balkan adventures. In his opinion, the Axis would do well to steer clear of non-essential distractions. Most notably Hitler made no mention whatsoever of his secret plans to invade the U.S.S.R.

Ciano favourably described the Axis dictators' second Brenner summit meeting:

> Rarely have I seen the Duce in such good humour and good shape as at the Brenner Pass today. The meeting was cordial and the conversations were certainly the most interesting of all that have taken place so far. Hitler put at least some of his cards on the table, and talked to us about his plans for the future. These are my general impressions: (1) there is no longer any talk about a landing in the British Isles and preparations already made remain where they are; (2) it is hoped to attract France into the orbit of the anti-British coalition, since it is now realized that the Anglo–Saxon world is still a hard nut to crack; (3) greater importance is given to the Mediterranean sector, which is good for us. Hitler was energetic and again extremely anti-Bolshevist. 'Bolshevism,' he said, 'is the doctrine of people who are lowest in the scale of civilization.' Ribbentrop, on the other hand, was very silent and in noticeably bad health.[58]

Although Hitler had acknowledged on multiple occasions that the Mediterranean and Adriatic lay in the Italian orbit, Mussolini knew that Hitler did not want to stir the Balkan pot, for German interests in the Balkans were economic, not military. But Mussolini was greatly put off by Hitler's habitual practice of taking decisive action without consulting him beforehand; German duplicity knew no bounds. The Nazi–Soviet Pact, which the Italians abhorred, was a case in point. And the most recent episode was the German occupation of Romania* without any advance notification to Italy. Mussolini therefore decided to turn the tables on Hitler and launch an independent *blitzkrieg* of his own. He fumed: 'Hitler always faces me with a *fait accompli*. This time I am going to pay him back in his own coin. He will find out from the papers that I have occupied Greece. In this way the equilibrium will be re-established.'[59]

In Mussolini's opinion, a Greek campaign was too grand a venture not to be undertaken. If successful, as Mussolini believed it would be—'In three days we will be in Athens!'—it would demonstrate that Fascist Italy, like her Teutonic ally, was also capable of lightning victories. Italian prestige would be elevated, and Mussolini's popularity would soar (he believed), as it did in 1936 after the Italian conquest of Ethiopia. Thus on 15 October, Mussolini ordered Marshal Badoglio and General Roatta to invade Greece. Ciano noted: 'A meeting with the Duce at the Palazzo Venezia, to discuss the Greek enterprise. Badoglio, Roatta, Soddu, Jacomoni, Visconti Prasca, and myself take part in it.'[60] The war council was held in Mussolini's study at 11 a.m. The Duce opened the proceedings with an introductory speech:

> DUCE: The object of this meeting is to lay down in broad outline the procedure to be followed in the attack I have decided to launch against Greece.
>
> This attack will have, first of all, to aim at both sea and land objectives.
>
> Our land objectives must be designed to give us possession of the whole South Albanian coastline. They are, therefore, the occupation of the Greek islands of Zante, Cephalonia, and Corfu; and the capture of Salonika.
>
> When we have reached these objectives, we shall have improved our position in the Mediterranean with regard to England.
>
> Either simultaneously or later, Greece must be occupied completely so as to get her out of the fighting and ensure that, whatever happens, she remains within our political and economic orbit.
>
> Having thus defined the problem, I have also settled the date which, in my opinion, should not be postponed even for an hour—namely, the 26th of this month.
>
> This is an operation I have been planning for a long time, for months and months, before we came into the war—before the conflict began, even.

* On 8 October, half a million German troops entered Romania, seized the Ploieşti oil fields, and marched into Bucharest. Casualties were relatively few. Dictatorial powers were granted to the pro-German Marshal Ion Antonescu and Romania signed the Tripartite Pact on 23 November, joining the Axis thereby.

> Having settled these essential points, we must now consider how to put this operation into effect. I have therefore sent for the Lieutenant-General of Albania [Jacomoni] and for the Commander of our Army [Visconti Prasca] to give us a picture of the political and military situation, so that we may decide on all the measures needed to attain our ends in the best way and in the shortest possible time.
>
> I should add that I foresee no trouble from the North. Yugoslavia has every interest in keeping quiet, as may incidentally be seen from public declarations from official sources, which rule out the possibility of complications arising except where the defence of the country is concerned.
>
> As to Turkish complications, I should discount them, especially now that Germany has planted herself in Romania, and Bulgaria has strengthened her position. The latter might be a pawn in the game, and I shall take the necessary steps to see that she does not lose this unique opportunity of realizing her claims to Macedonia and an outlet to the sea.
>
> Having fixed our objectives and the date, we must now look at the other aspects of the situation, so as to decide, on the basis of these, the measures to be taken and the means of carrying them out.

Mussolini's confederates then gave a military appraisal of the Greeks. Jacomoni interposed with the remark that the Greeks 'now appear determined to oppose our operations'. Visconti Prasca opined that as soldiers the Greeks were 'not the sort of people to enjoy fighting'. Although Mussolini and his abettors did not as yet have any inkling, the latter assessment was very soon to be proven incorrect.

A final detail remained. Mussolini felt it would be necessary to orchestrate a sham operation to make the Italian action in Greece appear justified to the outside world:

> DUCE: Now there is still another thing. Now the date has been settled, the question is, how to make this action appear necessitated by events. We have a general justification in the fact that Greece is an ally of our enemies, who use her bases, etc.; but there ought to be an 'incident' to enable us to say we are coming to keep order. If you can provoke this incident, well and good—if not, it doesn't matter.
>
> JACOMONI: I could manage something on the frontier—incidents between the Tsameri [an Albanian tribe] and the Greek authorities.
>
> VISCONTI PRASCA: We have already got French weapons and bombs ready for a feint attack.

> DUCE: All that does not matter to me in the slightest; the thing is to provide a little smoke. However, it would be a good thing for you to furnish a pretext for us to touch off the fuse.
>
> CIANO: When do you want the incident to occur?
>
> DUCE: On the 24th.
>
> CIANO: An incident will occur on the 24th.
>
> DUCE: No one will believe in this coincidence, but by way of metaphysical justification one might say that matters were bound to come to a head.
>
> What you need in operations of this kind is to act with the maximum resolution, for that is the secret of success, with regard, also to any outside help.
>
> Now we must provide an alibi in such a way that people will be able to say, 'There is nothing to be done. What is the use of going to the help of people who have been defeated already?' That is an argument which the Turks might well use, and which even the English might find it convenient to invoke.[61]

Due to a 'lack of preparations', the date for the invasion was later pushed back an additional two days, to 28 October (the eighteenth anniversary of the Blackshirts' March on Rome).

On 19 October, Mussolini wrote a letter to Hitler outlining the conclusions he had reached in the aftermath of their summit meeting at the Brenner a fortnight earlier. The communication was belatedly sent on 22 October and received by the Germans two days thereafter. The Duce began with an anti-French exposition. He complained that 'the French hate the Axis more than before, that Vichy and de Gaulle have divided their roles, and that the French do not consider themselves beaten because, as they say, they did not wish to fight'. Moreover, Mussolini accused, the double-dealing Vichy Government was 'in contact with London through Lisbon' and was counting on America to pull Britain's chestnuts out of the fire. Therefore, collaboration with the French was unthinkable. In a nutshell: the inclusion of France in an 'anti-English continental bloc' was not a viable option. Mussolini continued:

> I nevertheless believe that the moment has come for defining the shape of metropolitan and colonial France of tomorrow, reduced, as you justly wish, to proportions that will prevent her from beginning again

> to dream of expansion and hegemony.... The metropolitan and colonial acquisitions claimed by Italy [from France] are, as I have told you, rather modest: They are limited to Nice, Corsica, and Tunisia. I do not mention [French] Somaliland, which is pure desert country.... If then the financial and economic questions incident to the war are taken care of, Italy does not have any nor will she advance any further demands in regard to France.

In his uncharacteristically lengthy missive Mussolini also broached the subject of Greece, underscoring the fact that the Greeks were in the British camp and that he intended in the near future 'to launch operations simultaneously on the Greek and on the Egyptian front'. But the Duce purposefully neglected to specify an exact date, so as to leave Hitler in the dark:

> As regards Greece, I am resolved to end the delays, and very soon. Greece is one of the main points of English maritime strategy in the Mediterranean. The King is English, the political classes are pro-English, and the people are immature but trained to hate Italy. Greece has ordered the mobilization of her armed forces and, as early as last May, has made air and naval bases available to Great Britain ... English officials have recently taken virtual possession of all [air] fields in Greece. In short, Greece is to the Mediterranean what Norway was to the North Sea [a liability], and must not escape the same fate [invasion and occupation].

Mussolini concluded with an assessment of Spain. The assumption of the post of foreign minister by Suñer, the Duce reasoned, ensured 'that the tendencies hostile to the Axis are eliminated or at least neutralized'. However, Mussolini felt that Spain's 'internal economic situation' had not improved, and he added: 'Again I express my conviction that Spanish non-belligerence is more advantageous to us than her intervention. We ought to keep intervention as a reserve: It is a card that we ought to play at the most opportune moment ... such as prolongation of the war through 1941 or an overt intervention of the United States. Meanwhile Spain will have the time necessary to prepare herself.'[62]

Hitler's special train reached the French town of Hendaye, near the Spanish frontier, on the afternoon of 23 October. The occasion was a meeting with Franco held at the local railroad station. With both dictators comfortably seated in Hitler's parlour car, the Führer resolutely assured Franco that Britain was thoroughly defeated. Franco was skeptical of this presumptuous claim, for German efforts to eliminate the R.A.F. over the summer as a prerequisite to invasion had obviously failed. What Franco sought was the French colonial empire in North Africa, free and clear. Hitler proposed to Franco that Spain enter the war alongside the Germans and Italians in January 1941. German 'specialists' would seize Gibraltar from the British. The rock fortress would then be placed under Spanish control. But Franco declined, stressing that 'Spanish pride' precluded this possibility. If Gibraltar were to be captured, it would have to be done solely by Spaniards.

Although ideologically eye to eye with the Axis Powers, Franco was unwilling to commit himself. (Nor was Franco, who distrusted the Germans, willing to grant German troops passage through Spanish territory. In case the Germans might attempt to do so he positioned Spanish forces in the Pyrenees to interdict them.) Franco also observed, quite correctly, that even if the Germans succeeded in occupying England with land forces, the British Government and the Royal Navy would likely withdraw to the safety of Canada. From there, with American aid, they would continue the war at sea.

Lastly a secret protocol was signed (and later finalized in Vienna by the foreign ministers), but it was only of token value since neither party's requirements were met. The tedious conversation lasted for nine hours. Hitler was at his wits' end. He had been thwarted by the little Spanish revolutionary, whom he had been unable to draw into the Axis. The experience had been a most unpleasant one. 'Rather than go through it again,' Hitler confided to Mussolini in Florence several days later, he 'would prefer to have three or four teeth taken out.'[63]

Over the course of the next few days, Hitler and Ribbentrop learned of Mussolini's intentions concerning Greece, for large-scale military undertakings such as the Italians were planning could not remain entirely secret. At Hitler's behest, Ribbentrop contacted Ciano in Rome by telephone on 25 October to propose a conference between the two Axis chiefs. Perhaps Mussolini could be dissuaded. The Italians, although wary, agreed, and a meeting was scheduled for 28 October at Florence.

But the wheels were already in motion. At 3 a.m. on 28 October, Emanuele Grazzi, the Italian ambassador in Athens, delivered an ultimatum (see Appendix C for the full text) to Ioannis Metaxas, the Greek prime minister. Its final paragraphs read:

> It is obvious that the policy of the Greek Government has been and is directed towards transforming Greek territory ... into a base for [Allied] war operations against Italy....
>
> The Italian Government, therefore, has reached the decision to ask the Greek Government, as a guarantee of Greek neutrality and as a guarantee of Italian security, for permission to occupy with its own armed forces several strategic points in Greek territory for the duration of the present conflict with Great Britain.

> The Italian Government asks the Greek Government not to oppose this occupation and not to obstruct the free passage of the troops carrying it out....
>
> Wherever the Italian troops may meet resistance this resistance will be broken by armed force...[64]

For Metaxas, the Italian occupation of Greek territory, even if temporary, was out of the question. He laconically pronounced: 'Then, it is war!' Consequently, Italian troops in Albania, poised to attack, traversed the northwest Greek frontier at 5:30 a.m. (despite the ultimatum having a three-hour deadline). The Italo–Greek War had begun.

From the get-go, the invasion went badly for the Italian Army. In just days, tenacious Greek land forces, although facing a numerically superior foe of some 140,000 men, routed the Italian invaders. The Italian *Julia* Division attacked the Greeks in the Epirus region, aiming to take control of the Pindus mountain passes. The elite *Alpini* troops managed to advance some 25 miles, but the aggressors were encircled and driven back. Lasting a fortnight, the battle cost the lives of 5,000 Italians. Another decisive battle was fought during the first week of November at the Elaia-Kalamas River. There, the Greek Eighth Infantry Division (under Major-General Charalambos Katsimitros) formed a defensive line to hold back the Italians, and despite the enemy's numerical superiority, it succeeded. General Visconti Prasca was relieved on 8 November and replaced by General Ubaldo Soddu. Next day the Greek Army launched a great counteroffensive which ultimately succeeded in expelling Italian forces from Greece altogether. It was obvious that Mussolini had miscalculated, and on 18 November, he delivered a fiery speech in Rome lambasting the Greeks:

> After long and patient waiting, we have torn the mask from a country guaranteed by Great Britain, a perfidious enemy, Greece. It was an account which demanded settlement. One thing has to be said, and it will perhaps surprise certain out-of-date classical scholars. The Greeks hate Italy with a hatred which seems inexplicable at first sight; but it is general, profound, and incurable, in all classes, in the cities, in the villages, everywhere. The reason why is a mystery. Nevertheless, the fact remains. To this hatred, which can be described as absolutely grotesque, Greek policy adapted herself during recent years. It was a policy of absolute complicity with Great Britain....
>
> This complicity, shown in many ways which will be irrefutably proved in due course, was a continuous act of hostility against Italy. From maps discovered by the German General Staff in France, it has been established that as early as May, Greece had offered to the English and French all her naval and air bases. It was imperative to put an end to this situa-

> tion; and that was done on 28th October, when our troops crossed the frontier between Greece and Albania.
>
> The rugged mountains of Epirus and its muddy valleys do not lend themselves to a lightning war, as the incorrigible experts of a comfortable armchair strategy would suggest. No deed or word by myself, or the Government, or any other responsible quarter suggested a lightning war....
>
> Comrades, there are some among you who remember the unpublished speech I made in July 1935, before the Abyssinian War. I said that we would break the backs of the Negus. Now, with the same absolute, I repeat absolute, certitude, we shall break the backs of the Greeks, whether in two or twelve months makes little difference.[65]

Hitler reached Florence at 10 a.m. on 28 October for his summit meeting with Mussolini. According to interpreter Paul Schmidt, 'Mussolini greeted Hitler with a self-satisfied smile.' Brimming with triumph and swaggering along the railway platform as though he had the world in his pocket, Mussolini declaimed in a stentorian voice: 'Führer, we are on the march! Victorious Italian troops crossed the Greco–Albanian frontier at dawn today!'[66] Although Hitler was infuriated, he kept his composure. The Axis leaders conferred at the Palazzo Pitti, site of the Medici treasures. Hitler wished to inform Mussolini about the substance of his talks with Laval and Pétain at Montoire (on 22 and 24 October respectively), and Franco at Hendaye on 23 October. As for Italy's unexpected Greek campaign, Hitler pledged to back Mussolini unreservedly. He offered Mussolini parachute divisions; if the Duce saw fit, these could be employed in the conquest of Crete.

Regarding the talks with the French and Spanish leaders, there were no new developments. It was essential, Hitler stressed, that the Vichy Government remain master of the French colonies in North Africa. Above all, French Morocco had to be held. It was also imperative that de Gaulle's forces be kept at bay, preferably by the French themselves. It would be of great psychological value to have established 'a compact Continental bloc against England'.

Hitler held Pierre Laval in low esteem. To Mussolini, he characterized the former two-time French prime minister as 'a dirty democratic politician, a man who doesn't believe in what he says, who turns to us only to save himself'. In other words, a lying opportunist. Hitler had advised Laval that a speedy conclusion of the war would benefit France, for as long as hostilities went on the German occupation would continue. A few deluded Frenchmen still clung to the absurd notion that Britain would ultimately defeat Germany. That kind of thinking was nonsense. The Axis had triumphed; that much was plain for all to see. It was only the prospect of receiving American and Soviet aid that kept Britain from throwing in the towel. The Soviet Union need not be feared. Germany had 180 divisions available to keep the Slavic hordes in check. And as for the Americans, it would be 1942 before they were ready to intervene militarily. Laval conceded Hitler's points but emphasized the fact that swaying the French people to turn on England was not presently workable. Rather he had to focus on 'defending himself in Africa' and 'exploiting every incident' to foment anti-British sentiment.

With Pétain, it was much of the same. Hitler thought much more favourably of the eighty-four-year-old French marshal, or so he said. But politics were politics, and the bottom line was that France had declared war on Germany, was defeated, and would have to foot the bill. Hitler declared that he would not conclude a peace treaty of any kind with France until all Italian claims were fulfilled.

Franco had been a great disappointment. Hitler described Franco as 'a brave spirit, but a man who has become leader only by chance'. The *Caudillo* was unsuited for the political scene. Hitler acknowledged that it was the Spanish Government's prerogative to decide when to join the war. But Spanish material and colonial demands were excessive, so much so that the former would place 'too great a burden on the Axis' and the latter would 'cause the immediate alignment of the French Colonial Empire with the de Gaullist camp'. Suñer wanted 'frontier rectifications in the Pyrenees ... French Catalonia ... Oran and all Morocco up to the 20th Meridian'. Such a scheme was out the question. Hitler then handed Mussolini the German–Spanish–Italian Secret Protocol concluded at Hendaye for the Duce's approval.

When it was Mussolini's turn, he first spoke of France. The Duce expressed his gratitude to Hitler for ensuring that Italy's claims would be satisfied. It was true that they were remarkably moderate, Mussolini said, for Nice and Corsica were just 'a small part of French metropolitan territory' and were 'geographically Italian lands'. Italy's rights in Tunisia were 'well known' and the French Somaliland was 'merely a classic example of desert'. And from the Axis perspective, the collaborationist Vichy regime, with Pétain at its head, was preferred. As soon as France had compensated the Axis in full, it would be possible to have dealings with her. But all the Axis would receive from France, Mussolini predicted, was 'purely passive cooperation', nothing more. After the war, France could seek recompense from a defeated England. The issue at hand was whether France should pay her debts at once or later.

In connection with Spain, Mussolini stated that he was in accord with Hitler's outlook. The Duce then reviewed the secret three-power protocol and he found it satisfactory. It contained provisions for 'the secret adhesion of Spain to the Tripartite Pact'. It was Mussolini's opinion that the Secret Protocol should be publicized 'when all the Spanish military measures have been taken and the country is ready for intervention'. The talks concluded with both Italian and German parties in 'perfect agreement ... on all points'.[67]

The secret protocol read:

SECRET PROTOCOL

The Italian, German, and Spanish Governments have agreed as follows:

2. Spain declares her readiness to accede to the Tripartite Pact ... and for this purpose to sign, on a date to be set by the four [Axis] Powers jointly, an appropriate protocol regarding the actual accession.

3. By the present Protocol Spain declares her accession to the Treaty of Friendship and Alliance between Italy and Germany [the Pact of Steel] and the related Secret Supplementary Protocol of 22 May 1939.

4. ... Spain will intervene in the present war with the Axis Powers against England after they have provided her with the military support necessary for her preparedness ... Germany will grant economic aid to Spain by supplying her with food and raw materials, so as to meet the needs of the Spanish people and the requirements of the war.

5. In addition to the reincorporation of Gibraltar into Spain, the Axis Powers state that in principle they are ready to see to it ... that Spain receives territories in Africa...

6. The present Protocol shall be strictly secret...[68]

Hitler's interpreter, Schmidt, described the aftermath from the German point of view: 'He [Hitler] had been frustrated three times—at Hendaye, at Montoire, and now in Italy. In the lengthy winter evenings of the next few years these long, exacting journeys were a constant recurring theme of bitter reproaches against ungrateful and unreliable friends [Franco], Axis partners [Mussolini], and "deceiving" Frenchmen [Laval and Pétain].'[69]

But Hitler's dissatisfaction was only the tip of the iceberg. Mussolini's foolhardy initiative was certain to have serious negative ramifications, for history demonstrated that it took little to ignite the Balkan powder keg. The opportunistic Bulgars and Yugoslavs might be drawn into the conflict to acquire more territory, the Greeks might petition the formidable British for aid, and even the neutral Turks might be impelled to act.

That autumn, the Italians fared no better at sea than on land. On 11 November, British naval forces inflicted upon the Italians one of the most decisive defeats of the war. That evening at 9 p.m., the Fleet Air Arm of the British Royal Navy launched Operation Judgment, a devastating air attack upon the powerful Italian Fleet stationed at Taranto Harbour. Carried out in two waves approximately ninety minutes apart, a total of twenty-one Swordfish bomber planes took off from the aircraft carrier HMS *Illustrious*. Twelve of the aircraft carried an aerial torpedo, the others bombs and flares. The night-time raid on Taranto Harbour, hastily defended by anti-aircraft guns and shore batteries, caught the Italians—who were without radar—by surprise. In the space of a few minutes, Taranto Harbour was ablaze. Of the warships anchored there, three of six battleships (*Littorio*, *Duilio*, and *Cavour*), two cruisers, and two auxiliaries were put out of commission. Italian naval strength in the Mediterranean was reduced by one-half thereby. Next day the remaining warships relocated to safety at Naples. British losses included two downed aircraft, two fatalities, and two airmen taken prisoner. Ironically, Japanese military brass took notice of the successful British attack, analyzed it, and repeated it on a larger scale at Pearl Harbour less than thirteen months later.

On 12 November, Ciano documented the disaster: 'A black day. The British, without warning, have attacked the Italian Fleet at anchor in Taranto, and have sunk the dreadnought *Cavour* and seriously damaged the battleships *Littorio* and *Duilio*. These ships will remain out of the fight for many months. I thought I would find the Duce downhearted. Instead, he took the blow quite well and does not, at the moment, seem to have fully realized its gravity.'[70]

Addressing the House of Commons on 13 November, Churchill reported:

> The Royal Navy has struck a crippling blow at the Italian Fleet. The total strength of the Italian battle fleet was six battleships, two of them of the '*Littorio*' class, which have just been put into service and are, of course, among the most powerful vessels in the world, and four of the recently reconstructed '*Cavour*' class. This fleet was, to be sure, considerably more powerful on paper than our Mediterranean Fleet, but it had consistently refused to accept battle. On the night of 11–12 November, when the main units of the Italian Fleet were lying behind their shore defences in their naval base at Taranto, our aircraft of the Fleet Air Arm attacked them in their stronghold....
>
> I felt it my duty to bring this glorious episode to the immediate notice of the House. As the result of a determined and highly successful attack, which reflects the greatest honour on the Fleet Air Arm, only three Italian battleships now remain effective. This result, while it affects decisively the balance of naval power in the Mediterranean, also carries with it reactions upon the naval situation in every quarter of the globe....
>
> Our pilots of the Fleet Air Arm ... like their brothers in the Royal Air Force, continue to render the country services of the highest order.[71]

And Admiral Andrew Cunningham, commander-in-chief of the Mediterranean Fleet, later wrote: 'Taranto, and the night of 11–12 November 1940, should be remembered for ever [sic] as having shown once and for all that in the Fleet Air Arm the Navy has its most devastating weapon.'[72]

On 17 November, Ciano left for Salzburg to confer with Ribbentrop and Hitler. Arriving the following day, Ciano first had a discussion with 'a rather enigmatic Ribbentrop' at the latter's Fuschl residence. There Ribbentrop informed him that Hitler would 'speak on the situation created by the Greek crisis'. Lunch was taken with Ribbentrop and Suñer; the latter was garrulous and critical of 'the German effort to get together with the French'.[73]

In the afternoon, Ciano called on Hitler at the Berghof. Using a map Hitler described to Ciano the military situation in the Mediterranean sector. The British had managed to occupy Crete and were now in the process of establishing additional air bases on Greek soil, near Salonika and in Thrace. Consequently, 'the whole of southern Italy was now as much within the range of English bombers as were the Albanian seaports'. And although the Romanian oil fields of Ploieşti—crucial to the German war effort—had hitherto been beyond the reach of British bombers, the latter were now within 500 kilometres' range. The defence of oil fields, Hitler pointed out, was 'actually very hard', for they were easily set ablaze by incendiaries. Hitler advised that the Italians should conduct air raids 'in the main against military targets' and dispense with 'retaliatory raids on Athens or other cities'. The Blitz had demonstrated to the Germans that air attacks on 'purely civilian targets' were simply not worthwhile.

Furthermore, Hitler asserted, there had been extremely negative repercussions to the Axis of a psychological nature. These had manifested themselves in 'a resurgence of reserve in certain countries towards German plans for a coalition'. The Bulgars 'appeared less inclined than ever to join the Tripartite Pact'. The Russians were showing 'considerable interest in the Balkans', which was most unwelcome. The Turks, too—on account of the disastrous Greek campaign—were disinclined 'towards a *rapprochement* with the Axis'. The effect on the Yugoslavs had 'so far been impossible to determine'.

To reverse these negative trends, the British and their Mediterranean Fleet had to be dealt 'a severe blow'. British access to the Mediterranean had to be severed at Gibraltar and Suez, and Spain had to enter the conflict at the earliest opportunity. Gibraltar would be seized, and German divisions garrisoned in Spanish Morocco.* This decisive step would effectively deter French Morocco from attempting to break with the Vichy regime. The loss of Northwest Africa had to be avoided 'at all costs', for it would be 'disastrous' should the British ever gain the upper hand there. And should access to the Mediterranean via Gibraltar be closed off, the British would be forced to reroute their transports around Africa.

---

* Operation Felix, the planned German seizure of Gibraltar. The second article of Hitler's Directive No. 18 for the Conduct of the War (dated 12 November 1940) stated, in part:

> 2. *Spain and Portugal.* Political steps to bring about an early Spanish entry into the war have been taken. The aim of *German* intervention in the Iberian peninsula (code name Felix) will be to drive the English out of the Western Mediterranean. For this purpose:
>
> *a.* Gibraltar will be taken and the Straits closed.
>
> *b.* The British will be prevented from gaining a foothold at another point of the Iberian peninsula, or the Atlantic Islands.[74]

Other political measures to be taken included diverting Russia's attention away from the Balkan region and redirecting it southwards; arriving at 'an understanding' with Turkey; gaining the collaboration of Yugoslavia 'in the settlement of the Greek question'; persuading Hungary to 'permit the transit of additional German forces to Romania'; and getting Romania to 'assume maintenance of the German troops'. Should the British manage to 'actually establish themselves in Greece', German forces would proceed from Romania through Bulgaria to engage them. However, no action in the Balkans could be undertaken until spring due to 'the weather and terrain conditions and the lack of suitable roads'.

Thereupon Hitler inquired of Ciano precisely what concessions Italy was willing to make 'to neutralize Yugoslavia'. He proposed that Italy offer Yugoslavia a guarantee of her territorial integrity, plus Salonika. In exchange, Yugoslavia 'would have to acquiesce in [the] demilitarization of the Dalmatian coast'. Ciano was personally in favour of the proposal, but he pointed out that the Duce would have to make 'the final decision'. Having passed the buck, Ciano added: 'Yielding to Yugoslavia would not come easy for the Duce, because he "could not suffer" the Yugoslavs.'* Hitler replied that for himself, too, it was anathema to be 'compelled to cultivate relations with countries which were uncongenial to him at heart' but emphasized that Yugoslavia's cooperation would help expedite 'the liquidation of the Greek affair'.

Lastly Hitler discussed the 'military measures' to be taken in the eastern Mediterranean. In order for operations against the Suez Canal to succeed, Italian forces in North Africa first had to capture Mersa Matruh and there establish an air base. This would enable Axis bombers to expel the British Fleet from Alexandria and annihilate it 'on the high seas'. To achieve this end, the Italian Air Force and the German Luftwaffe would collaborate. The former would dominate the western Mediterranean—the Italian–Albanian–Greek triangle—and the latter would dominate the eastern Mediterranean. As a result, the British Mediterranean Fleet would be eliminated during the winter of 1940–41 and British forces expelled from Greece in the spring. Axis plans in connection with Egypt would be deferred until the autumn of 1941.

In response, Ciano expressed his total agreement with Hitler's assessment and assured the Führer that he would contact Mussolini at once. Ciano was certain that the Duce would be of the same mind.[75]

---

* According to Ciano's record of the conversation, Hitler had asked him: 'Do you think that Mussolini would be prepared to make a pact with Yugoslavia on these three points: Axis guarantee for the Yugoslav frontiers; cession of Salonika to Yugoslavia; demilitarization of the Adriatic by Yugoslavia?' After Ciano had replied in the affirmative, Hitler had said: 'But if that is so I am certain that we can have Yugoslavia on our side. The Greek affair will rapidly resolve itself into one of the greatest successes for the Axis. Yugoslavia will have Salonika, Bulgaria an outlet to the sea, Italy all the remaining part of Greece. Once Greece is lost [to the British] and Egypt threatened, England will be practically chased out of the Mediterranean.'[76]

In his *Diary*, Ciano set down his personal recollection of the interview:

> There was a heavy atmosphere. Hitler is pessimistic and considers the situation much compromised by what has happened in the Balkans. His criticism is open, definite, and final. I try to talk to him, but he does not allow me to proceed. Only in the second part of the conversation, that is, after Hitler gave his consent to eventual negotiations with Yugoslavia, does he become warm and cordial, at times almost friendly. The idea of an alliance with Yugoslavia excites him to the point that while his pessimism at first appeared too black now his optimism seems too rosy.[77]

On 20 November, Ciano was received by Hitler and Ribbentrop at Vienna's Hotel Imperial for 'a brief reception'. It was a continuation of their conversation two days earlier. Ciano informed Hitler that Mussolini had 'expressed his unqualified agreement with the Führer's proposals concerning Yugoslavia'. If the Yugoslavs were amenable to such a deal, the Italo–Greek War could be liquidated in just several weeks' time. 'Prince Regent Paul,' Ciano declared, 'would most certainly take an affirmative stand on [Italo–Yugoslav] cooperation.' The reasons for this were twofold: first, Paul had invested a substantial part of his fortune in Italy; and second, he had purchased a villa in Florence where he intended to reside 'entirely dedicated to his artistic interests'. Thus Paul would most certainly wish to avoid an Italo–Yugoslav war.

'Prince Regent Paul would go down as a great statesman,' Hitler interjected, 'if Yugoslavia were to acquire Salonika under his regency.' In fact, such a valuable acquisition could so elevate Paul's prestige that he might even opt to remain in power rather than abdicate at the expiration of his regency. Also, Princess Olga's ambitions were well known; undoubtedly, she would wish to rule as queen of Yugoslavia one day. Ciano agreed 'with great animation' to Hitler's points, then mentioned that Mussolini had advised him by telephone of an improvement on the Balkan Front. Italian forces would stand firm. No military aid from Germany would be required; only trucks, as previously negotiated.[78]

At the meeting's end, Hitler emotionally imparted to Ciano: 'From this city of Vienna, on the day of the *Anschluss*, I sent Mussolini a telegram to assure him that I would never forget his help. I confirm it today, and I am at his side with all my strength.' Ciano noticed that Hitler 'had two big tears in his eyes' and he thought: 'What a strange man!'[79] Before taking his leave, Ciano accepted from Hitler a sealed letter for the Duce.

In his letter, Hitler first explained that he had requested a summit meeting in Florence with the Duce in order 'to present my views … before the beginning of the threatening conflict with Greece'. Hitler had wished for the Italians 'to postpone the action a while longer, if possible until a more favourable season of the year'. He had also wanted the Italians 'not to undertake this action without a prior lightning-like occupation of Crete'.[80] The remainder of the lengthy letter was a repetition—almost verbatim—of the content of the Hitler–Ciano talks of 18 November.

On the same day as Ciano's meeting with Ribbentrop at Salzburg, a telegraph was sent to Mussolini by the Romanian dictator, General Ion Antonescu. It was an adulatory paean: 'The Romanian Chief of State sends to the Duce his heartiest and sincerest wishes and deep gratitude. He expresses his boundless admiration for the manner in which this member of the Roman family of nations prepares the way not only for the life of its own great people but also for other nations.'[81]

After the ratification of the Tripartite Pact in late September, the Hungarian Government had officially notified the Reich Government of its wish to sign it—and to do so prior to Romania. Once Mussolini had agreed and the Japanese did likewise, in October Ribbentrop had given Hungarian Ambassador Döme Sztójay the nod. Thus on 20 November, Hungary became the fourth power to accede to the Tripartite Pact (and the Axis). But Ciano was against the prospect of having lesser nations join the Tripartite Pact. He considered them to be of little value to the Axis cause and even detrimental: 'Signature of Hungary's adherence. Romanian and Slovakian adherences will follow. I do not attach much importance to the adherence of these states, which are vassals of Germany, or almost so. In fact, they weaken the Tripartite Agreement itself, and seem to be the useless bits of *ersatz* diplomacy of our victory.'[82]

Two days later, Mussolini sent Hitler a message in reply to his recent letter. The Duce began with a few palliative—and disingenuous—words concerning his belated communication of 19 October: 'I regret keenly that my letter of 19 October, that is, nine days before the outbreak of [Italo–Greek] hostilities, did not reach you in time to permit you to give me your opinion, which I would naturally have considered in all its importance.' This was a falsehood, for the Duce had been resolved to launch his Greek campaign come what may. Next, he offered a sugar-coated explanation for the debacle in Greece. Naturally, his version of events was intended to depict Italian military incompetence in as favourable a light as possible:

> After a promising and rapid start the advance of the Italian troops in Greece came to a standstill and permitted the Greeks to take the initiative, for the following reasons:
>
> a) A veritable flood irreparably blocked with torrents of mud the armoured division which was on the point of breaking through at Janina;

b) The desertion of almost all the Albanian troops, who threw away their arms and went over *en masse* to the enemy. The command has had to gather and disarm fully 7,000 Albanian soldiers;

c) The attitude of Bulgaria, which permitted Greece to withdraw almost the entire eight divisions which she had in Thrace and employ them all against the nine Italian divisions, which were weakened by the desertion of the Albanian elements.

Mussolini explained what he was doing to salvage the situation: 'This is now all a matter of the past. I am naturally aware of the unfavourable psychological repercussions which these events have caused, but I believe that these are passing phenomena. I am preparing a sufficient number of divisions (30) to annihilate Greece and am not worried about the bombings of the southern cities, where there are no important industrial plants.'

In connection with Spain, Mussolini was willing, in person, to attempt to persuade Franco to throw in his lot with the totalitarian Powers: 'I am of the opinion that the Spanish card can be played at the present moment. I do not know the results of your conversations with Suñer, but I am prepared to meet with Franco in order to exert the pressure necessary to make him enter the field on the side of the Axis.' As regards Yugoslavia, he disclosed the preconditions that would have to be met in order for Italy 'to guarantee the present boundaries of Yugoslavia and to recognize Yugoslavia's right to Salonika'. These were threefold:

a) that Yugoslavia adhere to the Tripartite Pact;
b) that she demilitarize the Adriatic;
c) that her military intervention be agreed on; in other words, that it occur only after Greece has received an initial blow from Italy.

Mussolini stressed the necessity to coordinate Italo–German aerial operations in the Mediterranean sector: 'With regard to an intensification of our collaboration in the air in the Mediterranean, I consider it indispensable. It is necessary that the two General Staffs of the air forces meet as soon as possible in order that all technical decisions may be made.' He assured Hitler that the Italian people were willing to do their all to secure victory: 'The Italian people are prepared to bear the heaviest sacrifices and, goaded by failure, will give everything that is asked of them.' Mussolini concluded by expressing to Hitler his 'greetings of faithful comradeship'.[83]

A significant personnel change was made at the highest levels of the *Comando Supremo* a fortnight later, when on 4 December Chief of Staff Marshal Badoglio resigned. He was made the scapegoat for the Italian Army's recent failures in Greece (for which he nursed a strong grudge). Two days later, General Ugo Cavallero, a man with considerable organizational ability but who was subservient towards the Germans, assumed the post.

A disconcerting communication from General Ubaldo Soddu, commander-in-chief of Italian forces in Albania (General Visconti Prasca's successor), was received by Mussolini the same day Badoglio stepped down. Soddu held the view that 'any military action has become impossible and the situation must be settled through political intervention'. Mussolini was dismayed and to Ciano he stated: 'There is nothing I can do. This is grotesque and absurd, but it is a fact. We have to ask for a truce through Hitler.'[84] On 6 December, Mussolini, still greatly displeased, inveighed against his commanders and especially the unmilitaristic Italian masses: 'If, when I was a Socialist, I had had a knowledge of the work of the Italian middle class, not purely theoretical as learned by the reading of Karl Marx, but practical, based on experience such as I have now, I would have launched a revolution so pitiless that, by comparison, the revolution of Comrade Lenin would have been child's play.'[85]

Ambassador Alfieri, who had been ill for three months, was called to the Palazzo Venezia where Mussolini instructed him to return to Berlin at once to request 'military and material aid' from the Germans. But when Alfieri met with Ribbentrop on 7 December at 5 p.m., the latter was especially abrasive. To make matters worse, Alfieri had been inadequately briefed—by both Mussolini and Ciano—as to the exact type of aid Italy required, and to his chagrin, he was therefore unable to provide Ribbentrop with specifics. Ribbentrop scolded Alfieri for his ignorance and harshly added that the Greek fiasco could have been avoided altogether if only the Italians had heeded Hitler's prudent advice not to upset the Balkan applecart.

Next day Alfieri was received by Hitler. The Italian diplomat began with a *tour d'horizon* of the events leading up to the Greek campaign and the military situation as it presently stood. The reasons he offered for the crisis in Albania, which was 'critical and acute', were twofold: '1) The Italian troops at the front faced superior forces of Greeks; [and] 2) The lines of communication between Italy and the front were restricted.' In short, the resilient Greeks had proven too tough a nut for the Italians to crack.

In turn, Hitler stated that 'in October he had still hoped to be able to advise the Duce in time about his doubts, reservations, and proposals'. Prior to the Italian invasion of Greece, Hitler complained, he had sent General Enno von Rintelen (the German military attaché in Italy) to inquire of General Roatta if any such plans were in the works, to which Roatta had given a negative reply. And now, as a result of the Italian reversals, the perceived might and stability of the Axis had been greatly undermined: 'Spain was hesitating; France was becoming refractory; and

Above left: Profile portrait of Benito Mussolini, Italian prime minister and Duce of Fascism. (*National Digital Archives, Poland*)

Above right: Galeazzo Ciano, Mussolini's son-in-law and foreign minister from 9 June 1936 to 6 February 1943. Thereafter ambassador to the Vatican. Executed 11 January 1944 at Verona for treason. (*National Digital Archives, Poland*)

Below: Anglo–Italian summit meeting at Rome. It was the British Government's final attempt to draw Fascist Italy into the Allied camp. From left to right: Foreign Minister Galeazzo Ciano, Foreign Secretary Lord Halifax, Prime Minister Neville Chamberlain, and Prime Minister Benito Mussolini, January 1939. (*Hoover Institution Archives*)

Above: The Duce on a visit to Turi Airfield in 1939. (*Keystone-Hulton-Getty*)

Below left: The Duce in a characteristic pose: delivering the Fascist salute in Rome, 5 July 1939. (*Keystone/Getty Images*)

Below right: Mussolini proclaiming to the Roman masses from the balcony of the Palazzo Venezia news of Italy's entry into the war against Britain and France, 10 June 1940. (*ilGiornale.it*)

TORINO
Anno 74 - Num. 140
Ogni numero 30 centesimi

LA STAMPA

MARTEDI'
11 Giugno 1940-XVIII
Edizione MATTINO

IL DUCE HA PARLATO

La dichiarazione di guerra all'Inghilterra e alla Francia

"Scendiamo in campo contro le democrazie plutocratiche e reazionarie dell'occidente,, Svizzera, Jugoslavia, Grecia, Turchia, Egitto, per quanto dipende da noi, non saranno coinvolti nel conflitto - "La parola d'ordine è una sola: vincere. E vinceremo,,

braccia contro gli affamatori che detengono ferocemente il monopolio di tutte le ricchezze, di tutto l'oro della terra.

« E' la lotta dei Popoli fecondi e giovani contro i popoli isteriliti e volgenti al tramonto; è la lotta fra due secoli e due idee.

« Ora che i dadi sono gettati e la nostra volontà ha bruciato alle nostre spalle i vascelli, io dichiaro solennemente che l'Italia non intende trascinare nel conflitto altri Popoli con essa confinanti, per mare o per terra. Svizzera, Jugoslavia, Grecia, Turchia, Egitto prendano atto di

evento di portata secolare, rivolgiamo il nostro pensiero alla Maestà del Re Imperatore (la moltitudine prorompe in grandi acclamazioni all'indirizzo di Casa Savoia) che, come sempre, ha interpretato l'anima della Patria, e salutiamo alla voce il Führer, il Capo della grande Germania alleata (il popolo acclama lungamente all'indirizzo di Hitler).

« L'Italia proletaria e fascista è per la terza volta in piedi, forte, fiera e compatta come non mai (la moltitudine grida con una sola voce: Sì!). La parola d'ordine è una sola,

The front cover of an Italian newspaper, 11 June 1940. The text, translated to English, reads: 'THE DUCE HAS SPOKEN/The declaration of war on England and France/Let us take the field against the plutocratic and reactionary democracies of the West. Switzerland, Yugoslavia, Greece, Turkey, Egypt, as far as it depends on us, will not be involved in the conflict—The watchword is only one: to win. And we will win.' (*La Stampa*)

The Fascist and Nazi dictators in Munich *en route* to the Führerhaus to discuss the armistice requested by the French Government, 18 June 1940. (*National Digital Archives, Poland*)

Candid photograph of the Axis leaders in excellent spirits at Munich, 18 June 1940. (*National Archives and Records Administration*)

Mussolini conducting an inspection in the Alps following the Battle of France, late June 1940. (*National Digital Archives, Poland*)

Above: Mussolini at the French Front; Alpine riflemen stand at attention with raised bayonets, July 1940. (*National Digital Archives, Poland*)

Right: Mussolini in dialogue with Hitler and Foreign Minister Joachim von Ribbentrop at the Sala Clemente of the Palazzo Vecchio, 28 October 1940. On the far left is Field Marshal Wilhelm Keitel, chief of the *Wehrmacht* High Command. (*National Digital Archives, Poland*)

Above: Ciano, Ribbentrop, Hitler, and Mussolini at the Sala Clemente of the Palazzo Vecchio in Florence, 28 October 1940. (*National Digital Archives, Poland*)

Below left: The Führer and the Duce on the balcony of the Palazzo Vecchio in Florence, 28 October 1940. (*National Digital Archives, Poland*)

Below right: The first and only summit meeting of the Latin dictators. At Bordighera, the Duce attempted unsuccessfully to convince the *Caudillo* to enter the war against Britain. From left to right: Foreign Minister Ramón Serrano Suñer, *Generalissimo* Francisco Franco, and Mussolini, February 1941. (*Washington Post*)

Above: The Duce, accompanied by the bespectacled General Ugo Cavallero (at left), reviews a line of troops standing stiffly at attention, April 1941. (*Archivio Centrale della Stato*)

Right: The Duce, frowning at the camera, with Francesco Jacomoni, the repressive ruler of Albania, in April 1941. Jacomoni was designated viceroy (*Luogotenente del Re*) in Albania following the latter's invasion and incorporation into the Italian Empire as a protectorate two years prior. (*Archivio Centrale della Stato*)

Mussolini and Achille Starace, then chief of staff of the Blackshirts (until May 1941), April 1941. On the far left: Francesco Jacomoni. (*Archivio Centrale della Stato*)

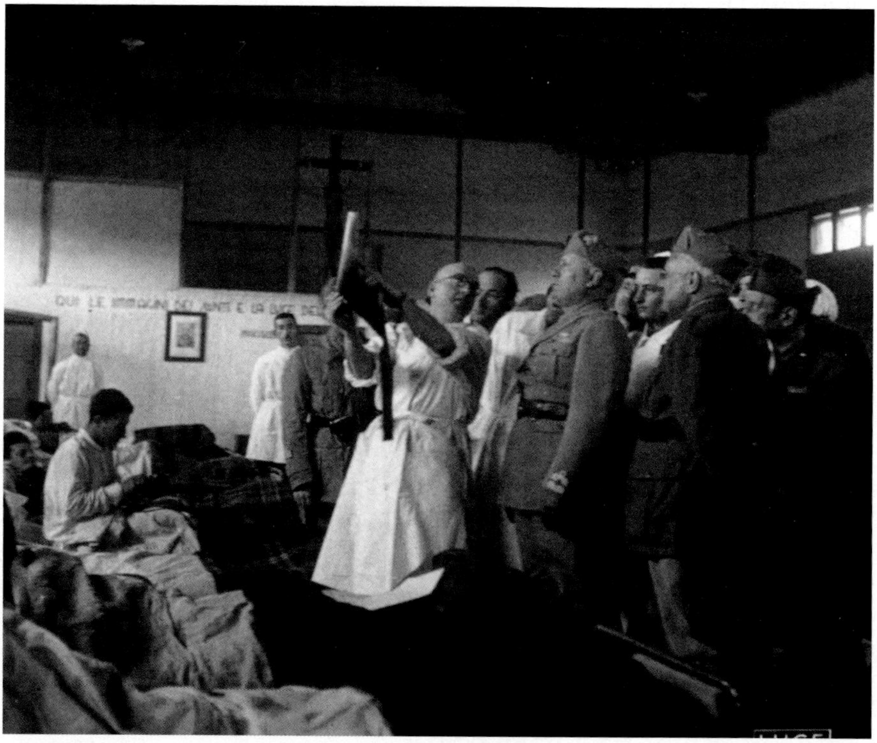

The Duce pays a visit to injured combatants at a field hospital, April 1941. (*Archivio Centrale della Stato*)

Above: A silhouetted Mussolini, striking an imperious pose, observes a procession of cavalry troops parading before him, April 1941. (*Archivio Centrale della Stato*)

Below left: The Duce examines a military map at Passo Lagora, Albania, April 1941. (*Archivio Centrale della Stato*)

Below right: Mussolini, with General Giovanni Messe trailing behind (far right), receives the Fascist salute by civilians at Passo Lagoria, Albania, April 1941. (*Archivio Centrale della Stato*)

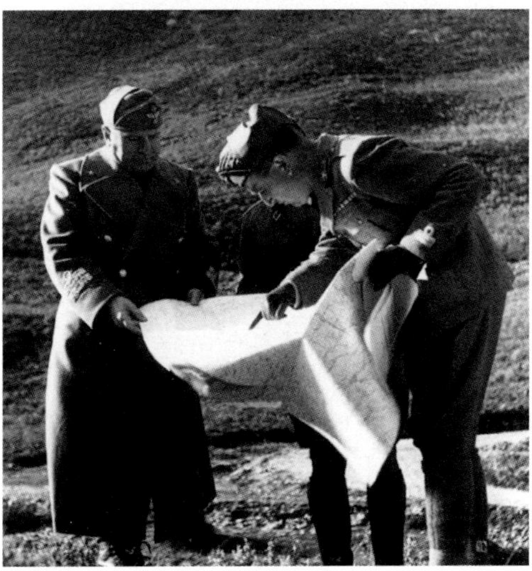

Mussolini amid frontline troops at an artillery site, April 1941. (*Archivio Centrale della Stato*)

A candid photograph of Mussolini intently examining the operational zone, April 1941. (*Archivio Centrale della Stato*)

The Duce peers through a telescope in order to more clearly survey the region, April 1941. (*Archivio Centrale della Stato*)

A beaming Mussolini in the presence of officers, civilians, and an Orthodox priest, April 1941. (*Archivio Centrale della Stato*)

The Duce, with Jacomoni on the far left, encounters the local population, April 1941. (*Archivio Centrale della Stato*)

Mussolini reviews soldiers standing solemnly at attention with bayonets raised, April 1941. (*Archivio Centrale della Stato*)

Above left: A contemplative Mussolini with street workers, April 1941. (*Archivio Centrale della Stato*)

Above right: Mussolini samples the rations while at the Balkan Front, April 1941. (*Archivio Centrale della Stato*)

Above left: Mussolini among frontline soldiers, April 1941. At the far right, facing the camera, is General Cavallero. (*Archivio Centrale della Stato*)

Above right: Mussolini accompanied by General Gastone Gambara, April 1941. In the centre, directly between the Duce and Gambera, is General Cavallero. (*Archivio Centrale della Stato*)

Mussolini with Fascist leader Achille Starace. On the far left, holding binoculars, is Roberto Farinacci, a pro-German and virulent anti-Semite who, in 1941, served as general inspector of the Blackshirt Militia in Albania. (*Archivio Centrale della Stato*)

Mussolini with the advisory council of the high commissioner's office from Ljubljana, Slovenia, 18 June 1941. (*Digital Library of Slovenia*)

The dictators *en route* to review Italian soldiers in Ukraine at the height of the Russian campaign. Behind the Duce, with arms folded, is Field Marshal Gerd von Rundstedt, 28 August 1941. (*National Digital Archives, Poland*)

THE SUN 8 A.M.

BALTIMORE, THURSDAY, DECEMBER 11, 1941

GERMANY, ITALY DECLARE WAR

HEAVY JAPANESE RAIDS MADE ON CAVITE BASE; LANDINGS BEATEN OFF

U. S. Communique Reports Some Enemy Forces Got Ashore On Luzon—Defenses On East And West Coasts Augmented

ADMIRAL KIDD DIES IN RAID ON PEARL HARBOR

Flash

Germany and Italy simultaneously declared war on the United States today.

New York, Dec. 11—Premier Mussolini today declared Italy at war with the United States, in a broadcast heard here by NBC.

RUBBER AT SEA MAY BE LOST, JONES FEARS

ROOSEVELT, CHIEF AIDES CONFER IN WAR'S FIRST GRAND STRATEGY COUNCIL

Group Expected To Meet Regularly—Hull Proposes All American Republics Meet To Act On Hemisphere Solidarity

KNUDSEN CERTAIN OF WAR PRODUCTION

TELLS OF SINKING OF H. M. S. REPULSE

ATTACK ON WAKE ISLAND DESCRIBED

Reaction In London

Roosevelt Talk Hailed

The Army's First Test

Above left: Nazi Germany and Fascist Italy declare war on the United States of America, 11 December 1941. (*Baltimore Sun*)

Above right: An American wartime anti-Axis propaganda poster featuring an aggressive quotation typical of Mussolini. (*National Archives and Records Administration*)

Above: Mussolini and Hitler at Klessheim Castle near Salzburg, Austria, 29 April 1942. On this occasion, the Axis leaders discussed plans for a joint invasion of Malta, then a British colony, code-named *Unternehmen Herkules* (German) aka *Operazione C3* (Italian). (*National Digital Archives, Poland*)

Below left: Mussolini in conversation with Field Marshal Wilhelm Keitel at Feltre Airfield, less than one week prior to being ousted from power, 19 July 1943. (*Walter Frentz*)

Below right: Late city edition of *The New York Times* the day following Mussolini's removal from office, 26 July 1943. Marshal Pietro Badoglio, former chief of staff (1925–1940), was appointed Mussolini's successor as Italian prime minister by King Victor Emmanuel III. (*The New York Times*)

"All the News That's Fit to Print."

The New York Times.

LATE CITY

NEW YORK, MONDAY, JULY 26, 1943.

MUSSOLINI OUSTED WITH FASCIST CABIN

BADOGLIO, HIS FOE, MADE PREMIER BY KI

SHIFT BELIEVED FIRST STEP TOWARD PE

PEACE INITIATIVE URGED BY WALLACE ON AMERICA NOW

For 'Common Man' He Asks Full Production, Employment and Security

WITH DEMOCRACY FOR ALL

Vice President, at Detroit, Accuses 'Fascists' of Trying to Undermine Roosevelt

Cheers Halt Games As Duce Strikes Out

NORTH JERSEY OPA DROPS DRIVING BAN

Maze of Rulings, Plus Vacation Permits, Is Too Confusing—Inspectors Tired of Abuse

RUSSIANS PUSH ON

Drive 2½ Miles Closer to Orel and Take 30 More Villages

NAZI STAND STIFFER

Enemy Counter-Attacks Desperately to Hold Escape Corridor

LONDON IS CAUTIOUS

Evidence of Crack in the Rome-Berlin Axis Is Viewed With Joy

BADOGLIO 'WAR HERO'

Britons See Possibility of His Being 'Front' for Fascist Deal

ONE IS OUT, THE OTHER IN

British Eighth Army Opens New Drive to Take Catania

ITALY SEEN MAKING FIRST PEACE STEP

Observers in Washington Look for Similar Action by Axis

Bulgaria was even more fearful than before of committing herself...' And as for Yugoslavia, she was 'cool in her attitude'.

Hitler's proposed solution was characteristically draconian. At the Albanian Front, order had to be restored at all costs. This was to be achieved by 'the shooting of generals and colonels who abandoned their positions and by the decimation of troops'. Hitler pointed out 'that decisive help could not be given before March because of the weather'. He declared that meanwhile what was urgently needed was 'a man with "iron nerves and barbaric determination" who would not shrink from serious measures and would, above all, mete out exemplary punishment to the elements responsible for the retreat of the Italians'. With regard to immediate aid, the Führer advised Alfieri that German transport aircraft would be dispatched to Albania. The number provided would be contingent 'on the Italian ground organization in Albania'. Lastly Hitler requested another conference with Mussolini 'as soon as possible', either at the Obersalzberg or the Brenner Pass.[86]

For Fascist Italy, the war was about to take a turn for the worse. On 9 December, after nearly three months, the British counterattacked at Sidi Barrani. General Henry Wilson, commander of British forces in Egypt, launched Operation Compass. An overwhelmingly successful raid dislodged Graziani's Tenth Army from its encampment at Sidi Barrani, which was captured on 10 December, and drove it back over the Libyan frontier out of Egypt. Ciano recorded his early assessment of the British assault:

> News of the attack on Sidi Barrani comes like a thunderbolt. At first it doesn't seem serious, but subsequent telegrams from Graziani confirm that we have had a licking. Mussolini, whom I see twice, is very calm. He comments on the event and with impersonal objectivity. It almost seems that what has happened doesn't concern him in the least.... But it is serious, at home and abroad. It is serious outside of Italy because from the tone of Graziani's telegrams it does not appear that he has sufficiently recovered from the blow to prepare a counterattack. Inside of Italy, because it makes matters worse. Public opinion had already been shaken and too much divided to receive this new and heavy blow.[87]

In spite of his calm demeanour, Mussolini was appalled, and on 12 December, he bitterly commented to Ciano: 'In Libya we have suffered a real defeat. This time it will not be said that politics is to blame. I have left the military authorities the most ample of freedom.' That evening Mussolini received 'a catastrophic telegram' from Graziani, who was contemplating a withdrawal all the way to Tripoli! The Duce was 'very much shaken', and for good reason.[88]

By this time Hitler had decided to destroy the Soviet Union by force of arms, and his unpleasant talks with the intractable Commissar Molotov on 12–13 November had only strengthened his resolve. The Führer was determined not only to eradicate the Soviet State, but Bolshevism itself. On 18 December, he issued his fateful Directive No. 21, Operation Barbarossa. The preamble read:

> *Directive Nr. 21*
> *Case Barbarossa*
>
> The German Armed Forces must be prepared *to crush Soviet Russia in a quick campaign* before the end of the war against England (Case Barbarossa).
>
> For this purpose the *Army* will have to employ all available units with the reservation that the occupied territories will have to be safeguarded against surprise attacks.
>
> For the Eastern campaign the *Air Force* will have to free such strong forces for the support of the Army that a quick completion of the ground operations may be expected and that damage of the eastern German territories will be avoided as much as possible....
>
> Concentration of the main effort of the *Navy* remains unequivocally against England also during an Eastern campaign.
>
> If occasion arises I will order the concentration of troops for action against Soviet Russia eight weeks before the intended beginning of operations.
>
> Preparations requiring more time to start are—if this has not yet been done—to begin presently and are to be completed by 15 May 1941.[89]

Hitler believed that he had learned from the lessons of history, and he was resolved not to commit the same fatal error as Napoleon. Unlike the latter's *Grande Armée*, the *Wehrmacht* would invade Russia in mid-May. And by the end of summer 1941, if the Führer was to have his way, the Soviet juggernaut would be no more, and the Teutonic dream of *Lebensraum* in the East would be a reality.

In a letter dated 17 December, Ciano prompted Ambassador Alfieri to contact Ribbentrop and request an appointment with Hitler. The purpose was for Alfieri to communicate to the Führer Italy's critical need for large quantities of raw materials for her armaments industry, without which 'industry would come to an inevitable and immediate stop'.[90] The request was granted, and on 19 December, Alfieri was received by Hitler at the Reich Chancellery. In the name of the Duce, Alfieri expressed the fervent hope that the Führer would be willing, on the basis of Axis solidarity, to supply the items required. Alfieri then handed over a list, prepared by Ciano, of the particulars.

Hitler was receptive to Alfieri's *démarche* for raw materials—up to a point. He informed Alfieri that in instances 'where raw materials were available in normal amounts, it was better to send adequate quantities [of these] to Italy'. Alternatively, in cases where Italy lacked 'the necessary machinery' to process certain raw materials, it would be preferable 'to produce the goods in Germany and deliver the finished products to Italy'. Hitler would submit the list to his economic experts to determine how best to handle Italy's paucity of raw materials. But the Führer stipulated a condition: in exchange, Italy would be obliged to provide the Reich with a supply of Italian workers for her own armaments industries, owing to Germany's labour shortage. Thereupon Hitler expressed his wish for another *tête-à-tête* with Mussolini 'as soon as possible' and advised that he would shortly transmit to the Duce a letter containing an assessment of 'the general situation'. Hitler also touched upon Spanish intractability:

> Spain had taken a very cool and negative attitude.... Italy and Germany might have expected more gratitude from Franco after what the Duce and the Führer had done for the *Caudillo*, who in the last analysis owed his whole political existence to them. They would have to remember that attitude.... Spain had now withdrawn completely and the military operations in this connection [Operation Felix] could no longer take place.

Hitler concluded with a few tactful words: 'Italy should not take the present setbacks too seriously. Every nation had certain "streaks of bad luck"; Frederick the Great, the greatest general Germany ever had, during some years had suffered nothing but defeats in his campaigns.'[91]

In an unsparing radio broadcast to the Italian population on 23 December, Churchill affirmed how it was Mussolini—and Mussolini alone—who had committed the folly of plunging the country into war against England alongside the bloodthirsty jackbooted Germans. The Fascist dictator had done so on his own initiative and contrary to the will and interests of the Italian people, and he had betrayed them thereby:

> One man, and one man alone has ranged the Italian people in deadly struggle against the British Empire, and has deprived Italy of the sympathy and intimacy of the United States of America. That he is a great man I do not deny, but that after eighteen years of unbridled power he has led your country to the horrid verge of ruin can be denied by none. It is one man who, against the Crown and Royal Family of Italy, against the Pope and all the authority of the Vatican and of the Roman

> Catholic Church, against the wishes of the Italian people, who had no lust for this war, has arrayed the trustees and inheritors of ancient Rome upon the side of the ferocious pagan barbarians [Germans].[92]

On the last day of the year, Hitler sent Mussolini a sympathetic letter intended to bolster his morale. It was a thorough recapitulation of where the Axis presently stood *vis-à-vis* their neighbours, client states, and those nations whom the Axis were attempting to draw into their camp.

Hitler declared that in the West, the war had 'actually been decided'. In order to crush England, all that was necessary was 'a powerful final thrust'. This would be carried out 'by strong German forces ... when the conditions are right for success'. In France, Laval had been dismissed from office. Hitler believed that the reason for this was General Weygand's 'extortionist demands from North Africa to the Vichy Government'. In any event, the potential disloyalty of Vichy France's unreliable leaders made it imperative, at the very least, 'to maintain a sharp scrutiny of what is going on'.

Hitler was very critical of Spain's unwillingness to throw in her lot with the Axis: 'Spain, under the impression of what Franco considers to be the changed situation [i.e. Axis military reversals], has for the time being refused to cooperate with the two Axis Powers. I fear that Franco is committing here the greatest mistake of his life.' Above all, Spain's recalcitrance had effectively torpedoed Operation Felix. Hitler explained how the undertaking was to have unfolded:

> ... we had made all the preparations for crossing the Spanish border on 10 January [1941] and attacking Gibraltar at the beginning of February. In my opinion the attack would have led to success in a relatively short time. The troops for this were excellently selected and trained, and the weapons were especially designated and readied for the purpose. From the moment in which the Strait of Gibraltar was in our hands the danger of any kind of untoward behaviour on the part of French North and West Africa would have been eliminated.

As regards Bulgaria, she 'has shown herself disinclined to accede to the Tripartite Pact and to assume a clear, resolute attitude...' Hitler wrote favourably of Hungary and Romania; these two nations had taken 'The clearest stand in this conflict'. For the Balkans, Hitler stated: 'It only necessary, Duce, that your front in Albania be consolidated, so that at least essential parts of the Greek or Greek–English Army are tied down there.' Yugoslavia's attitude was presently 'one of watchful waiting'. Yugoslavia would consider acceding to the Tripartite Pact only when 'the psychological situation has been generally improved once more by military successes'.

'I do not believe,' Hitler declared, 'there will be any Russian step to our detriment so long as Stalin lives and no very special crises occur on our side.' Nevertheless, to ensure that the situation remained so, Hitler deemed 'the existence of a German *Wehrmacht* that is strong enough to oppose any conceivable eventuality from the East as a prerequisite for any safe conclusion of this war. The more obviously strong this power is, the less will be the likelihood that it will have to be used...'

The Führer had nothing positive to say about the situation in North Africa. In his view, it was not possible to initiate 'any sort of large-scale counterattack ... at the moment'. The reason for this was that 'preparations of such operations requires a period of at least 3 to 4 months'. The measures to take in Libya for the time being—in Hitler's opinion—was 'to bring about a reinforcement of anti-tank defences'.

In closing, Hitler averred that Italy's reversals would have a beneficial effect: they would, in fact, strengthen and unite the *popolo Italiano*: 'Your people, Duce, will only emerge hardened from the first reverses. The British attempt to separate the Italian people from you will lead to their being bound to you more strongly than ever before.' Lastly, Hitler gave Mussolini an assurance of German support: 'Everything that is in my power and the power of my people will be done to make this the year of final victory.'[93]

But in spite of his German ally's exhortations, for Mussolini the year 1940 ended on a sour note. The British, despite being forced to go it alone, showed no sign of faltering. On the contrary, their determination to hold out had stiffened. Mussolini was perfectly aware that the more protracted the war, the less certain its outcome. And the ever-present danger of American and Soviet intervention dangled over the Axis like the sword of Damocles. In early June, it had appeared to the Duce that Italian entry into the war would swiftly yield substantial gains with minimal risk. The elimination of a principal enemy, France; the subjugation of the Balkans and North Africa; and the expulsion of the British Fleet from the Mediterranean basin—all had seemed within easy reach. Instead, Mussolini's irredentist claims—Nice, Corsica, Tunisia, and Djibouti—had not been satisfied; his Greek campaign had been an utter failure; his own fleet, moored at Taranto Harbour, had been ravaged; and his desert legions had been routed from Egypt back into Cyrenaica.

If the past six months were any indication of what lay ahead, the future did not bode well.

4

Catastrophe, 1941

... today the Axis is master of the Continent and allied with Japan.... Europe therefore, with the exception of Portugal, Switzerland and, for a little while yet, Greece, is all outside the orbit of Britain and against Britain.[1]

Mussolini to Blackshirts in Rome, 23 February 1941

The German people are dangerous because they dream collectively. But history teaches that all attempts to unify Europe under a single rule have failed.[2]

Mussolini to General Luigi Marras, 15 October 1941

The Powers of the Steel Pact, Fascist Italy and Nationalist Socialist Germany, ever closely linked, participate from today on the side of heroic Japan against the United States of America.[3]

Mussolini from the balcony of the Palazzo Venezia, 11 December 1941

In early January 1941, there occurred, for the Italians, a disagreeable diplomatic incident *vis-à-vis* the Germans. Several weeks earlier, Mussolini had envisaged that it might be profitable—both politically and economically—for Italy to enter into a partnership with an unlikely ally, the Soviet Union. Thus on 26 December, Ciano—in accordance with the Duce's wishes—had made the following overture to the Soviet Ambassador in Rome:

> Referring to earlier conversations, the Fascist Government believes that the time has come to intensify the examination of the relations between Italy and the Soviet Union both in the political and economic spheres. In the opinion of the Italian Government there is no ground for differences of opinion between Italy and Russia. The interests of both countries present no frictions of any sort and can even be regarded in many respects as complementary.
>
> This having been assumed, Italy acknowledges and is ready to recognize formally the predominance of Russian interests in the Black Sea as well as the new frontiers attained by the Soviets. On her part Italy demands that the predominance of her Mediterranean interests be recognized. On the basis of these general principles and with the addition of possible questions which the Soviet Government would present as subjects for discussion, Italy is ready to bring the pact of friendship, non-aggression, and neutrality of 1933 up to date and to give to it a more substantial content.[4]

The Soviet Government was receptive to these proposals, and consequently, four days later, Ambassador Augusto Rosso conferred with Foreign Commissar Molotov. There were, however, three issues which troubled the Soviets: '[1.] guarantee of Romania; [2.] Italian attitude in the Danube matter; [3.] question of the Straits with respect to Russian security in the Black Sea'. Before proceeding further, the Soviet Government wished to know where the Italian Government stood on these matters. The Italian official reply read:

> 1) The guarantee given to Romania has no anti-Soviet meaning, but represents instead a compensation given by the Axis to Romania for the mutilations which she suffered and at the same time sets a limit to Hungarian, and possibly also to Bulgarian, violation.
> 2) In view of the gesture of understanding which was made by the U.S.S.R., Italy is prepared, within the limits of what is possible, to meet halfway the Soviet demands in the Danube question, since the participation of Italy in supervision of traffic on the river itself has been accepted.
> 3) The question of the Straits is fundamental. It is therefore necessary that the Moscow Government define the exact outline of the problem; the solutions could vary from simple demilitarization to the annexation of territory—the latter is from the outset to be ruled out.[5]

But in Berlin on 6 January, when Ambassador Alfieri notified Ribbentrop about the Italian approaches to the Soviets, Ribbentrop flew into a rage.

Ribbentrop sharply stated 'that the Balkan policy must not be shackled by too hasty an agreement with the Russians'. The Soviets, Ribbentrop fumed, were undoubtedly attempting 'to get into the Balkans again through the window by the roundabout way of an agreement with Italy'.[6]

Although the Balkan sector lay in the Italian orbit, it was obvious that the Germans did not want the Italians to interfere there. And after consulting with Hitler at Obersalzburg, Ribbentrop peremptorily advised the Italians—who acquiesced at once—to discontinue their negotiations with the Soviets.

Mussolini left for Foggia on 13 January to consult with his generals from Albania. Upon his return three days later, after having spoken with General Cavallero, Mussolini was 'sombre and pessimistic'. As far as he was concerned, the military had let him down: 'Greece,' Mussolini said, 'was a political masterpiece; we succeeded in isolating that country and in having it fight us all alone. Only the Italian Army failed us completely.'[7]

Ciano had pre-arranged with Mackensen a conference between the Axis dictators, scheduled for 19 January, at Berchtesgaden. But because of the Italian Army's abysmal performance, Mussolini was hardly eager to see Hitler. As Ciano put it: 'He [Mussolini] feels that he will meet Hitler under conditions of obvious inferiority.'[8]

On 18 January, a 'frowning and nervous' Mussolini entrained to Salzburg for his summit meeting with Hitler. The Duce was 'shaken' by negative reports about the fighting in the Balkans. An elite division known as the *Lupi di Toscana* (Wolves of Tuscany), only recently landed in Albania, had received 'a kick in the pants'. Many had been taken prisoner. Unfortunately, the *Comando Supremo* had placed high hopes on these seasoned fighters. Mussolini repeatedly grumbled, 'If anyone had predicted on 15 October what actually happened, I would have had him shot.'[9]

The Italian party, including Ciano and General Alfredo Guzzoni (an unimpressive paunchy man with a dyed toupée), arrived on the morning of 19 January. Ciano described the occasion:

> We arrive at a small station. I think it is Puch. Hitler and his chiefs of staff are waiting for us on the platform in the snow. The weather is fair and the cold not too intense. The meeting is cordial, and, what surprises me most, spontaneously cordial. There are no hidden condolences in the air—condolences that Mussolini feared. There is, without delay, a meeting between Hitler and the Duce, and also one between me and Ribbentrop.[10]

Hitler spoke to Mussolini of France and made plain his concerns in connection with 'the stability of the situation'. He emphasized that there was considerable animosity between Pétain, Weygand, and de Gaulle, but noted that for the three of them, the common denominator was one and the same: antipathy towards the Axis. One could not 'rule out a surprise in the French attitude', and he was therefore keeping a close eye on French North Africa.

As regards Spain, Hitler deemed her alignment with the Axis and her entry into the war 'a factor of fundamental importance'. But Franco's 'hesitant and faithless attitude' had frustrated his plans for Operation Felix. According to Hitler, this was the fault of Suñer and the subversive influence of the Catholic Church upon the Spanish Government. Hitler therefore proposed that Mussolini personally meet with the *Caudillo* to persuade him to bring Spain into the war. He also denied the Spaniards' claim that he had turned down their requests for material aid and stated that he was prepared to fulfill them. Mussolini agreed to confer with the *Caudillo* by the month's end, although he knew that the obstinate Spaniard would not easily be won over. But if he managed to draw Franco into the Axis camp, his stock in Germany and abroad, which had been plummeting for some time, would rise. He would then have succeeded where Hitler, at Hendaye, had failed. German intervention to stabilize the crisis in the Balkans was also discussed.[11]

The Führer then turned to the subject of Operation Marita. This undertaking, Hitler's Directive No. 20 for the Conduct of the War (dated 13 December 1940), was intended for the *Wehrmacht* to step in and bail out the Italians on the Albanian Front. The first two articles of Operation Marita specified:

> 1. The result of the [Italo–Greek] battles in Albania is not yet decisive. Because of a dangerous situation in Albania it is doubly necessary that the British endeavour be foiled to create airbases under the protection of a Balkan front, which would be dangerous above all to Italy as well as to the Romanian oil fields.
> 2. My plan therefore is:
> *(a)* To form a slowly increasing task force in Southern Romania within the next months.
> *(b)* After the setting in of favourable weather, probably in March, to send this task force for the occupation of the Aegean North coast by way of Bulgaria, and if necessary to occupy the entire Greek mainland (Operation Marita). The support of Bulgaria is to be expected.

The ensuing relevant articles stipulated that a total of twenty-four divisions were to be assembled in southern Romania. In March, the German divisions, passing through Bulgaria, were to occupy both the Aegean coast and the Bay of Salonika. If necessary, they were to further proceed across Larissa, capital of Thessaly, and the Isthmus of Corinth. The German divisions were to be reinforced by the Luftwaffe, which would be tasked with 'liquidating the opposing Air Force, and … to occupy British strongpoints on the Greek Islands through airborne landings'. The Bulgars were to protect the flanks in case the Turks intervened. The extent of participation of the Bulgars, Yugoslavs, and Italians in the attack was yet to be determined.[12]

Ciano jotted down his overall impression of the conversations:

> Mussolini … says that he found a very anti-Russian Hitler, loyal to us, and not too definite on what he intends to do in the future against Great Britain. In any case, it is no longer a question of landing in England. Hitler said that the undertaking would be extremely difficult and that if it failed the first time it could not be attempted again. Added to this there is the fact that, while England now fears the loaded pistol of invasion, after a failure she would know that Germany holds only an empty pistol.…
>
> Hitler talked for about two hours on his coming intervention in Greece; he dealt with the question primarily from a technical point of view, placing it in the general political panorama. I must admit that he does this with unusual mastery. Our military men are impressed.…
>
> Results of the visit, generally good. There is absolute solidarity between the countries of the Axis, and we shall march together in the Balkans.[13]

Before Mussolini's summit meeting with Franco, on 6 February Hitler dispatched to the *generalissimo* a lengthy communication. The Führer did not mince his words:

> The entrance of Spain into this struggle has certainly not been conceived of as exclusively to the benefit of the interests of Germany and Italy. Spain herself has advanced very great territorial claims for the fulfillment of which the Duce and I had declared ourselves ready in every degree which could at all be reconciled with an acceptable new arrangement of the African colonial possession for Europe and its countries. And I may point out in this regard that in this struggle up to now first Germany and then Italy, have suffered the most prodigious blood sacrifice, and that both, in spite of this, themselves made very modest claims.…
>
> Spain will never get other friends than those given in the Germany and Italy of today, unless it becomes a different Spain. This different Spain however would only be the Spain of decline and of final collapse. Even for this reason alone, *Caudillo*, I believe that we three men, the Duce,

> you, and I, are bound to one another by the most rigorous compulsion of history that is possible, and that thus we in this historical analysis ought to obey as the supreme commandment the realization that in such difficult times, not so much an apparently wise caution as the bold heart, rather, can save nations.[14]

The Duce, meanwhile, was not optimistic about his forthcoming encounter with Franco. He did not believe that the cautious Spanish dictator would allow himself to be drawn into the war under the present military circumstances:

> The participation of Spain at this time would have effectively ended the war. I'll talk to Franco today as if I were a lawyer; yesterday I could speak to him as friend. The Greek campaign will never encourage him to enter the war; Franco is careful about the fate of his people ... I will tell him all that has to be said, but I have no illusions—he'll have made up his mind before I open my mouth. Had General Visconti Prasca taken Greece in the time frame we had set for ourselves, Spain would have forgotten Hitler's refusals. The war against England will be won in the Mediterranean: at Suez and Gibraltar. This will not be the time Franco comes into the war with us.[15]

On 12 February, Mussolini met with Franco and Suñer at Bordighera, a small Ligurian town. It was the first and only encounter between the two Latin dictators. (A second was to take place after the Axis had won the war.) The morning conference took place at the Villa Margherita. Ciano was not present;[*] on this occasion, Filippo Anfuso, one of his subordinates, filled in for him.

Mussolini exercised his considerable powers of persuasion to induce Franco to throw in his lot with the Axis. But Franco—although tactful to his Italian interlocutor—once again abstained, as he had done with Hitler at Hendaye in October. Mussolini opened the meeting with an expression of goodwill. He mentioned that Spain had been 'much discussed' by himself and the Führer during their talks at the Berghof several weeks ago. Mussolini reiterated Hitler's asseveration that the capture of Gibraltar by German forces would be of great strategic advantage to the Axis. He and the Führer had deliberated on 'the reasons why Spain has not entered the

* A month earlier, on 26 January, Ciano had departed for Bari. There he would command an air squadron until late April. He and other Fascist leaders, including ministers and Fascist Party bosses, had—to their great displeasure—been conscripted and sent to the Albanian Front. The previous day Ciano had bid farewell to Mussolini, who had been less than cordial. Ciano ruefully noted: 'In saying farewell he made certain observations which he might very well have omitted.'[16]

war'; the subject of grain had arisen. The Germans stated that at Hendaye they had been prepared to provide Spain with grain but that the Spanish 'had been evasive'. Therefore, Mussolini said, the Führer had asked him to personally discuss the matter with the *generalissimo*.

The Duce continued with an assessment of the war's progress. It was, Mussolini declared, 'his profound conviction that the Axis will win the war'. Most of Europe's nations were either conquered by the Reich, in her sphere of influence, or pro-German. The British were pinning their last hopes on Soviet Russia. But Germany had positioned eighty-five divisions on her Eastern border to keep the Russians at bay if necessary. Such a mighty barrier would effectively deter the Bolshevik hordes. In the Balkans the Bulgars were favourably disposed, the Turks would not attack if left alone, and the Romanians could mobilize land forces to the strength of thirty divisions if need be. American intervention might well pose a substantial threat later on, but the Americans would be facing powerful Italo–German naval and aerial forces.

As for Germany, she was continuing to rearm; submarines and airplanes were being produced at a rapid rate. Within Germany there were no issues. The Reich was determined and confident of winning the war. Nations under the German jackboot were being kept in line. Revolts would be mercilessly crushed. If France 'attempted anything' she would be completely occupied by the Germans save for the Italian zone. Italo–German relations were 'clear, straightforward, intimate'. Neither partner would forsake the other by concluding a separate peace. Italy's aerial and naval contributions to the Axis cause were great; the setbacks in Africa were insignificant. The Axis would send reinforcements to set things right. Opposition on the Albanian Front would 'soon be liquidated'. German forces would 'shortly descend on Salonika, and then the situation throughout the Eastern Mediterranean will be changed'. British resistance would go on for some time, but Germany would do all in her power 'to end it in 1941'.

Mussolini again emphasized that 'if the Axis could pass through Gibraltar and enter Morocco' it would compromise French North Africa to their benefit. Italo–German warships could then conduct a 'raiders war' through the Gibraltar Strait. Mussolini cautioned Franco that in the event of an Allied victory 'the first nation to be hit would be Spain'. Spanish aspirations in North Africa would be quashed and Britain 'would attempt to disintegrate Spanish unity to prevent Spain from following an independent policy'.

It was now Franco's turn to speak. He thanked Mussolini for Italy's valuable contributions to his Nationalist forces during the Spanish Civil War, then broached the subject of the Gibraltar stronghold. Unlike the

Germans, Franco did not believe that Gibraltar could be taken by an aerial attack. Only mortar bombardment would do the trick, for it had a 'continuous effect' whereas aerial bombardment only had an 'intermittent effect'. The Spanish General Staff intended to 'increase the calibre of the mortars from 101 to 120 mm'. 'With these,' Franco averred, 'she [Spain] will destroy the siege-works of Gibraltar, which are strong internally but on the other hand weak inside, and by blocking it, will force the entrance canal.' But the *Caudillo* was adamant on one point: that Spain seize Gibraltar 'with her own resources'.

Spain's North African colonial aspirations were a crucial factor, said Franco. Morocco was the case in point. It had been 'torn from her' by France, Spain's 'age-old enemy'. And prior to joining the war, Franco declared, Spain required grain. This was due to the year's poor harvest which had yielded only half its projected output due to lack of seed, manure, and mules. The people were starving. A deficiency of this type meant that Franco had to limit the Spanish Army to 300,000 soldiers since otherwise they could not be adequately fed. Spain's contribution to the war would be nil if she could not 'succeed in bringing real aid'.

Suñer then interjected to dispel the mistaken belief held in certain German circles that Spain had chosen to stay out of the war due to recent Axis reversals. These included the failure of the Germans to successfully invade England, the defeats sustained by the Italians in Libya, and the looming danger of American entry into the conflict. There was no truth to these allegations, Suñer insisted. He also expressed his dissatisfaction with the ambiguity of the recently concluded Vienna Protocol.*

Mussolini then summarized, as he understood them, Franco's dual prerequisites for Spain's entry into the war: '1. The dispatch of sufficient grain [to Spain by Germany]. 2. Acceptance of her colonial aspirations.' Franco agreed. Thereupon Mussolini attempted to 'define Spain's grain requirements'. In response, Franco referred the Duce to the lengthy memorandum given to Ambassador Stohrer in Madrid. The upshot of the conference was that Spain would enter the war if the requirements for 'grain, armaments, transport, etc.' in the Stohrer memorandum were partially fulfilled at once, and if Article 5 of the Vienna Protocol was amended in Spain's favour. Mussolini concluded by advising Franco that he would notify Hitler of the Spanish terms.[17]

A fortnight later, from his grandiloquent residence (the El Pardo Palace), Franco drafted an assertive response to Hitler rebutting the points the Führer had made in his letter of three weeks prior:

* The German–Spanish–Italian protocol done at Hendaye on 23 October 1940. Ciano and Ribbentrop had later appended their signatures at Vienna.

> I have made clear to you since the beginning of these negotiations the conditions of our economic situation, the only reasons why it has not been possible up to now to determine the date of Spain's participation....
>
> Furthermore, it must be acknowledged that in this question of the supply of foodstuffs, Germany has not fulfilled her offers of effective support until very recently....
>
> One observation I must repeat to your Excellency ... in order that the closing of Gibraltar may have a decisive value it is also necessary that the Suez Canal be closed at the same time. If this last circumstance should not take place ... the situation of Spain in the event of an inordinately prolonged war would then become extremely difficult....
>
> The protocol of Hendaye—permit me to express it—is ... extremely vague and Your Excellency remembers the conditions (today so changed) of this vagueness and lack of preciseness. The facts in their logical development have today left far behind the circumstances ... of October ... and the protocol then existing must at the present be considered outmoded.[18]

Thus German–Spanish diplomacy had come to naught. In Ciano's view it was the boorish Germans who had alienated the Spanish, and he wrote that 'if Spain falls away the fault rests in great part with the Germans and their uncouth manners in dealing with Latins ...'[19]

Meanwhile, on the Libyan Front, the relentless British drive westwards was gaining steam. After capturing Bardia on 5 January—'This is a washing for the drying of which at least a week is necessary,' said Mussolini—British and Commonwealth forces continued to advance along the Libyan coast towards Tobruk.[20] An Italian naval base of great strategic value, Tobruk was captured on 22 January. Of the Italian defenders, some 2,000 men were killed in action and 25,000 were captured. Allied losses were comparatively light, only 400. Thereafter the British and their allies pushed on towards Derna.

In the wake of the disaster at Tobruk, Ciano said reprovingly to Mussolini:

> At Sidi Barrani they spoke of surprise. Then, you counted upon Bardia, where [Lieutenant-General Annibale] Bergonzoli was, the heroic Bergonzoli. Bardia yielded after two hours. Then you placed your hopes in Tobruk because [Lieutenant-General Enrico] Pitassi Mannella, the king of artillerymen, was there. Tobruk has also been easily wrested from us. Now you speak with great faith of the escarpment of Derna. I beg to differ with your dangerous illusions. The trouble is grave, mysterious, and deep.[21]

Less than a fortnight later, on 3 February, Hitler—who had been attentively following the Anglo–Italian clashes in Libya—commented to his generals: 'The loss of North Africa could be acceptable militarily, but it would have disastrous psychological repercussions in Italy. Great Britain would then have a loaded gun drawn against Italy itself ... British forces would not be engaged. The British, having about twelve divisions, could use them effectively in Syria. We must be sure to avoid all this.'[22]

The Allies forged ahead and in the space of nine days captured Derna (30 January), Benghazi (6 February), and Beda Fomm (7 February). Graziani's Tenth Army was largely destroyed. In total, the British operation netted some 133,000 prisoners. What was left of Graziani's Tenth Army was pursued to El Agheila. But on 9 February (in what some strategists deem to have been a serious error), Churchill called a halt and ordered the transfer of British forces to the Balkans to assist the Greeks.

By the end of the first half of 1941, the Italians would lose their East African Empire—Eritrea, Ethiopia, and Italian Somaliland. On 19 January, the Sudan Defence Force, commanded by Lieutenant-General William Platt, initiated operations against Italian East Africa. The latter was defended by Italian and Ascari forces under the duke of Aosta, viceroy since 1937. Platt's forces took the town of Keren on 27 March and captured the remainder of Eritrea soon thereafter—the capital city, Asmara, and the seaport of Massawa—on 3 and 8 April respectively.

That winter, the British launched another offensive (Operation Canvas), advancing from Kenya into Italian Somaliland. The invaders received assistance from the locals, who turned on their Italian occupiers, harassed them, and otherwise created for them a plethora of difficulties. Mogadishu, capital of Italian Somaliland, was captured on 25 February.

Addis Ababa was recaptured on 6 April, wherefrom the Italians had withdrawn the previous day, and on 5 May, Emperor Haile Selassie triumphantly returned. The duke of Aosta and his troops made a final stand at the Amba Alagi stronghold in northern Ethiopia but succumbed to the enemy on 19 May. Consequently, Italian domination of the Red Sea area was at an end. Mussolini grumbled: 'We have lost our empire, while the French still retain theirs.'[23]

Meanwhile, the British sought to recapture British Somaliland, annexed to Italian East African since late August. Operation Appearance was thus launched from Aden on 16 March. The Aden Striking Force, a detachment consisting of some 3,000 Allied invaders, landed at Berbera before sunrise. The city was captured by mid-morning and the Italians hastily withdrew. Four days later, the Allies also took Hargeisa, and the Italian occupation of the distant British protectorate, which had lasted only seven months, was over.

On 9 February, British naval forces bombed Genoa and La Spezia (Operation Grog), causing great destruction. Churchill declared to Roosevelt in a broadcast these stirring words: 'Put your confidence in us. Give us your faith and your blessing, and, under Providence, all will be well. We shall not fail or falter; we shall not weaken or tire. Neither the sudden shock of battle, nor the long-drawn trials of vigilance and exertion will wear us down. Give us the tools, and we will finish the job.'[24]

In a speech to Blackshirts at the Teatro Adriano (Adrian Theatre) in Rome on 23 February, Mussolini posited that Italy had been in a continuous state of war against the Western plutocracies—not since 10 June 1940, or 1 September 1939—but since 1922, from the very beginning of the Fascist regime:

> We have actually been at war since 1922—that is, from the day when we lifted the flag of our [Fascist] revolution, which was then defended by a handful of men against the Masonic, democratic, capitalistic world. From that day world liberalism, democracy, and plutocracy declared and waged war against us with press campaigns, spreading libelous reports, financial sabotage, attempts and plots even when we were intent upon the work of international reconstruction which is and will remain for centuries, as the undestroyable documentation of our creative will.

Midway through his speech, the Duce alluded to the British bombardment of Genoa and extolled Fascism and Italian nationalism. The British, Mussolini vowed, would never succeed in eroding the morale of the indomitable Italian people:

> Churchill has not the least idea of the spiritual forces of the Italian people or of what Fascism can do. We can understand Churchill's ordering the shelling of industrial plants at Genoa to disrupt work, but to shell the city in order to break down its morale is a childish illusion. It means that the British do not at all know the race temperament of the Ligurian people in general and the Genoese in particular. It means that they are ignorant of the civilian virtues and proud patriotism of the people who gave the fatherland Columbus, Garibaldi, and Mazzini.[25]

Pressured by the Germans, at the beginning of March the hitherto neutral Bulgars joined the Axis. Prime Minister Bogdan Filov, a Germanophile, signed the Tripartite Pact. Shortly thereafter German troops began to assemble on Bulgarian soil in preparation for the Balkan campaign. Expecting the Germans to strike soon, a contingent of British and Commonwealth land forces arrived in Greece.

Ciano met with Hitler at the Hotel Imperial in Vienna on 1 March. The Führer began by stating that as far as he was concerned 'the crises of the past winter could now probably be considered as having been overcome'. He was certain that the Albanian Front had at last been 'consolidated'. And in North Africa, in a fortnight the Germans—who several weeks prior had dispatched an expeditionary force to Libya to take matters in hand—would have enough armoured units at their disposal to hold the British in check.

The French Colonial Empire was another important factor to take into consideration. 'Stabilization of the situation in North Africa ... would be advantageous towards the French,' Hitler reasoned, 'especially in connection with the relationship between Vichy and French North Africa.' Why? Because at present 'the consolidation of the Axis position in North Africa was the sole means of pressure on French North Africa that Italy and Germany possessed'. This was due to the fact that their fair-weather friends, the Spaniards, had unequivocally stated that they were unwilling to enter the war. The Spanish, Hitler complained, were now claiming that Gibraltar, as a matter of Spanish honour, could only be taken by Spanish forces. Hitler was of the opinion that the Spaniards' chances of achieving this were 'slight' at best; it would probably take them a decade. Nevertheless, although the Spanish could not be relied on, aerial warfare directed against the British in the Mediterranean from Tripolitania would gradually make it 'extremely difficult' for them to remain there.

Every effort, Hitler added, had to be directed towards the ultimate aim of 'breaking down England'. It would be of great psychological benefit if all the nations of Continental Europe formed 'an anti-English bloc'. In connection with Bulgaria, her recent accession to the Tripartite Pact was a most satisfactory development. It would also be desirable 'to bring about Yugoslavia's accession to the Tripartite Pact', for this would be yet another psychological blow against the British. Ciano interposed to point out that in connection with Yugoslavia, Mussolini was less interested in an Italo–Yugoslav agreement now that Bulgaria had joined the Axis. In any event, the Italo–Yugoslav Treaty of 25 March 1937, signed in Belgrade, still remained in effect.

Hitler then asserted that it was absolutely essential for Italy to keep a firm grip on Rhodes. He had recently received reports informing him that Italian forces had succeeded in retaking the Dodecanese island, which the British had captured several days prior. Ciano replied 'that Rhodes was extremely well fortified and had two airfields'. In his opinion, any attempted incursion by the British was bound to fail. The British had, however, managed to 'cut off the supply of both gasoline and food'. But once Greece was liquidated, it would be possible for Rhodes to 'be rescued'.

As regards Greece, Hitler's 'only concern' was that the British might launch an aerial attack from there against the Romanian oil fields. If they should attempt such an undertaking, he would send long-distance Luftwaffe bombers to retaliate against the Iraqi oil fields at Mosul. For this purpose, it was imperative that Rhodes remain in Axis hands to serve 'as an intermediate landing place and refuelling station'. Thereupon Hitler outlined on a map 'the probable course of the operations against Greece'. There would be Greek resistance, Hitler predicted, but from a psychological standpoint it would be devastating for the Greeks once Salonika was taken by Axis forces.

Ciano declared that in East Africa matters had come to a head. 'It was impossible,' Ciano explained, 'for the Italians to offer resistance in the flat country because the psychological powers of resistance of the coloured troops there did not stand up against modern motorized weapons.' The Italians would therefore fall back 'to the high plateau' and from there continue the struggle. In these mountainous regions it would be possible to hold out for a lengthy duration. Hitler then spoke of 'the imminent entry of German troops into Bulgaria'. Luftwaffe units would soon reach Bulgarian airfields; and anti-aircraft artillery had been strategically positioned in Romania and Bulgaria at 'vulnerable points'.

The subject of Spain was once again raised. Hitler stated that Franco had told him that if the Germans and Italians had not contributed to the Spanish Civil War, the conflict would still have been won, but 'would only have been more "lengthy"'. Ciano replied that this was 'absolutely untrue'. On the contrary, Ciano declared, the *Caudillo* had dispatched two generals to Italy in the summer of 1936 and had admitted that unless he were to receive aircraft from the Italians immediately, his Nationalist cause would be irretrievably lost, and he would then have no recourse but to seek refuge in Africa.

Hitler remarked that the past several months had demonstrated 'that Franco was not a good comrade'. When the Italians had experienced military reversals in the Balkans, the *Caudillo* should have lent assistance accordingly. Ciano asserted that the blame for this could be attributed to none other than Suñer, 'a 150 percent Jesuit'. Moreover, Spain still maintained close relations with Britain. In fact, the Spanish duke of Alba (Jacobo Fitz-James Stuart), himself a relation of the British royal family, was pro-British. The Spanish, Ciano accused, had been involved in all sorts of underhanded activity. The Duce had even threatened to arrest the Spanish ambassador in Rome for espionage, his diplomatic immunity notwithstanding. It was only then that this shady character had been recalled by his government.[26]

Meanwhile, in the Balkans, the Italo–Greek war had reached an impasse. The Italians had augmented their forces and by February had managed to stabilize the Albanian Front thereby. Twenty-eight Italian divisions faced half as many Greek divisions. Mussolini wished to inflict a devastating blow upon the Greeks prior to the planned German invasion of the Balkans, and on 2 March he reached Tirana to personally oversee the forthcoming Spring Offensive (*Operazione Primavera*). It was to be the final solo attempt by the Italians to crush the Greeks. Launched on 9 March, it was headed by General Carlo Geloso, commander of the Eleventh Army. Italian forces rained destruction down upon the Greeks with intense aerial and artillery bombardments, but ultimately little progress was made. The Greeks counterattacked effectively and held out against all odds. By 14 March, General Cavallero recognized that the offensive was a lost cause and he recommended to Mussolini that it be discontinued.

Four and a half months after the disaster at Taranto Harbour, the Italian Navy sustained another major defeat at sea. After Italian signals were intercepted by British code-breakers at Bletchley Park, Mediterranean Fleet forces led by Admiral Andrew Cunningham set forth to intercept Italian warships commanded by Vice-Admiral Angelo Iachino. The Italian vessels were preying on British convoys. Contact was made on the morning of 28 March south of the Peloponnese peninsula, off Cape Matapan. The battleship *Vittorio Veneto* attacked first but before long was on the run, having sustained torpedo damage. It managed to escape but three heavy cruisers—*Fiume*, *Pola*, and *Zara*—and two destroyers—*Vittorio Alfieri* and *Giosue Carducci*—were sunk, dealing the Italian Navy a heavy blow. Over 2,300 Italians perished, whereas British losses were minimal—one torpedo bomber with a crew of three. Italian prospects for attaining naval supremacy in the Mediterranean sector were now all but nil.

On 4 March, Prince Regent Paul of Yugoslavia arrived at the Berghof in secret for a meeting with Hitler. In exchange for Salonika and a German guarantee of Yugoslavia's territorial integrity (contrary to Italian interests), Yugoslavia was to accede to the Tripartite Pact. Succumbing to German coercion, on 25 March Yugoslav Ministers Dragiša Cvetković and Aleksandar Cincar-Marković journeyed to Vienna where, in conformance with German expectations, Cvetković signed the Tripartite Pact at the Belvedere Palace.

After the formalities with the Yugoslavs were concluded, Hitler conferred with Ciano at the Hotel Imperial. The Nazi dictator pointed out to Ciano that Yugoslavia's entry into the Axis camp would facilitate German military operations against Greece. Thereupon Ciano advised Hitler that at a meeting with Mussolini in Bari, the Duce had instructed him to put several questions to the Führer.

But first, Ciano had a few points to cite from Mussolini's personal notes. Regarding Albania, the Duce wished only to convey 'that the front was quiet and the situation was stabilized'. As for the Italo–Greek war, it could, from a certain standpoint, even be considered desirable, for 'it had clarified the entire Balkan situation in favour of the Axis'. Bulgaria and Yugoslavia had joined the Axis camp chiefly to gain their share of 'Greek booty'. Without this incentive, both Balkan nations 'would otherwise have persisted in their ambiguous positions'. Such an equivocal attitude on their part would have posed an ongoing threat to the Axis. In the Duce's view 'the entire Danube Basin had to be liberated from Franco–English influence', and it was the Italo–Greek war that had accelerated this development. The elimination of Greece would also 'open up important strategic possibilities in the aerial and naval war'. Another Italian offensive in Albania was projected for the end of March; it 'would occur at the central part of the Albanian Front (Këlcyrë)'. Having finished reading, Ciano then requested that Hitler share his current views on Spain, France, Russia, and Turkey. Ciano also mentioned that the Duce desired another conference.

In connection with the four aforementioned countries, Hitler replied that:

1. Franco had no intention of waging war against Britain and had all but denounced the Hendaye Protocol;
2. The Vichy Government was not to be trusted, and the French Colonial Empire had to be prevented from being lost to the Allies;
3. The Soviets' attitude had become increasingly hostile due to the Germans' unwillingness to abandon Finland to them; and
4. He would attempt, with judicious care, to bring about a *rapprochement* with Turkey.

Lastly, Hitler stated that a summit meeting between himself and the Duce would be possible after Foreign Minister Yōsuke Matsuoka's visit to Germany was over.[27]

Yugoslavia's accession to the Tripartite Pact was destined to be very short-lived. This development was so poorly received in Belgrade that it prompted a clique of officers, led by Army General Dušan Simović, to carry out a *putsch*. The government was ousted, Prince Paul's regency was terminated, seventeen-year-old King Peter II (Paul's nephew) was installed onto the throne, and General Simović succeeded Cvetković as prime minister. Hitler, infuriated at the unexpected turn of events and above all recognizing that the Balkan sector had to be secure before he could launch his Russian campaign, had the day of the *coup d'état* issued Directive No. 25 (Operation Punishment). The first article stated: 'The military *putsch* in Yugoslavia has changed the political situation in the Balkans. Even if Yugoslavia at first should give declarations of loyalty, she must be considered as a foe and therefore must be destroyed as quickly as possible.'[28] The invasion of Russia, originally fixed for 15 May, was pushed back five weeks.

In a conference with his generals on 30 March, Hitler divulged that unlike in the West, the war in Eastern Europe would be genocidal in nature. The ideological archenemies of National Socialist Germany—Jews and Commissars—would be ferreted out and liquidated by *Einsatzgruppen* (Special Action Groups) trailing behind the Wehrmacht. The Führer believed that the U.S.S.R. would collapse in just several weeks, and he later said contemptuously to General Jodl: 'We have only to kick in the door and the whole rotten structure will come crashing down.'[29]

The German assault on Yugoslavia began on 6 April. Hungarian and Bulgarian auxiliaries also took part. The Italians penetrated into Croatia on 11 April. Belgrade was mercilessly bombarded by the Luftwaffe (6–8 April), and on 17 April, the Royal Yugoslav Army capitulated. A week prior to the surrender, on 10 April, the Independent Croat State was established. It was ruled by the Ustaše, an extremist nationalist movement patterned on Italian Fascism. At its head was Ante Pavelić, who held the title of Poglavnik (Leader). The murderous regime—whose unspeakable crimes against humanity rivalled even those of Himmler's S.S.—persecuted those of Serbian, Jewish, and Roma origin, plus Bosniaks.

The Germans simultaneously launched Operation Marita through Bulgar territory. The Greeks now had to fight a second deadlier foe on yet another front, and they were overwhelmed by the German onslaught. Defended by an insufficient number of troops, the Metaxas Defensive Line was swiftly bypassed. Allied forces had no alternative but to stage a fighting retreat southwards. The great Greek cities fell: Salonika (9 April), Larissa (19 April), Thermopylae (25 April), and Athens (27 April). Victorious German soldiers hoisted the swastika flag above the Acropolis, symbol of ancient Greek civilization. Three days later, the entire Peloponnese was in German hands. Before they could escape the Greek mainland, some 7,000 Allied troops were taken prisoner.

In the first half of June, the Italians occupied the Peloponnese and the regions of Thessaly and Attica. For their minor contribution to the Axis cause—namely, providing the Germans with a jumping-off point and trailing behind the German Army—the Bulgars on 14 May received Greek Thrace and a slice of Macedonia. The Germans in three weeks had achieved what the Italians had failed to do in over five months.

Their defeat notwithstanding, Hitler himself praised the tenacity of the Greek combatants. In a speech to the *Reichstag* on 4 May, he admitted: 'Historical justice ... obliges me to say that of the opponents that have taken up arms against us, most particularly the Greek soldiers, have fought with the greatest bravery and contempt of death. He only capitulated when further resistance became impossible and therefore useless.'[30] With the Balkan campaign concluded, Hitler fixed the date for Operation Barbarossa to start on 22 June, as evidenced by a top secret military document dated 1 May which denoted the following: '*Timetable Barbarossa:* The Führer has decided: *Action "Barbarossa"* begin[s] 22 June.'[31]

Next was the turn of Crete, the largest of the Greek islands. German paratroopers launched an airborne invasion (Operation Mercury) on 20 May. It was fiercely resisted by Greek, British, and Commonwealth forces. Cretans also partook in the defence of their island. German losses were initially severe, but on 22 May, the Maleme Airfield was captured. Additional German assault troops were thus able to access the island and overrun northern Crete. The Greeks and the Allies retreated to the south of the island, where they were either rescued by the Royal Navy or taken prisoner by the Germans. Some linked up with local Cretan resistance groups. After ten days the German conquest of Crete was complete.

By early April the Italians, with German aid, had managed to reacquire much of the Libyan territory lost to the British during the winter. On account of the Italians' dismal performance in Cyrenaica, on 9 February Hitler had informed his generals that he intended to send the newly established German *Afrika Korps* under Lieutenant-General Erwin Rommel to Libya to help the beleaguered Italians (Operation Sunflower). The *Afrika Korps* reached Tripoli on 14 February, and two days before Rommel, an expert tactician who was soon to be famously known to friend and foe alike by the sobriquet 'Desert Fox', had himself arrived. He was tasked with defending the province of Tripolitania.

Rommel's forces took the initiative at once. German units reached Sirte (15 February) and Nofilia (18 February). Under Rommel's capable leadership, Italo–German forces captured El Agheila (24 March), Mersa Brega (1 April), Benghazi (4 April), Derna (7 April), and Mechili (8 April). And on 10 April, Rommel's forces struck at Tobruk, beginning a major siege. That spring General Wavell launched two Allied operations* in an attempt to relieve the Tobruk stronghold, but both British undertakings were brief and unsuccessful, and by late May Axis troops had penetrated into Egypt. In the North African theatre, the tide had turned in favour of the Axis.

---

* Operations Brevity and Battleaxe, 15–16 May and 15–17 June 1941 respectively.

On 20 April, Ciano met with Hitler once again, this time at Munich. The war in the Balkans was first discussed; as usual, the Führer monopolized the conversation. He was very satisfied with the progress of the Balkan campaign which, in his view, was nearly at an end, for at this point Hitler considered 'any further Anglo–Greek resistance improbable'. The war in the Balkans had enabled the Axis to gain greater control over the Mediterranean sector; this brought Axis forces 'considerably nearer to the Suez Canal'. Ciano interjected to state that Mussolini deemed 'the probable action against the Canal zone just as important as military cooperation against the British Isles'. Hitler concurred; however, the question of how best to attack Egypt had yet to be determined. Hitler spoke very critically of General Franco in this regard. Had the disloyal Spaniard shown greater solidarity with his Italo–German benefactors, British control of Gibraltar would be no more and the action against the British in North Africa would have been 'extremely easy'. This undertaking no longer appeared to be in the cards.

Another possible route from which to attack Egypt was through Turkey. However, carrying out the attack 'by force', i.e. without the Turks' consent, was not an option. The Turks would have to be offered some sort of inducement in order to permit this, but precisely what was uncertain—perhaps Syria? The other available route from which to attack Egypt was via Libya, and it was therefrom that Hitler recommended the Italo–German assault be launched. There would be, to be sure, 'many difficulties', in particular the transportation of Axis divisions across the Mediterranean.

The recent advances made thus far in Libya were the result of Rommel's 'brilliant action'. Nevertheless, Hitler preferred to have 'at least five more divisions' to throw into the battle to supplement those already engaged. Due to 'the hot season ... now approaching', such operations would not likely begin until October. On the subject of submarine warfare against the British, Hitler said little, most likely because 'the results obtained' had been below expectations.

Both the Axis successes in the Balkans and the recent Russo–Japanese Pact (13 April) had intensified isolationist sentiment in the United States. Prior to 1942, Hitler predicted, American deliveries to Britain would 'not be of any great magnitude'. But after 1942, it would be a different matter; one which would then warrant 'the most careful consideration'. Hitler felt that 'the Japanese card' would be most useful in offsetting 'any American action'. Thus he wished for the Tripartite Pact 'to be kept continually in evidence as an active and operative factor in international policy'. The Führer concluded by advising Ciano that he wished to meet with Mussolini again in the near future, this time in Italy.[32]

In a letter dated 4 May, Ciano attempted once more to persuade his opposite number in Spain to enter the war on the Axis side. He wrote to Suñer:

> You know how much the Duce and Italy have respected and still respect Spain's complete independence in deciding on its attitude towards the conflict. You alone can judge how much it is possible to do for the good of your country and when it can be done. But it is certain that Spain can have no other place than at the side of Italy and Germany, and past as well as future events are destined to make this union ever more intimate and effective. The great new destiny of Spain is to be found in the certain victory of the Totalitarian States.[33]

Unknown to the Third Reich's upper echelons until it was too late, on 10 May Deputy Führer Rudolf Hess boarded a Messerschmitt and flew to Scotland alone on an ill-conceived peace mission. The muddled Hess had apparently been under the erroneous impression that even at this late stage he might be able to personally broker a peace agreement between Germany and Britain. Under the circumstances, both the British and Germans considered his well-intentioned but temerarious endeavour to be an act bordering on lunacy, and Hitler took great pains to distance Hess from the Nazi regime thereafter. Ribbentrop hastily journeyed to Italy in a desperate attempt to put as positive a spin on the Hess scandal as possible. On 13 May, Ciano wrote:

> Von Ribbentrop unexpectedly arrives in Rome. He is discouraged and nervous. He wants to confer with the Duce and me for various reasons, but there is only one real reason: he wants to inform us about the Hess affair ... Mussolini comforted von Ribbentrop, but afterwards told me that he considers the Hess affair a tremendous blow to the Nazi regime. He added that he was glad of it because this will have the effect of bringing down German stock, even with the Italians.[34]

The pride of the German Navy, the battleship *Bismarck*, was sunk in the North Atlantic by British naval forces on 27 May. Just three days prior, the *Bismarck* had destroyed the British battlecruiser *Hood* and, seeking revenge, the British had zealously pursued it. Over 2,000 Germans perished at sea, and the loss of the Third Reich's greatest capital ship—823 feet long, armed with 15-inch guns, and capable of a speed of 30 knots—was irreplaceable. And on 8 June, British forces invaded Vichy Syria from Palestine (Operation Exporter). Damascus was captured on 21 June, and three weeks later the French sued for peace. For the Germans, the possibility of launching attacks from the French mandate against Egypt and Suez was lost thereby. These events proved that Britain was still a formidable adversary and would remain so for the foreseeable future.

Mussolini did apparently have some inkling that war between Germany and the Soviet Union might be in the cards, and that the Italians, for ideological reasons, would have to take part. On 30 May, General Cavallero wrote in his *Diary*: 'The Duce told me that he foresaw the possibility of a conflict between Germany and Russia. He said that we could not stay out of this because it involved the struggle against Communism.'[35]

On 2 June, the Axis dictators met once more at the Brenner Pass. During Mussolini's preliminary, confidential session with Hitler, the Führer raised the embarrassing matter of Hess's unauthorized flight to England; spoke of the recent sinking of the battleship *Bismarck* by the British; and assured the Duce that Admiral Dönitz's U-boats, unleashed in wolfpack formation against British convoys, would turn the tide in the Atlantic. The Führer was affable, but he made no mention of Germany's invasion plans against the Soviet Union. The conversation was, as usual, monopolized by Hitler, who droned on almost uninterruptedly for five hours. In spite of the tedium, Mussolini 'was satisfied with the meeting, especially because he was able to note that for us [the Italians] there was no lowering of tone on the matter of Italo–German relations'.[36]

Ciano also had a private conversation with Ribbentrop. In connection with Russia, the latter mendaciously assured him that the rumours of an impending German attack were 'devoid of foundation, or at least excessively premature'. All the Germans had done, Ribbentrop clarified, was to position a 'concentration of forces' at the German–Russian frontier in response to the Russians having done so first. Ribbentrop did not believe that Stalin would be foolhardy enough to actually attack the Reich, but should the unthinkable happen, the *Wehrmacht* would destroy the Russian armies. Ribbentrop's primary concern (so he said) was that a Russo–German war 'would interrupt supplies which … are now developing at a satisfactory pace'.[37]

Next day Ciano penned another letter to Suñer. He posited that soon British naval power in the Mediterranean would cease to be a factor. Spain, Ciano argued, could not afford to remain inactive and should openly demonstrate its solidarity with Italy and Germany by acceding to the Tripartite system:

> I am writing to you on my return from the conversation on the Brenner. I think that you will be happy to learn that Spain was discussed with lively interest both by us and by the Germans and that the Axis attributes fundamental importance to friendship with your country.

> The events of the last weeks have had an important effect on the course of the war. The Balkans are now liberated from English influence. The British Navy has lost many of its bases and is caught in an ever tightening vise by the forces of the Axis. A day will come—and it is not far distant—when the entire Mediterranean will be liberated from the presence of the British Fleet.
>
> Can Nationalist and Falangist Spain remain indifferent and absent in the face of events of such great import for our life and our future as Mediterranean Powers? As a sincere and proved friend of Spain I do not think so....
>
> But today it seems to me that Spain, even without throwing herself into the conflict, should publicly show that the banner of Falangism is side by side with that of the Fascist and Nazi revolutions at this decisive moment of history.[38]

Mussolini endorsed Ciano's earnest missive with a brief handwritten note appended: 'I confirm the above. Spain must *at least* adhere to the Tripartite Pact and that before other adhesions take place. By subscribing to the Tripartite Pact, Spain comes once more into line as far as tomorrow's European settlement is concerned. I take the occasion to remember myself to you and to add my most cordial expressions of friendship.'[39]

By 10 June, however, Mussolini's feelings towards the Germans had taken a sharp turn. The Duce was having second thoughts. He inveighed to Ciano about Hitler's inconsiderate behaviour and of their recent conference at the Brenner, which he now felt had been a waste of time:

> Personally, I've had my fill of Hitler and the way he acts. These conferences called by the ringing of a bell are not to my liking.... And besides, what kind of conferences are these? For five hours I am forced to listen to a monologue which is quite fruitless and boring. He spoke for hours and hours of Hess, of the *Bismarck*, of things more or less related to the war, but he did not propose an agenda, he did not go to the bottom of any problem, or make any decisions.[40]

Mussolini also felt that the Germans were hindering Italian designs in the pro-Axis puppet state of Croatia:

> It is no importance that the Germans recognize our rights in Croatia on paper, when in practice they take everything and leave us only a little heap of bones. They are dirty dogs, and I tell you that this cannot go on for long. I do not even know if German intrigue will permit Aimone [duke of Spoleto] to ascend the Croatian throne.... For the moment

> there is nothing to be done. We must howl with the wolves. Today at the Chamber I will cajole the Germans, but my heart is filled with bitterness.[41]

The tenth of June was also the first anniversary of Italy's entry into the war, and on this historic date, Mussolini spoke to the Chamber of Fasces and Corporations. He would not address the chamber again for eighteen months. The Duce first spoke of Greece: 'Since August 1940, I had proof that Greece no longer was keeping even the appearance of neutrality.... Thus, on 15 October, it was unanimously decided to break hesitancies and take to the field at the end of the month. It was absolutely mathematical that in April, even if nothing happened to change the Balkan situation, the Italian Army would have broken through and annihilated the Greek Army.'

As regards the brutal liquidation of Yugoslavia, Mussolini declared: '... Yugoslavia revealed through a *coup d'état* its real sentiments. The Axis war against Yugoslavia, therefore, was rendered inevitable. Axis armies acted together with lightning rapidity.... The Yugoslav Army for which Paris and the Little Entente circle had created a reputation of "invincibility" was put out of action with the first blows.' The Duce characterized Yugoslavia as 'the third mosaic State artificially created at Versailles'. 'With exclusively anti-Italian function,' he declared with satisfaction, 'it falls to pieces at the first shock.'

Mussolini also asserted that American intervention in the European conflict against the Axis Powers would be no great cause for concern:

> It is well that it be known that American intervention does not bother us excessively. Specific declaration of war would not change the present situation, which is one of *de facto* war, if not *de jure*. American intervention, when employed completely, would be late, and if it were not later would not remove the terms of the problem. American intervention will not give victory to Britain but will prolong the war; will not limit the area of war but will extend it to other oceans; will change the United States regime into an authoritarian, totalitarian one in comparison with which the European forerunners—Fascist and Nazi—will feel themselves far surpassed and perfected.[42]

Two days later, Churchill spoke at a conference of Dominion High Commissioners and Allied Ministers at St. James Palace. It was before these notables that the eloquent British statesman made a disparaging yet comical reference when he alluded to 'Hitler, with his tattered lackey Mussolini at his tail and Admiral Darlan frisking by his side...'[43]

On 15 June, the ceremony for the adhesion of the new Croat State to the Tripartite Pact was held at the Ducal Palace in Venice. In the privacy of a gondola, Ciano inquired of Ribbentrop about the circulating rumours of imminent German aggression against the U.S.S.R. To his Italian interlocutor's query, Ribbentrop replied: 'Dear Ciano, I cannot tell you anything as yet because every decision is locked in the impenetrable bosom of the Führer. However, one thing is certain: if we attack them, the Russia of Stalin will be erased from the map within eight weeks.'[44]

Six days later, in a shocking letter dated 21 June, Hitler at last provided Mussolini with an explanation for the impending German invasion of the Soviet Union. The Soviets, Hitler claimed, were massing their armies along the Russo–German frontier in preparation for an attack on the Reich, and the latter had to strike pre-emptively in order to forestall it. The document was truthful insofar as it contained justifications—as Hitler perceived them—for unilaterally abrogating the Nazi–Soviet Non-Aggression Pact:

> Since the liquidation of Poland, there is evident in Soviet Russia a consistent trend, which, even if cleverly and cautiously, is nevertheless reverting firmly to the old Bolshevist tendency to expansion of the Soviet State.... The concentration of Russian forces ... is tremendous. Really, all available Russian forces are at our border....
>
> I have decided under these circumstances ... to put an end to the hypocritical performance in the Kremlin....
>
> As far as the war in the East is concerned, Duce, it will surely be difficult, but I do not entertain a second's doubt as to its great success....
>
> If I have waited until this moment, Duce, to send you this information, it is because the final decision itself will not be made until 7 o'clock tonight....
>
> Whatever now may come, Duce, our situation cannot become worse as a result of this step; it can only improve.

Hitler ended his message by admitting that Germany's alliance with the Bolsheviks had been anathema to him, for it had long felt like a betrayal of his ideological principles. He was pleased to once more have peace of mind:

> In conclusion, let me say one more thing, Duce. Since I struggled through to this decision, I again feel spiritually free. The partnership with the Soviet Union, in spite of the complete sincerity of the efforts to bring about a final conciliation, was nevertheless often very irksome to me, for in some way or other it seemed to me to be a break with my whole origin, my concepts, and my former obligations. I am happy now to be relieved of these mental agonies.[45]

At 3:30 a.m. on 22 June, Hitler's vast armies poured across the German–Russian frontier, advancing rapidly into enemy territory. Four and a half months earlier, on 3 February, the Führer had boasted to his generals: 'When Barbarossa commences, the world will hold its breath and make no comment!'[46] The Axis invasion force consisted of over three million men, the largest in all history. Also participating in Operation Barbarossa were hundreds of thousands of Italians, Romanians, Hungarians, Slovaks, and Croats. And several days later the Finns, seeking to reacquire East Karelia, initiated joint operations with the Germans in the north.

The Soviets were caught completely off guard. Although there had been indications that the Germans were planning a double-cross, the Soviet Government had failed either to recognize them or to act on them. At noon, a flustered Commissar Molotov broadcast an address to the peoples of the Soviet Union:

> Today ... without any claims having been presented to the Soviet Union, without any declaration of war, German troops attacked our country, attacked our borders at many points, and bombed from their airplanes our cities.... The Red Army and our whole people will again wage a victorious patriotic war for our country, for honour, for liberty.... Ours is a righteous cause. The enemy will be routed. Victory will be ours.[47]

Stalin remained in denial for a time, but before long the hard fact of the *Wehrmacht* penetrating deep into the Soviet heartland forced him to deal with the crisis.

Churchill proclaimed that Britain would henceforth be allied with the Soviet Union in a collective effort to eradicate Nazism, Anglo–Soviet ideological differences notwithstanding:

> No one has been a more consistent opponent of Communism than I have for the last twenty-five years. I will unsay no word that I have spoken about it. But all this fades away before the spectacle which is now unfolding.... We have but one aim and one single, irrevocable purpose. We are resolved to destroy Hitler and every vestige of the Nazi regime. From this nothing will turn us—nothing.... Any man or state who fights on against Nazidom will have our aid. Any man or state who marches with Hitler is our foe.... It follows, therefore, that we shall give whatever help we can to Russia and the Russian people.[48]

Mussolini replied to Hitler's recent letter on 23 June. He outlined the benefits to the Axis of liquidating Soviet Russia and underscored the 'enthusiastic approval' expressed by his Fascist Party stalwarts to the bold German move:

> I fully appreciate that your decision [to attack Russia] must have been preceded by long reflection, because the war against Russia is primarily a struggle against the breadth of space. But all those who would point to historical precedents should be reminded that today the motors of tanks and airplanes, and the extraordinary manoeuvring skill of both your generals and your soldiers, have overcome space.
>
> The solution of the Russian problem results, I believe, in the following advantages:
>
> *a.* It deprives Great Britain of her last hope on the European Continent;
>
> *b.* It relieves us of any concern for the immediate future;
>
> *c.* It brings us back to our political doctrine, which for tactical considerations we temporarily abandoned;
>
> *d.* All anti-Bolshevist tendencies throughout the world, including the Anglo–Saxon countries, will again turn toward the Axis;
>
> *e.* The new Russia, diminished in territory and liberated from Bolshevism, may be returned to the practice of sincere economic collaboration with the rest of Europe, and make raw materials which we need available to us, especially if the Anglo–Saxons should impose upon us a war of unforeseeable duration.
>
> Everything I have said will show you, Führer, what enthusiastic approval your decision to take Russia by the throat has met with in Italy and especially among the old guard of the party, which would have accepted with a heavy heart any other solution of the [Russian] problem.[49]

Embittered by the Italian misadventures of the past year in Greece and North Africa, on 1 July Mussolini spitefully expressed to Ciano the hope that the Germans would have a tough time of it in Russia: 'I hope for only one thing, that in this war in the East the Germans will lose a lot of feathers.'[50] But the Duce still wished to contribute to the anti-Bolshevik crusade, and to General Giovanni Messe he declared: 'We cannot count less than Slovakia and the other minor states. I must be at the side of Hitler in Russia as he was at mine in the war against Greece, and is henceforward in Africa. The destiny of Italy is intimately bound up with that of Germany.'[51]

Mussolini accordingly issued orders for the formation of an Italian unit to serve alongside the Germans on the Russian Front. The C.S.I.R. (Italian Expeditionary Corps in Russia), comprising three divisions—the *Torino*, the *Passubio*, and the *Principe Amadeo Duca d'Aosta*—was established on 10 July. Led by General Messe, it was deployed to southern Russia.

On 12 July, representatives of the U.S.S.R. and Britain concluded the Anglo–Soviet Accord,* a military alliance. Its purpose was for the two nations 'to grant each other all assistance and mutual support against Hitlerite Germany and not to negotiate or conclude an armistice or peace except by mutual consent'.[52] But when news of the Anglo–Soviet Accord came to Mussolini's attention, he felt it unlikely that the Germans would be capable of concluding their Russian campaign prior to the onset of winter. 'This,' predicted the Duce (referring to the accord), 'will open the door to many unknown factors.' But Mussolini at once made the following pronouncement: 'We must hope for two things: that the war will be long and exhausting for Germany and that it will end in a compromise, which will preserve our [Italian] independence.'[53]

Accompanied by his entourage, on 24 August Mussolini entrained to East Prussia for another summit meeting with Hitler. To Filippo Anfuso, who was filling in for his superior Ciano (on account of the latter's throat infection), Mussolini stressed the absolute necessity of Italy contributing materially to the war against Bolshevism: 'If we are absent, the circumstance that I was the first to combat Communism will count for nothing against the fact that the Italians were not in Russia. That is why our participation is of capital importance.'[54]

The Axis chiefs conferred at the *Wolfsschanze* (Wolf's Lair), Hitler's remote headquarters at Rastenburg, on 25 August. Mussolini complained to Hitler about the 'abnormality' of Italo–French relations. These were governed by the Armistice Convention which, Mussolini professed, had ceased to function and had been rendered obsolete 'by the development of events'. But in Hitler's view, it would be inopportune to 'deal with' France while the Russian campaign was in progress. Nevertheless, he too distrusted the French, whom he was watching with a close eye. 'The French question,' Hitler assured his Italian ally, 'will be re-examined at the end of the war.' Hitler also inveighed against General Franco for having not been amenable to German operations against Gibraltar in the early months of 1941, and added that Spain had been 'a real disappointment to him'. Mussolini replied that while he was in accord 'with the Führer's way of thinking', he believed that due to the idiosyncrasies of Spain as a nation it would be 'useless to exercise further pressure to induce her to intervene'. As regards Russia, Hitler stated that he intended to 'annihilate the Soviet military forces' in order to remove once and for all 'the recurring threats of conflict' to Germany and to Europe. And after operations in the East were concluded he would 'deal the final blow to England by invading the island'.

* It was superseded by the Anglo–Soviet Treaty, signed in London on 26 May 1942.

Towards the end of the conversations, Mussolini advised Hitler that he wanted Italian forces to 'take part on a larger scale in the operations against the U.S.S.R.' Mussolini explained that Italy's 'abundance of men' made it possible for him to 'send another six, nine, or even more divisions'. Hitler expressed his gratitude to the Duce for his generous offer but cited 'difficulties of a logistical nature' as an excuse to decline. Mussolini, however, would not let the matter drop so quickly. Hitler reluctantly agreed to give the matter further consideration, and spoke of using Italian troops—who naturally were accustomed to warmer climates—in Soviet Ukraine, 'where the average winter temperature is not, generally, lower than six degrees below zero'.[55]

Next day the dictators flew to Brest Litovsk. There they were received by Field Marshal Kluge, commander of the German Fourth Army, who gave an account of the battle resulting in the capture of the Byelorussian city. The Axis leaders continued their tour, and on 28 August, they flew to the Ukraine where they were met by Field Marshal Rundstedt at Uman, and at the Tekucha crossroads by Generals Messe and Cavallero. Further on the dictators reviewed the *Torino* Division, which made a favourable impression. After a simple lunch of meat and vegetable soup, black bread, and oranges, Hitler left Mussolini's side to converse with German soldiers, shaking hands and fraternizing.

Piqued at being left out of the spotlight, Mussolini later declared to Alfieri: 'Hitler might have taken me with him when he went to speak to the troops, instead of leaving me with old Rundstedt. Did you notice how unsoldierly the Führer looked when he was among his men?'[56] It was the petulant gripe of a *prima donna*.

To the Führer's consternation, on the return trip Mussolini requested to pilot the airplane, a Condor, himself—and did so for approximately a half-hour. Hitler, who had never learned to drive an automobile, let alone fly an aircraft, was most anxious, as were the rest of the passengers aboard. Mussolini performed the feat with boyish enthusiasm and afterwards even wished to have it included in the official *communiqué*. Very self-satisfied, to Alfieri he said cheerfully: 'Don't forget to mention that for a considerable part of the way I piloted the Führer's four-engined plane myself. You can add that according to my reckoning I have travelled altogether 3,300 miles by rail, 1,250 by air, and several hundred by road. And, as you can see, I'm quite ready to do it all over again.'[57]

By late summer, after having undergone an operation, Ciano had at last recovered from his throat affliction. On 24 September, he received from Emilio Cecchi, the Italian attaché in Berlin, a disturbing report concerning the mistreatment of Italian labourers in Germany. Not only were they being beaten for minor infractions, but large, trained watchdogs were being unleashed upon them. Ciano reported the matter to the Duce, who was troubled and angered. He had received the news from other quarters as well. 'These things,' Mussolini fumed, 'are bound to produce a lasting hatred in my heart. I can even wait many years, but in the end I shall square this account. I will not permit the sons of a race which has given to humanity Caesar, Dante, and Michelangelo to be devoured by the bloodhounds of the Huns.'[58] Mussolini advised Ciano to arrange a meeting with Ribbentrop to address the issue.

It came to Mussolini's attention in mid-October that during his visit to the Eastern Front, a German had snidely commented in reference to him, 'There goes our *Gauleiter* [district leader] for Italy.' An embassy staff member purportedly overheard the wisecrack. Mussolini tasked Alfieri with uncovering the truth of the matter, and Ciano documented the Duce's bitter remarks concerning the alleged belittlement:

> I believe it. In Germany there exist certain phonograph records. Hitler makes them; the others play them. The first record was the one about Italy being the loyal ally, on an equal footing with Germany, mistress of the Mediterranean as Germany was of the Baltic. Then came the second record, that of the victories, that Europe would be dominated by Germany. The conquered states will be colonies. The associated states will be confederated provinces of Germany. Among these the most important is Italy. We have to accept these conditions because any attempt to rebel would result in our being reduced from the position of a confederated province to the worse one of a colony. Even if they should ask for Trieste tomorrow, as part of the German *Lebensraum*, we would have to bow our heads.[59]

A fortnight later, Ciano set off for Rastenburg to confer with Hitler and Ribbentrop. During this interview, which took place on the morning of 25 October, Ciano raised two key points. The first was in relation to the incidents of inexcusable abuse inflicted upon Italian workmen, and the second concerned the Duce's wish for increased Italian participation in the Russian campaign.

As regards the maltreatment of the Italian workers by German overseers, Hitler merely stated 'that he understood the difficulties which inevitably arise when such a huge mass of men is moved to areas so different in climate, habits, and customs ... the incidents which have occurred between the Italians and the Germans and the shortcomings of the workmen should not be dramatized'. Hitler added that one had to bear in mind that amongst the Italian workers and local Germans 'there are still anti-Fascist and anti-Nazi elements which have every interest in creating reasons for difficulties and distrust between the two allied countries'. In the end, the Führer met Ciano halfway; those disruptive elements who were 'more harmful than productive' would be repatriated.

Ciano found the Führer most receptive to the proposal for 'larger scale [Italian] participation in operations in Russia'. 'After the crossing of the Caucasus,' Hitler stated, 'larger use will be made of intervention by the Italian forces.' This would be especially applicable to areas with a warmer climate in which the Italians would be better suited for combat than the Germans. And when Ciano suggested the dispatch of Italian Alpine divisions to partake in the conquest of the Caucasus region, Hitler declared: 'I know that we are talking of excellent divisions.' The Italian and German general staffs could 'make contact on the subject', and Ciano did not foresee any obstacles in this regard.

Hitler also spoke of a European New Order. This concept, under the catchphrase of 'European Solidarity', was one that attracted him. The Führer recognized its propagandist value as a counterweight to the Allies' Atlantic Charter* and he was now trumpeting it to his subalterns, who were in turn parroting it ceaselessly. Its chief features included the destruction of the Bolshevist creed and the collaboration of the European Axis nations. In his letter to Mussolini, Ciano elaborated on it:

> Now the fashionable slogan is that of 'European solidarity'. Europe—the Führer said—besides being a geographical expression is a cultural and moral conception. In the war against Bolshevism the first signs of continental solidarity have shown themselves.... Once Russia is beaten, the whole of Europe, under the guidance of Germany in the North and Italy in the South, will be able to organize itself politically and economically and constitute the great unity which is destined to bar the way to tomorrow's real danger which is American imperialism. This is what the Führer puts forward. This is what all those near him repeat.

Ciano wrapped up his report to Mussolini by describing the affability of his German hosts: 'I had up until now never found in the Germans such a lively, attentive, comradely interest in our affairs, nor had I for long heard the Führer and Ribbentrop express themselves in such explicit terms on the importance of our participation in the conflict and on the role which Fascist Italy will play in the world of tomorrow. And this is the asset of the situation today.'[60]

---

* The 'Joint Declaration' of 14 August 1941 by Churchill and Roosevelt containing eight articles specifying Anglo–American postwar aims.

On 6 November, Mussolini was in another one of his anti-German moods, and to Ciano he railed: 'We can do nothing against Germany for the time being. We must bide our time. It is a country that no one can vanquish militarily, but it will collapse through lack of internal equilibrium. For us, it is a problem of "holding out" and waiting until this takes place.'[61]

Ciano returned to Berlin on 24 November, having been invited by Ribbentrop six weeks earlier to attend the 'formal celebration' and renewal of the Anti-Comintern Pact along with 'representatives of all the signatory States'. But Ciano saw through it, for under the guise of 'European solidarity' the true purpose of the gathering was to affirm 'Nazi hegemony over the Continent'.[62]

The ceremonies were held over the next few days, and Ciano took stock of where the Italians stood relative to the Germans: 'The Germans were the masters of the house, and they made us all feel it even though they were especially polite to us. There is no way out of it. Their European hegemony has now been established. Whether this is good or bad is neither here nor there, but it does exist. Consequently, it is best to sit at the right hand of the master of the house. And we are at the right hand.'[63]

Back in Rome on 29 November, Ciano submitted his lengthy report to Mussolini. He took care to underscore the special courtesies extended towards himself personally and the accolades given—both privately and publicly—to Italy and the Duce: 'Special treatment was reserved for Italy.... All possible attentions were paid to us, and not only formally. While in conversation with me, Hitler and Ribbentrop reaffirmed with great clarity our right to territorial claims and policies. In public too, they continually praised Italy and the Duce, and, for the first time, I heard Italian military valour spoken of with enthusiasm.'[64]

Ciano concluded with a vivid personal recollection of his time in Berlin:

> I found the city markedly more sluggish in its movement and in its traffic. Many more disabled men are to be seen in the streets and many fewer party uniforms. There are also few young men to be seen. The crowd did not show any particular interest in the ceremonies which took place. The square in front of the Chancellery, which on other similar occasions filled with applauding or at least inquisitive people, was this time almost deserted. If one speaks to people one finds that there is a feeling—it is widespread—of war-weariness, but it cannot be said that there is any fatigue and even less that faith in victory has diminished. Morale is high even if external signs of enthusiasm are lacking. It is true that the prospect advanced by Ribbentrop of a war which may even last many years has certainly not been the cause of rejoicing, but neither has it worried or shaken any of the numerous people from various classes and of different outlooks whom I chanced to meet during these days.[65]

On 3 December, the Japanese ambassador was received by Mussolini and Ciano at the Palazzo Venezia. There he dropped a bombshell on the Italians. Reading from a lengthy document, he solemnly explained that the talks between Japan and the United States—ongoing for nearly a half-year—had deteriorated. As a result of this breakdown in diplomatic relations, the Japanese ambassador advised, conflict between Japan and the United States—and by extension, Britain also—was not only likely, but imminent!

The Japanese ambassador then requested, per the Tripartite Pact, that Italy declare war on the United States upon the outbreak of Japanese–American hostilities. He also proposed that Italy sign a protocol stipulating that she would agree to not enter into a separate peace with either the United States or Britain. To these two requests Mussolini 'gave general assurances', pending his prerogative to first consult with the German Government to coordinate their plans. After the Japanese ambassador had departed, Mussolini, who already considered the United States to be in a *de facto* state of war with Italy, was content. To Ciano, he declared with an air of satisfaction, 'Thus we arrive at the war between continents, which I have foreseen since September 1939.'[66]

On the morning of 7 December, a Sunday, the Japanese attacked the American naval base at Pearl Harbor, Oahu. Scores of aircraft, with the stark red symbol of the Rising Sun emblazoned on their wings, mercilessly bombarded the warships moored in the harbour. They struck without warning. The Americans were caught utterly unprepared, and in the space of ninety minutes the Japanese air raiders succeeded in substantially crippling the American Pacific Fleet, achieving a tremendous tactical victory thereby.

Ciano was dismayed at the prospect of American intervention, which he believed (correctly) to be inevitable and formidable: 'One thing is now certain: America will enter the conflict, and the conflict itself will be long enough to permit her to put into action all her potential strength.' But Mussolini felt differently, and Ciano described the Duce's personal satisfaction: 'Mussolini was happy. For a long time now he has been in favour of clarifying the position between America and the Axis.'[67] As expected, next day the United States declared war on the Empire of Japan.* In his memorable address to Congress, Roosevelt described 7 December as 'a date which will live in infamy'.

---

* On 8 December, Britain also declared war, for in addition to attacking Pearl Harbor, the Philippines, Guam, and Wake Island, the Japanese also invaded Malaya and bombarded Singapore and Hong Kong, then British possessions. Four weeks earlier, in his speech at the Mansion House, Churchill had declared that 'if Japan attacked the United States, a British declaration of war would follow "within the hour"'.[70]

Ciano arrived at Turin on 9 December to meet with François Darlan, Pétain's deputy. Next day he conferred with the anti-British admiral. His impressions were positive:

> He is a small man, energetic, willful, and rather boastful, who talks without reticence, and calls a spade a spade. He is a military man, who is beginning to develop a taste for politics, and because he is French, he does it with a certain finesse. Is he sincere? I can't say, except for one thing: he hates the British. Some ways of speaking and some expressions cannot be simulated. On the other hand, there is no choice for him, and he declares it: if the British should win the war, his fate would not be a happy one.

Mussolini, however, displayed scant interest in Ciano's conversation with Darlan; instead, the outbreak of American–Japanese hostilities weighed heavily on his mind.[68]

At 2:30 p.m. on 11 December, Ciano received the American *chargé d'affaires* and broke the news that Italy was now at war with the United States. The diplomat visibly paled and replied, 'It is very tragic.' He then presented Ciano with a telegram from U.S. Ambassador Phillips, who had perceived that 'zero hour was approaching' and had wished to convey his personal regards while there was still time.[69]

As on the occasion of the declaration of war on Britain and France eighteen months earlier, the Duce addressed the Roman masses from the balcony of the Palazzo Venezia. His speech was bellicose yet brief—much more so than Hitler's violent anti-American harangue to the *Reichstag* lasting some eighty-eight minutes. Mussolini proclaimed:

> This is another day of solemn decision in Italy's history and of memorable events destined to give a new course to the history of continents.
>
> The Powers of the Steel Pact, Fascist Italy and Nationalist Socialist Germany, ever closely linked, participate from today on the side of heroic Japan against the United States of America.
>
> The Tripartite Pact becomes a military alliance which draws around its colors 250,000,000 men determined to do all in order to win.
>
> Neither the Axis nor Japan wanted an extension of the conflict.
>
> One man, one man only, a real tyrannical democrat [Roosevelt], through a series of infinite provocations, betraying with a supreme fraud the population of his country, wanted the war and had prepared for it day by day with diabolical obstinacy.
>
> The formidable blows that on the immense Pacific expanse [at Pearl Harbor] have been already inflicted on American forces show how prepared are the soldiers of the Empire of the Rising Sun.

> I say to you, and you will understand, that it is a privilege to fight with them.
>
> Today, the Tripartite Pact, with the plenitude of its forces and its moral and material resources, is a formidable instrument for the war and a certainty for victory.
>
> Tomorrow, the Tripartite Pact will become an instrument of just peace between the peoples.
>
> Italians! Once more arise and be worthy of this historical hour!
>
> We shall win.[71]

Ciano concisely described the momentous event: 'Mussolini made a speech from the balcony—a brief and cutting speech, which fell on a great crowd. A very pro-Japanese setting. News of the naval victories has excited the Italian imagination. The demonstration, however, was not very enthusiastic.'[72] Also that day, representatives of the Axis Powers signed the 'No Separate Peace Agreement'. The trilateral compact had been prepared three days prior. Each nation pledged to refrain from concluding a separate peace or armistice with either America or Britain. With such a policy, the fates of Italy, Germany, and Japan would be indissolubly bound together:

> ARTICLE I
>
> Italy, Germany, and Japan will henceforth conduct in common and jointly a war which has been imposed on them by the United States of America and England, by all means at their disposal and until the end of hostilities.
>
> ARTICLE II
>
> Italy, Germany, and Japan undertake each for himself that none of the parties to the present accord will conclude either armistice or peace, be it with the United States or with England without complete and reciprocal agreement [of the other signatories to this pact].
>
> ARTICLE III
>
> Italy, Germany, and Japan, even after the victorious conclusion of this war, will collaborate closely in the spirit of the Tripartite Pact, concluded 21 Sept. 1940, in order to realize and establish an equitable new order in the world.
>
> ARTICLE IV
>
> The present accord is effective immediately on its signature and remains in force for the duration of the Tripartite Pact, signed 27 Sept. 1940. The high contracting parties of this accord will at an opportune moment agree among themselves the means of implementing Article III above of this accord.[73]

Several weeks earlier, on the North African Front, the British Eighth Army had struck from Mersa Matruh. On 18 November, General Claude Auchinleck (Wavell's successor as of 5 July) launched Operation Crusader, and after nine days of intense combat, Commonwealth forces at last succeeded in relieving Tobruk, which had been besieged since 10 April—a total of 231 days. On 7 December, Italo–German forces under Rommel's command fell back to Gazala, and eight days later, to avoid being outflanked, Rommel authorized a withdrawal to El Agheila. Thus by mid-December, the Axis armies had once more been ejected from East Libya.

Mussolini felt that responsibility for the debacle lay with Rommel. Ciano observed: 'Things are not going well in Libya. Even Mussolini is beginning to admit it, and he blames Rommel, who, he believes, spoiled the situation with his recklessness.'[74] As for Rommel, the *Afrika Korps* commander was contemplating a general retreat all the way into Tunisia in order to avoid being captured by the enemy: 'Rommel announces that he, with his slender armoured resources, will break into Tunisia, because he does not wish to be made prisoner by the British.'[75]

Grasping at straws in an attempt to salvage the situation on the Libyan Front, Mussolini drafted an ill-advised letter to Hitler 'on the question of the Tunisian ports'. The Duce proposed that 'either Vichy France comes to an agreement with us and grants them [the ports], or it will be necessary to take them by force'.[76] Such a step would, Mussolini reasoned, facilitate the supplying of Axis forces in North Africa. Hitler, however, was unwilling to entertain this measure, for he did not wish to disaffect the French.

Ciano left Rome on 14 December to confer with Pavelić, dictator of the Independent Croat State. The meeting was held in Venice over the next two days. Accompanying Pavelić were his foreign and finance ministers, Mladen Lorković and Vladimir Košak respectively. The Croatian party's agenda was to convince the Italians to withdraw their occupation forces.

The talks began with Pavelić elaborating on internal Croatian affairs. 'In those areas not infested by war,' Pavelić explained, 'the powers of the State are gradually being organized and asserting themselves.' The main problem—namely, the Jews—was 'being dealt with'. Pavelić pointed out that when the Ustaše 'took power', there were 35,000 Jews; now, eight months later, there were 'not more than 12,000'. The term used by the Croatians to account for this reduction in number was 'emigration', a euphemism for liquidation.

Pavelić informed Ciano that the lower echelons of the Catholic clergy were maintaining 'a very favourable attitude' towards the Ustaše regime; the upper ranks less so, particularly the bishops. The Poglavnik also spoke of the monarchy. Most Croatians, himself included, believed it to be essential and were pleased 'that the Crown is to be entrusted to a prince* of the House of Savoy'.

On the subject of the German minorities in Croatia, Pavelić declared that 'it is out of the question that the Statute granted to them may put them in a condition such as to constitute a state within the State and to form in any way a pole of attraction for Croatian elements which are not of German origin'. Pavelić stated that in fact the reverse was happening; Croatian representatives from villages populated by ethnic Germans were requesting to be excluded from being counted among the latter.

Pavelić advised Ciano that relations with Hungary were negative; the latter country 'continued to pursue an unfriendly policy towards Croatia'. And to ameliorate Italo–Croatian relations, the return of civil powers to the Ustaše in the second (Italian) zone, Pavelić felt, would go a long way. He complained that numerous Italian officers, particularly the lower echelons, were deficient in their 'ability to exercise civil powers in places where they know neither the people, the language, nor the customs'.

The Poglavnik was 'convinced of the necessity of using strong measures against the Chetniks† and Communists'. 'Decisive operations,' he added, would be initiated against these fractious elements during the winter. Pavelić further advised the Italians 'to reinforce their military forces', especially in the area of Southern Bosnia and Montenegro. There, Pavelić averred, could be expected 'the most dangerous surprises'.

Lastly, Pavelić discussed the measures being taken 'to bring about an increasing *rapprochement* between Croatia and Italy'. The Italian language would be made mandatory in Croatian schools; in many institutions this had already been implemented. Nearly two-thirds of the pupils preferred learning Italian to German. But the lack of teachers was a concern. Pavelić expressed the wish for teachers to be sent to Croatia providing that they were 'of Italian race and not Croats from Istria, or worse still, of Slovenes'.[77]

Ciano diarized his impressions of the Croatian dictator: 'Pavelić is growing more and more confident as he continues to rule. He is more resolute, casual, and calm. He has complete domination over his ministers and even treats them harshly. In my presence he reproached his Minister of the Treasury [Košak], who blushed to the roots of his hair and hung his head.'[78] In general, the meeting itself was satisfactory, but Ciano found his brief sojourn in the 'City of Canals' to be a depressing experience: 'Venice was sad, empty, tired. Never have I seen it so squalid. Empty hotels, deserted streets, Fog. Misery. Darkness.'[79]

---

* Prince Aimone, brother of the duke of Aosta (Prince Amedeo).

† A resistance group of nationalist Serbian guerrilla fighters commanded by Draža Mihailović. (A wanted poster dated 9 December 1941 offered a reward of 200,000 dinars for his capture.)

On 5 December, Soviet forces launched a great counteroffensive to hurl back the Teutonic invaders, who were by this time nearing Moscow. Two days later, Hitler responded by issuing a directive ordering the *Wehrmacht* to take up defensive positions along the battlefront and hold the line:

DIRECTIVE NO. 39

> The surprisingly early arrival of severe winter weather in the East and the supply difficulties resulting therefrom call for the immediate cessation of all major offensive operations and a shift to the defensive.
>
> The conduct of this defensive will be determined by the *objective* to which it is directed, namely:
>
> (*a*) To retain such areas as are of great importance to the enemy with respect to his operations and armament production.
>
> (*b*) To make possible for the *Wehrmacht* forces committed in the East the greatest possible measure of recuperation and rehabilitation.
>
> (*c*) To bring about by the foregoing the prerequisites for resuming major offensive operations in 1942.[80]

Hitler also took the drastic step of dismissing Walther von Brauchitsch, commander-in-chief of the German Army, on 19 December. Hitler blamed the field marshal for the German Army's failure to take Moscow, and he personally assumed Brauchitsch's former post in order to imbue the German Army with National Socialist fervour. Three months later, Minister Goebbels jotted down in his *Diary* what Hitler truly thought of Brauchitsch: 'The Führer spoke of him only in terms of contempt. A vain, cowardly wretch who could not even appraise the situation, let alone master it.'[81] This sensational news did not worry the Duce, however. Ciano wrote: 'Mussolini does not attach very great importance to the matter. He believes, in fact, that in the last analysis it will be advantageous because "this war has proven that only political armies have something to say, and now Hitler is making his army more political"'.[82]

Meanwhile, Mussolini was taking some malicious pleasure at the Germans' tribulations in the East. Ciano recorded: 'Mussolini is satisfied with the way the war is going in Russia. He talks about it openly. The failure of the German troops cheers him.'[83] The Germans were not, apparently, the invincible supermen that Nazi propaganda had so impressed upon the world. But by Christmas Day, the Italians perceived that the situation was getting out of hand. Ciano noted: 'Alfieri writes that the disasters on the Russian Front have gone farther than is desirable for us. I glean this from the Germans of the Embassy. They are very much discouraged. The Duce, who is beginning to understand the problem, now affirms that it is serious and that perhaps it will have further consequences.'[84]

In spite of Mussolini's earlier affirmations that Italy was incapable of enduring a protracted conflict, by this point he was soberly contemplating a war of at least three- or four-years' duration. In a speech to the Council of Ministers on 27 December, Mussolini predicted: 'The war will last long—three to four years. The situation at the Eastern Front will gradually be stabilized. Germany will occupy those territories which she regards as essential. Russia will be liquidated as an opponent. To win the war, Great Britain must be defeated; either by invasion or the capture of her world bases. The key is the Suez Canal...'[85]

But this was pure fantasy. It was highly unlikely that even the combined, overwhelming might of the entire Axis coalition could—or would—defeat the Soviet colossus. German intelligence had grossly underestimated the actual strength of the Soviet armies. In the dark times ahead, Mussolini would begin to entertain the notion of the Axis concluding a separate peace with the U.S.S.R. If such a diplomatic masterstroke could be achieved, it would enable the bulk of Axis forces to be withdrawn from the Russian Front and dispatched to North Africa to deal with the troublesome and formidable Anglo–Saxons. It was a pipe dream that, unfortunately for Mussolini, would go unfulfilled.

5

Empire Lost, 1942–1943

I would like to convey to you personally my impression that we must make a separate peace with Russia as soon as possible.[1]

Mussolini to General Enno von Rintelen, 6 November 1942

Italy has only one alternative: to conquer or fall at the side of Germany.[2]

Mussolini to Ministers Alfredo De Marsico and Vittorio Cini, 19 June 1943

In early 1942, the focus of the Italians was directed eastwards, where deep in Russian territory German forces were being routed by the Soviets' winter counteroffensive. On 2 January, the Italians received word from their embassy in Berlin that the situation in Russia was worsening, but Mussolini took the news with a grain of salt. Next day Ciano returned from Bologna, where he had delivered a lengthy speech to Fascists at the Medica Theatre; aboard the train speeding its way to Rome, he encountered Ambassador Mackensen. Ciano noted that the diplomat was despondent and said little, for the *Wehrmacht*'s recent failure to take Moscow had taken a heavy psychological toll on all Germans, civilian and military alike.

Ten days later, Ciano recorded in his *Diary*:

> From the military point of view attention has turned toward the Russian Front, where difficulties continue for the Germans. Alfieri, too, who as a rule paints everything in rosy colors, begins to admit openly that in Russia they are swallowing a bitter pill. The retreat continues under the growing pressure of the enemy. The Duce does not seem to be exces-

> sively worried, but considers the situation very serious. He criticizes Hitler for the entire Russian campaign and says that he has falsified his *communiqués*. 'He [Hitler] has used big figures to impress people like that jackass of a Roosevelt,' he said, 'and the results have been sinister. In fact, they are both big jackasses and belong to kindred races.'[3]

Elsewhere, the war situation was, for the Axis, about to take a turn for the better. On 21 January, from El Agheila, Rommel struck back; and eight days later, the *Afrika Korps* succeeded in recapturing Benghazi. A thousand Allied troops were taken prisoner. When the Duce sent Rommel a communication urging him to take the initiative and seize Benghazi, Rommel abruptly replied: 'Benghazi already taken.' The *Afrika Korps* pressed onwards, arriving at Gazala on 4 February. 'Mussolini,' Ciano had written two days earlier, 'is very happy about operations in Libya.'[4]

Ciano left for Budapest on 14 January for a conference with Regent Miklós Horthy and other Hungarian notables. During the conversations, Horthy mainly discussed 'the situation on the Eastern Front'. Despite the Axis military reversals caused by the recent Soviet counteroffensive, he believed that 'a winter line not too far back' could be established that would permit Axis forces to renew offensive operations in the spring. Horthy was 'willing to intensify [Hungarian] participation in the war', but in spite of undue pressure exerted by Ribbentrop, he was opposed to ordering a general mobilization owing to a lack of surplus labour and the 'most serious effect' mobilization would have on the Hungarian economy. And moreover, Horthy stated, 'the attention of Hungary is still principally taken up with Romania.' Although Italy and Germany had, per the Vienna *Diktat* (1940), guaranteed Transylvania's altered frontiers, Horthy was certain that should 'some unpredictable event ... modify the military situation in Europe profoundly, the Romanians would not hesitate to turn their coats for the *n*th time and would attack the Hungarians'. Thus it was crucial for Hungary to maintain 'a strong military force' in order to ward off any potential Romanian aggression. From Horthy's 'way of speaking', Ciano was able to perceive the elderly Regent's 'deep-seated bias' against the Germans. Lastly, Horthy expressed his hope that, after the war, Italy would continue 'to exercise an effective influence in Central Europe and the Danube region', thereby assuring the Hungarians the greatest prospects for a 'political and moral independence'.

For Mussolini's benefit, Ciano evaluated the Hungarians' disposition *vis-à-vis* their Italo–German partners:

> The Hungarian attitude towards us [the Italians]—excellent. Where the Germans are concerned, formally perfect; in actual fact, bad. Two things

> have gone to make them so: (1) fear of growing German influence on Hungary such as to destroy—at least *de facto*—that national independence to which the Hungarian people is attached with frenzied patriotism; (2) the preferential attitude shown to Romania by the Germans on more than one occasion. The Hungarians are incapable of understanding how the Germans can now forget Romania's policy of hostility to Germany, which lasted twenty years, and how they can show such faith in a nation which, in Hungarian opinion, is ready to betray them at the first crowing of the cock.[5]

Back in Rome on 20 January, Ciano reported to Mussolini the details of his visit to Budapest. The Duce appeared to be interested and, on his part, informed Ciano of recent developments. In his *Diary*, Ciano wrote candidly about the Hungarians' anti-Germanism: 'The truth is that the Hungarians are exasperated with the Germans. You can't remain long with any Magyar before he speaks ill of Germany. All of them are like this, from the Regent to the last beggar on the street. Admiral Horthy said, "The Germans are a courageous people, and I admire them for this, but they are also an unbearable, tactless, and boorish people."'[6]

On 28 January, *Reichsmarschall* Göring arrived in Rome for a comprehensive military discussion with Mussolini. Upon alighting at the railway station, Göring declared to his Italian hosts: 'We are having hard times.' It was a gross understatement, for the winter of 1941–42 dashed permanently the Germans' hopes for a speedy conquest of the U.S.S.R. At the Palazzo Venezia, Göring spoke with the Duce for nearly three hours. Göring was embittered by the *Wehrmacht*'s reversals on the Russian Front. He spitefully attributed the blame to Hitler's irresolute generals, whose enthusiasm for National Socialism was lukewarm at best. Extreme temperatures as low as -40 degrees had also taken their toll. Nevertheless, the *Reichsmarschall* was certain that the Soviet Union would be liquidated in 1942, and England in 1943. Göring did not believe, however, that 'an understanding with France' was possible, for the French sought to undermine the armistice at every turn and were, at their core, implacably opposed to their Italo–German conquerors.[7]

Ciano's personal revulsion towards Göring was strong. At a luncheon with the 'bloated and overbearing' *Reichsmarschall* and Cavallero on 2 February, Ciano noted that the former 'said nothing that is especially worthy of mention'. Moreover, the obsequious behaviour of Italy's military chiefs towards Göring—who 'strutted blissfully'—thoroughly disgusted him.[8] Two days later, Ciano again dined with the vainglorious Göring, on this occasion at the Excelsior Hotel. He observed that 'during the dinner Göring talked of little else but the jewels he owned'. Ciano also described—not without humour—the *Reichsmarschall*'s departure from Rome: 'To the station he wore a great sable coat, something between what automobile drivers wore in 1906 and what a high-grade prostitute wears to the opera. If any of us tried a thing like that we would be stoned in the streets. He, on the contrary, is not only accepted in Germany but perhaps even loved for it.'[9]

At a meeting of the Council of Ministers on 7 February, Mussolini delivered 'a rather brief statement on the progress of the war in Libya'. About Italy's generals, the Duce spoke negatively. Conversely, Mussolini praised Rommel, 'who is always in his tank at the head of the attacking columns'. So keen were the *Bersaglieri* (Italian infantry) about Rommel, Ciano wrote, that they 'give him their feathers, bearing him in triumph on their shoulders, shouting that with him they are sure they can reach Alexandria'.[10]

The war in the Far East was also progressing in favour of the Axis. Singapore, a stronghold of the British Empire in Southeast Asia, the so-called 'Gibraltar of the East', surrendered unconditionally to the Japanese on 15 February. The battle had lasted one week and the entire garrison of 80,000 defenders was taken prisoner. Churchill delivered a grave thirty-minute broadcast about 'the worst disaster and largest capitulation of British history'.[11] To the British people, he announced that 'Singapore has fallen, and the Malaya Peninsula has been overrun':

> I speak to you tonight under the shadow of a heavy and far-reaching military defeat. But it is one of those moments when the British race can show that it can draw from reverses and turn them into victory. Japan has struck a hard blow, but what will be the verdict of 1942 or 1943? She struck under the cloak of negotiation, and her warlords have planned this for 20 years. I am sure, even in these dark hours, that 'criminal madness' will be the verdict of history when the events of 1942 or 1943 are written in history's pages. The whole of the time the American and British people were discussing peace, the Japanese were planning for war. Our shield of seapower in the Pacific has been temporarily dashed to the ground. Nobody must underrate any more the efficiency of the Japanese war machine.[12]

Next day Mussolini commented sardonically on the British capitulation: 'I should like to know the effect four English officers, presenting themselves with a white flag to surrender, has had upon those whimsical Orientals. If it had been us, no one would have attached any importance to it, but they are English.'[13]

A week later, Ciano received a report from the Consul General in Prague that Reinhard Heydrich, the ruthless deputy ruler of Bohemia–Moravia, was 'treating our [Italian] nationals if not worse than the Czechoslovaks certainly not much better'. Ciano brought the report to the Duce's attention, who expressed indignation and insisted that Alfieri protest to Ribbentrop to redress the situation.[14]

Around this time, Mussolini was in an anti-German frame of mind and, troubled about the limited availability of raw materials—steel and coal in particular—complained about the fact that the Germans fulfilled their obligations to their Italian allies in part only: 'Among the cemeteries I shall someday build the most important of all, one in which to bury German promises. They have delivered nothing, or almost nothing, of what they promised.'[15]

The Italians were not the only ones displeased with the Germans, for recently they had observed certain 'signs of friction between the Germans and Japanese'. One of the reasons for the discord was attributable to 'some proposals made by von Ribbentrop'. The presumptuous German foreign minister had antagonized his East Asian counterparts by 'arrogat[ing] to himself the role of Grand Master of the Tripartite Alliance'. The pro-Japanese Mussolini was pleased to hear of it, for he was all too familiar with the Germans' peremptory and inconsiderate behaviour: 'The Japanese are not a people with whom the Germans can take liberties such as calling the Emperor or the Prime Minister out of bed at two o'clock in the morning in order to announce to them decisions that they have already made and carried out.'[16] And just three days prior, in comparing the Japanese with the Germans, the Duce had said: 'I much prefer the yellow people, even if the Japanese were to arrive as far as the Persian Gulf.'[17]

Despite a report by Ambassador Alfieri advising that the Eastern Front had 'stabilized', additional notifications were received by the Italians at the beginning of March 'of continual offensive thrusts by the Russians, which at some points are quite deep'. As a result, Mussolini was concerned, and he questioned the quality of Axis forces in Russia: 'It's all right that the Germans have said that we had three hundred divisions. But even admitting that this is so, of what human material are these divisions composed? What is their real morale? Everything depends on the answers to these questions.'[18]

On 7 March, the Duce was once more in a contemplative mood, and he bemoaned the unsuitability of the Italians for the present global conflict: 'This war is not for the Italian people. The Italian people do not have the maturity or the consistency for a test so grave and decisive. This war is for the Germans and the Japanese, not for us.'[19] And a fortnight later, Mussolini spoke of Italy's 'internal situation'. The Italian people were 'not in the least for the war', he said, and the reason for this was that the commonfolk lacked 'immediate incentives'. Under the circumstances, therefore, Fascist propaganda 'should simply be to flaunt the banner of defeat as a threat'. For if Italy were vanquished, Mussolini reflected, the Allies would show her 'no generosity' and the Italian people would 'be reduced to slavery for a century'.[20]

On 24 April, the Italians received an invitation from the Germans for another summit meeting, this time at Klessheim Castle, near Salzburg. It lasted two days, beginning on 29 April, and its predominant theme was an Axis occupation of British-controlled Malta (Operation Hercules, or *Operazione C3*). The aim of this operation (tentatively projected for mid-July 1942) was to be twofold: firstly, to eliminate Malta as a naval base; and secondly, to obtain an unrestricted supply route across the Mediterranean Sea to the Italo–German forces in North Africa. Although Mussolini would have preferred for the talks to take place later—in early May—Hitler remained inflexible as regards to the date and Mussolini reluctantly agreed.

Ciano first had a private discussion with Ribbentrop concerning Axis difficulties on the Eastern Front. The subject of British obduracy was also raised. Ribbentrop refrained from divulging the particulars, but he hinted to Ciano that the German Army would not drive on towards the twin pillars of Bolshevism, Leningrad and Moscow. Instead, it would proceed southwards to the Caucasus to capture the oil fields, and once 'deprived of her indispensable source of fuel', the Soviet Union would be 'practically strangled'. The corollary would be the end of the *Ostkrieg* (Eastern war). With Russia 'immobilized', Ribbentrop continued, the British would perforce recognize that further opposition to the Axis on the continent would be futile, for the Soviet Union was Britain's last hope. American intervention, previously perceived by the British as 'decisive', seemed to be at this stage 'a colossal bluff'. And once the Anglo–Russian alliance was no more, Ribbentrop reasoned, Britain would 'realize the necessity of asking the Axis for the conditions of peace'.[21]

Ciano recapitulated in his *Diary* his personal recollection of his *tête-à-tête* with Ribbentrop:

> Hitler talks with the Duce, I talk with Ribbentrop, but in two separate rooms, and the same record is played in both. Ribbentrop, above all, plays his usual record.... Napoleon, the [Battle of] Beresina, the drama of 1812, all this is brought to life in what he says. But the ice of Russia has been conquered by the genius of Hitler. This is the strong dish that is served up to me. But what of tomorrow? What does the future hold? On this matter Ribbentrop is less explicit. An offensive against the Russians in the south with the oil wells as a politico-military objective.
>
> When Russia's sources of oil are exhausted she will be brought to her knees. Then the British Conservatives, and even Churchill himself ... will bow in order to save what remains of their mauled Empire. Thus spoke Ribbentrop.[22]

Ciano also described—not without some humour—the dull meeting between Mussolini and Hitler, during which the Führer monopolized the entire conversation without respite:

> Hitler talks, talks, talks, talks. Mussolini suffers—he, who is in the habit of talking himself, and who, instead, practically has to keep quiet. On the second day, after lunch, when everything had been said, Hitler talked uninterruptedly for an hour and forty minutes. He omitted absolutely no argument: war and peace, religion and philosophy, art and history. Mussolini automatically looked at his wrist watch, I had my mind on my own business, and only Cavallero, who is a phenomenon of servility, pretended he was listening in ecstasy, continually nodding his head in approval. Those, however, who dreaded the ordeals less than we did were the Germans. Poor people. They have to take it every day, and I am certain there isn't a gesture, a word, or a pause which they don't know by heart. General Jodl, after an epic struggle, finally went to sleep on the divan. Keitel was reeling, but he succeeded in keeping his head up. He was too close to Hitler to let himself go as he would have liked to do.[23]

Worn down by Hitler's interminable monologue, in the end Mussolini agreed to send additional Italian soldiers to the Russian Front to assist the Germans. On the return journey, Mussolini was in good spirits, as he always was in the aftermath of a conference with the Führer. Nevertheless, the Duce had a sense of foreboding, and he made the following sombre pronouncement: 'The German war machine is still formidably powerful, but has suffered great wear. Now it will make a new and imposing effort. It must attain its goal.'[24] The Axis dictators would not meet again until April 1943, when the military situation would be far more dire.

On 20 June, an 'incisive and vivacious' Mussolini received Foreign Minister Suñer at the Palazzo Venezia for a discussion. To his Spanish guest, Mussolini spoke negatively of monarchies, which were 'potentially the natural enemies of totalitarian revolutions'. The Duce was convinced that it was just matter of time before the Spanish king would 'want to stifle Falangism' and he shared with Suñer several 'Italian precedents' to support his argument. In connection with the war, Mussolini forecast with 'absolute certainty' that the Axis Powers would prevail, but that the conflict would last 'four or five years'.[25] A few days later, Mussolini met with Suñer again. Little of importance was said, save that Suñer confirmed 'that if Portugal should be attacked by the Anglo–Saxons, Spain [per the Iberian Pact of 1939] would not hesitate to come into the war'.[26]

After a lengthy period of stalemate on the North African Front, Rommel retook the offensive and opened the three-week Battle of Gazala (Operation Venice) on 26 May, forcing the British Eighth Army (under General Neil Ritchie) southeast of Tobruk. On the morning of 20 June, Rommel launched an assault on Tobruk itself and next day succeeded in taking it from its British garrison defenders, for which an exultant Hitler bestowed upon him the field marshal's baton.* Egypt, the Suez Canal, and even the oil-rich lands of the Middle East now appeared to be in reach of Axis forces. 'Tobruk has fallen,' Ciano noted with much satisfaction, 'and the British have left twenty-five thousand prisoners in our hands. This is a great success for us and opens new developments.'[28]

After the war, Churchill ruefully wrote in connection with the loss of Tobruk: 'This was one of the heaviest blows I can recall during the war. Not only were its military effects grievous, but it had affected the reputation of the British armies.'[29] Britain's political leaders were profoundly shocked, and in the House of Commons on 25 June, a vote of censure was brought against Churchill by John Wardlaw-Milne. The influential conservative politician brought forward a serious motion: 'That this House, while paying tribute to the heroism and endurance of the Armed Forces of the Crown in circumstances of exceptional difficulty, has no confidence in the central direction of the war.'[30]

A week later, Churchill delivered a lengthy, earnest speech before the House, to whom he admitted:

> The military misfortunes of the last fortnight in Cyrenaica and Egypt have completely transformed the situation, not only in that theatre, but throughout the Mediterranean. We have lost upwards of fifty thousand men, by far the large proportion of whom are prisoners, a great mass of material, and, in spite of carefully organized demolitions, large quantities of stores have fallen into the enemy's hands. Rommel has advanced nearly four hundred miles through the desert, and is now approaching the fertile Delta of the Nile. The evil effects of these events, in Turkey, in Spain, in France, and in French North Africa, cannot yet be measured. We are at this moment in the presence of a recession of our hopes and prospects in the Middle East and in the Mediterranean unequalled since the fall of France.[31]

Wardlaw-Milne's motion of 'No Confidence' was defeated; the results were 475 votes in favour of the Churchill Government, 25 against. Rommel, at the pinnacle of his success, confidently advised his superiors that the vast amounts of war materiel seized from the British at Tobruk would permit his forces to press onwards and capture Egypt and Suez.

---

* Rommel was elevated to field marshal on 22 June, but his promotion did not sit well with Mussolini, for it placed Rommel above the other Italian commanders in the field. The Duce railed against Graziani 'who has always been seventy feet underground in a Roman tomb at Cyrene while Rommel knows how to lead his troops with the personal example of the general who lives in his tank'.[27] Thus on the Italian side—'to offset the impression produced by the promotion of Rommel' (as Ciano put it)—Generals Ugo Cavallero and Ettore Bastico (the latter was commander-in-chief for Libya) were bumped up to the rank of marshal of Italy on 1 July and 12 August respectively.

In an extremely persuasive letter which Mussolini received on 23 June, Hitler made two recommendations: that, under the circumstances, Operation Hercules be deferred, and that, instead, Rommel's *Afrika Korps* should seize the golden opportunity now available to eliminate the remainder of British forces in Egypt once and for all:

> Destiny has offered us a chance which will never be repeated in the same theatre of war. The main military objective must be, in my opinion, to exploit it as totally and rapidly as possible. So far I have always had every defeated enemy followed as far and as completely as our forces allowed. The British Eighth Army is practically destroyed. In Tobruk, whose port installations are almost intact, you possess an auxiliary base, Duce, which is all the more important since the British themselves have built a railway from there almost as far as Egypt. If the remnants of this British Army are not now followed by every soldier to his last breath, the same thing will happen which deprived the British of success when [in 1941], within a very short distance of Tripoli, they suddenly stopped in order to send troops to Greece. Only this capital error on the part of the British Command made it possible for our efforts to be crowned with the reconquest of Cyrenaica....
>
> Therefore, Duce, if in this historic hour, which will not be repeated, I can give you a piece of advice straight from my eager heart, it would be: 'Order operations to be continued until the British forces are completely annihilated, as far as your Command, and [Field] Marshal Rommel, think that they can do it militarily with their forces.'
>
> The goddess of fortune passes only once close to warriors in battle. Anyone who does not grasp her at that moment can very often never touch her again.[32]

The Duce found Hitler's dramatic pitch irresistible and, seduced by the prospect of Egypt being added to the Italian Empire, he enthusiastically agreed. Thus the decision was made to pursue the severely mauled British Eighth Army into Egypt (Operation Aïda) and defer Axis operations against Malta to September. (But later, parachute divisions intended for the Malta undertaking were employed in Egypt, and in November Operation Hercules was cancelled permanently.)

The military situation at this stage appeared most promising. Next day Axis forces traversed the Libyan frontier into Egypt, and at his headquarters on 26 June, Rommel made an optimistic prediction: 'If today the army succeeds in breaking the enemy position, we shall be at Cairo or Alexandria on 30 June.'[33]

During this period of Axis successes, Ciano's *Diary* was replete with glowing entries briefly describing the Italo–German advances:

> In Libya, Rommel's action is progressing at full speed. The rosiest forecasts can now be made.—24 June 1942.[34]

> Victory has encouraged our forces in Libya and they are now preparing to besiege Mersa Matruh.—25 June 1942.[35]

> In Libya we are doing well, and our information gives the impression that the English are going through a grave crisis.—30 June 1942.[36]

Believing the capture of Cairo by Rommel's forces to be imminent, on 29 June Mussolini arrived at Derna with his arabesque ceremonial accoutrement, the Sword of Islam. Marshal Badoglio wryly commented on the Duce's vanity: 'Mussolini, who never missed a chance for self-glorification, went to Cyrenaica, taking with him an Arab horse and the Sword of Islam, so as to be ready for a triumphal entry into Alexandria.'[37]

In preliminary diplomatic discussions, it was proposed that Serafino Mazzolini, former governor of Montenegro, was to head the civil administration of Egypt which, the Germans agreed, would fall into the Italian sphere of influence. Hitler readily assented to the Italians' suggestion that Rommel be designated military commander but equivocated on the nomination of an Italian civilian delegate. But these considerations were premature, for within a short time Rommel was halted at El Alamein, and on 20 July, a disgruntled Mussolini was compelled to return to Rome empty-handed. He had been relishing the notion of entering Cairo at the forefront of his troops in a victory procession. Nevertheless, the Duce believed that within two to three weeks Axis forces would be able to renew their advance into Egypt and 'reach the great goals of the [Nile] Delta and the [Suez] Canal'.[38] But it was not to be. El Alamein—a bare 65 miles from Alexandria—was as far as Italo–German forces were destined to reach in the North African campaign.

Next day the Duce wrote to Hitler to explain the setback:

> The battle which began on 26 May and which can be called the battle of Tobruk, ended in the first days of July in front of the line of Bir el Alamein. The results of the battle were impressive, for a whole enemy army was destroyed, but the objectives hoped for—Cairo and Alexandria—were not attained because, after chasing the enemy for over five hundred kilometres, the Axis troops arrived exhausted.... The battle of Tobruk is over: the battle of tomorrow will be the battle of the Delta. The time needed to prepare for this new battle must be counted in weeks, but not a single moment must be lost in this competition of speed between the enemy and ourselves.[39]

A fortnight later, Hitler replied: 'However long it takes to consolidate our position [in Egypt], I have, like you, given orders to throw into North Africa everything of value in the way of support, reinforcements, and replacements...'[40]

That summer, Mussolini was afflicted with severe, debilitating stomach disorders. Several specialists were summoned to diagnose him, but their opinions varied, and the Duce ended up losing some 40 pounds. It was ultimately determined that the Duce was suffering from an ulcer aggravated by dysentery. Nevertheless, for many months, and notwithstanding the expertise of his physicians and the attentive medical treatment he received, the Duce had to endure constant pain. So intense was his suffering that Mussolini was occasionally incapable of carrying out the functions of his offices. To a certain degree, his illness was psychosomatic, brought on by the extreme stress—continually amplified—of ongoing military setbacks. Rommel's recent failure to take Cairo rankled deeply, and in his heart Mussolini knew that it had been the last chance for the Axis to deal the British a knockout blow in North Africa. All the Duce could do was wallow in his misfortune, and to Ciano he grumbled: 'The people are now wondering which of the two masters is to be preferred, the English or the Germans.'[41]

General Ambrosio, the Army chief of staff, shared with Ciano on 4 August the Italian General Staff's assessment of the military-political situation. Ciano entered in his *Diary*:

> (1) in Libya we shall not be able to resume our movements until the end of October; however, the prospects are good because English reinforcements are slower than had been foreseen while our reinforcements, especially the Germans ... are arriving regularly;
> (2) operations in Russia are developing well, and it is foreseen that German operations against the Caucasus will continue even during the winter;
> (3) personally, he [Ambrosio] does not believe in a victory that will liquidate our enemies. However, he thinks that Russia will probably be detached from the Allied camp, after which Great Britain and America will be obliged to come to terms.[42]

At the end of August, Rommel launched an offensive (Operation Surf) against the British Eighth Army, south of El Alamein. Ciano commented briefly on the timing of Rommel's initiative, the Duce's general sentiment, and Cavallero's ill-concealed opportunism:

> Yesterday evening [30 August] at eight o'clock Rommel attacked in Libya. He has chosen the day and the hour well, at a time when no one

> was expecting the attack and whisky has begun to appear on the English tables. Mussolini expresses no opinion, but is substantially optimistic. Cavallero ... telephones to give me news of the operation. As usual he wavers between 'yes' and 'no'. He does not wish to compromise himself, but intends to remain sufficiently near to gather the fruits of victory, if there are any.[43]

But by 5 September, Rommel had been routed back to his starting position, and on 9 September, Mussolini, alluding to 'operations in Libya', divulged to Ciano that 'the idea of an offensive is now given up, at least for some time'. The Duce was also angry with Rommel, 'who, according to English sources, has telegraphed accusing several of our [Italian] officers of having revealed some of his future plans to the enemy. As always, victory finds a hundred fathers, but defeat is an orphan. Now in Libya they are quarrelling, and Kesselring ran to Berlin to complain about Rommel. They are talking about a possible recall of Rommel.'[44] In late September, Rommel, who was returning to Germany for an overdue rest, made a stopover in Rome. Ciano wrote: 'I have had a visit from Rommel, who said that he is leaving on a six weeks' furlough. Mussolini is convinced that Rommel will not come back. He finds Rommel physically and morally shaken.'[45]

On 8 October, Mussolini spoke critically of the unduly oppressive treatment meted out by the Germans in the occupied nations, Greece in particular. This illogical and counterproductive policy, in the Duce's view, had the effect of undermining the stability of Europe: 'I have no qualms about the military course of the war. There will be neither surprises nor second fronts, but if we lose the war it will be because of the political stupidity of the Germans, who have not even tried to use good sense and restraint, and who have made Europe as hot and treacherous as a volcano.'[46]

Before the Council of Ministers two days later, Mussolini expressed his optimism for the future and spoke favourably of the Italian people: 'We cannot expect enthusiasm from a people who know that they must still face long sacrifices before victory, and must show discipline, obedience, tenacity—virtues which they have beyond all measure.'[47]

Reichsführer-S.S. Himmler arrived in Rome for a three-day visit on 11 October. He had received numerous reports of the Duce's deteriorating health and wished to take measure of the political climate in Italy himself. He was personally met at the station by Ciano. The S.S. chief had recently taken a trip to the front, the memory of which was (to him) 'a nightmare'. A lengthy conversation *à deux* followed. Ciano described the encounter in general terms:

> He [Himmler] says nothing very important, but what counts is the extremely reserved tone of his conversation. He ... speaks of all the difficulties, all the sacrifices, of what has been done, and above all, what remains to be done. He wanted to find out a good deal about Italy. In particular he wanted to know about the Monarchy and about the Vatican. He praised the loyalty of the first and the discretion of the second.[48]

Himmler also spoke with Mussolini, giving the Italian dictator a distorted account of Germany's handling of the Jewish question. Himmler claimed that because Jewish elements were engaged in all manner of subversive activity, it was necessary to remove them—without any regard for their gender or age—from the Reich, the General-Government, and other German-occupied areas. According to Himmler's notes of the interview, the Duce recognized the necessity for such measures and approved. Himmler stated that Jewish elements were either concentrated in camps or employed in construction projects in the East. Their high mortality rate, Himmler explained, was due to the fact that they were unaccustomed to heavy manual labour. Himmler did not expressly admit that the Reich was endeavouring to systematically annihilate all European Jewry, but Mussolini was nonetheless aware of the Germans' true intentions.[49]

In the second half of October, Göring took another trip to Italy in order to discuss with Mussolini the progress of the war in Russia and North Africa. A two-hour interview was held at the Palazzo Venezia on 23 October. Naturally the Duce was primarily concerned with the North African arena: 'In the event of an Anglo–American landing in French [North] Africa ... he would occupy Tunis at once.' Otherwise, Mussolini reasoned, 'there arose the possibility of an English landing in Italy'. Thereupon Göring bemoaned the fact 'that Tunis was not in the hands of the Axis' and inquired why, in June 1940, the occupation of Tunis had not been a condition imposed upon the vanquished French. Mussolini regretfully conceded that this had been a mistake: 'Italy had been too modest.' Nevertheless, Mussolini 'was optimistic as to the outcome of the war. The next year [1943] would be decisive.'[50]

On 26 October, Ciano met with Mussolini for a discussion; he had not seen the Duce in a fortnight. Ciano observed that Mussolini 'has lost a great deal of weight, but his eyes are clear, his voice firm, and he looks bold'. To Ciano, Mussolini's malady had the effect of making him appear 'more youthful'. On this occasion, Myron Taylor, Roosevelt's ambassador to the Holy See, had incurred the Duce's displeasure. Mussolini felt that the American diplomat's reports were responsible for the Allied bombing of Italy's northern cities, and he lambasted Taylor for his presumptuousness:

'This buffoon went back to America to report that the Italians are on their last legs, and that with one or two hard blows they can easily be beaten.' The Duce vowed that should Taylor again set foot on Italian soil he would find himself 'put in handcuffs', diplomatic immunity notwithstanding. But Ciano did not believe, as Mussolini did, that Taylor's reports were the underlying cause of the Allied air attacks. On the contrary, Ciano felt it was 'rather that the whole offensive plan of the Americans and the British is being applied'.[51]

Next day Robert Ley, the German Labour Front leader, arrived in Italy 'to head the National Socialist Mission of the Twentieth Anniversary of the March on Rome'.* Party Secretary Aldo Vidussoni escorted Ley into Ciano's presence; the latter found both Ley's appearance and mentality 'vulgar'. The German toper was 'such a bum' that Ciano could scarcely imagine how the man had managed to land the top job of Reich organization leader. Ciano noted that Ley had 'nothing new' to contribute, but merely told the falsehood that 'the whole Stalingrad action has cost the Germans only three thousand dead'. Even if the boorish Ley had increased the figure tenfold, Ciano would still not have bought it.[52]

To Mussolini, Ley presented a letter from the Führer:

> ... I wish above all to express my own indissoluble links with you and those of the National Socialist and the Fascist movements. I am quite clear that your historic March, twenty years ago, introduced a turning point in world history.... I am perfectly convinced, Duce, that you were the first man to succeed in combatting Marxism not by police methods, but by overcoming it through a force able to create a new state and community. You removed the mass of its followers and bound them to a new idea. I have often studied in retrospect the phases of your Fascist revolution, and I am always convinced anew that fate must have willed that two men and two revolutions in Europe should determine the features of the New Age.[53]

The Duce replied: 'The arrival of the mission headed by Doctor Ley, and the participation of the German Press and the people in our twentieth anniversary celebrations, created a profound and welcome impression not only in Fascist circles, but among the Italian people at large.'[54] The 'Twentieth Anniversary celebration' was held on 28 October, as scheduled. Ciano described it thusly:

* Mussolini, who now only infrequently appeared in public, did not deliver a speech on 28 October 1942.

> It was a single ceremony, the inauguration of the new quarters for the Exhibit of the Revolution. Mussolini appeared in public for the first time since his illness. In the open, in uniform, surrounded by many people, he seemed thin and more tired than two days ago at the Palazzo Venezia. He was welcomed in a way that I would call affectionate. But the organization of the ceremony was far from coming up to par, lacking even the least sense of camaraderie among its members. The fact is that the present secretariat of the party is made up of unknown men, to whom we are, in turn, unknown. This explains the coolness of the ceremony. It explains also a good many of the serious difficulties of the internal situation. On this very day of the recurrence of the Fascist celebration, the inefficiency of the party is felt more strongly than ever, because the party is headed by incapable, discredited, and questionable men.[55]

That autumn, the British inflicted upon Axis forces their biggest defeat thus far. The Second Battle of El Alamein was one of the great turning points of the war, coinciding with the Battle of Stalingrad and, in the Pacific theatre, the Battle of Guadalcanal. On 23 October, Lieutenant-General Bernard Montgomery, a crafty, ferret-like man, issued a personal notice to all his men:

> 1. When I assumed command of the Eighth Army I said that the mandate was to destroy ROMMEL and his Army, and that it would be done as soon as we were ready.
> 2. We are ready NOW.
> The battle which is now about to begin will be one of the decisive battles of history....
> All that is necessary is that each one of us, every officer and man, should enter this battle with the determination to see it through—to fight and to kill—and finally, to win.[56]

The British Eighth Army, a massive heterogeneous force of 195,000 Commonwealth troops, opened the attack at 9:40 p.m. with a devastating artillery barrage. Rommel, having resumed his command on 24 October after a period of convalescence, counterattacked on 31 October, but it made little difference. A few days later, Marshal Cavallero communicated to Rommel an optimistic message on Mussolini's behalf: 'The Duce authorizes me to convey to you his deep appreciation of the successful counterattack personally led by you. The Duce also conveys to you his complete confidence that the battle now in progress will be brought to a successful conclusion under your command.'[57] And on 3 November, the Führer personally exhorted Rommel, in typical Hitlerian style, to fight to the last man:

> I and the German people are watching the heroic defensive battle being fought in Egypt. We have loyal confidence in your powers of leadership as well as in the courage of the German and Italian troops under your command. In the situation in which you now find yourself, there can be no other consideration than to hold fast, never retreat, hurl every gun and every man into the fray. During the next few days there will be important air reinforcements transferred to the Commander-in-Chief South [Kesselring]. The Duce and the *Comando Supremo* will also strain every muscle to see to it that you are supplied with the means to continue the battle. The enemy has numerical superiority, but he, too, will come to the end of his resources. It would not be the first time in history that the stronger will has prevailed against the stronger battalions of the enemy. You can show your troops no other way than that which leads to victory or death.[58]

But the reality was that Rommel lacked the wherewithal to hold out. To avoid the wholesale destruction of his forces, Rommel messaged Hitler on 4 November for authorization to withdraw to Fouka. But with no response forthcoming, by late afternoon Rommel could delay no longer, and at 5:30 p.m. he issued the necessary orders on the Führer's behalf. The beleaguered *Afrika Korps* made its escape, withdrawing westwards towards Tunisia with the British in pursuit. Rommel's legions were driven out of Egypt, never again to return.

Over the next six weeks, the British Eighth Army pressed onwards like a steamroller, capturing Tobruk (11 November), Benghazi (20 November), Sirte (25 December), and Tripoli (23 January). And on 4 February, the British Eight Army traversed the Libyan–Tunisian frontier. The harried Italo–German troops fell back to the Mareth Line, a 25-mile section of French Tunisian fortifications. The 1,600-mile retreat dashed permanently all Italian plans for hegemony in North Africa and galvanized Allied spirits. The danger of Axis forces overrunning British Egypt and capturing the Suez Canal and the oil fields of Iraq and Iran—at one time a genuine possibility—was over. Churchill gave a succinct assessment: 'It may almost be said, "Before Alamein we never had a victory. After Alamein we never had a defeat."'[59]

The Allied blows continued to fall. Before dawn on 8 November, an Anglo–American expeditionary force of some 107,000 men landed in French Morocco and Algeria. The joint undertaking (Operation Torch) was intended to expel Axis forces from North Africa once and for all. In overall command and the operation's mastermind was General Dwight Eisenhower, future Supreme Commander of the Allied Expeditionary Force. The initial phase of the plan involved the seizure of three strategic seaports: Casablanca, Oran, and Algiers. Once in Allied hands, the plan was for the Anglo–Americans to speedily push forward to Tunis (the 'Run for Tunis'), trapping Rommel's *Afrika Korps* between them and Montgomery's Eighth Army.

General Eisenhower had prudently anticipated resistance to the Allied landings in Morocco and Algeria by Vichy French colonial forces. In a scheme to gain their loyalty, Eisenhower enlisted the cooperation of General Henri Giraud, an Alsatian. It was intended that Giraud take over command of French North African forces. But Giraud's broadcast of 9 November urging Frenchmen to cease fighting and side with the Allies fell on deaf ears.

Although the Giraud gambit had failed, Eisenhower had another ace up his sleeve. He concluded with Admiral François Darlan, Vichy France's Navy minister, a controversial deal. This was the so-called 'Darlan Deal' endorsed by Churchill and Roosevelt. It was essentially a bribe: the Allies would recognize Darlan as commander-in-chief of French forces in North Africa if he would order a ceasefire ending French resistance to the Anglo–American invasion. This he did on 10 November. Darlan was promptly relieved by his superior Pétain, but it was too late; the deed was done. Eisenhower also agreed to elevate Darlan to the lofty post of high commissioner of French North Africa. Giraud was placed in charge of French forces under the new Darlan administration.

General de Gaulle was incensed by the Eisenhower–Darlan deal. The Free French leader was revolted by the Allies' willingness to do business with such a turncoat. In a letter to Admiral Harold Stark, former chief of Naval Operations, he bitterly wrote: 'I understand that the United States buys the treachery of traitors if this appears profitable, but payment must not be made against the honour of France.'[60] Darlan was gunned down at point-blank range less than six weeks later, on Christmas Eve, by a twenty-year-old anti-Vichyist.

In the wake of the Anglo–American landings in French North Africa, Ribbentrop contacted Ciano by telephone. An urgent meeting was to be held in Munich for the Axis 'to consider our line of conduct towards France'. Mussolini was indisposed, for he was feeling unwell. It was decided that Ciano would go in his stead. The Duce imparted to Ciano his instructions: if France was 'ready to collaborate loyally', she would be rendered full assistance. Conversely, if France continued to remain non-committal, the Axis would perforce have to 'adopt preventative measures'. This would entail a German occupation of the Free Zone and an Italian occupation of Corsica.

Ciano had a preliminary discussion with Hitler on the evening of 9 November. Pétain's deputy, Laval, would arrive by automobile later. Hitler had no 'illusions on the French desire to fight'. Plus, the Axis also had to contend with General Giraud, a man with 'brains and courage'. Thus it was necessary to act now. The Führer intended to hear Laval out; nevertheless, nothing the Frenchman had to say would deter him from his chosen course of action, *viz.* 'the total occupation of France, landing in Corsica, [and establishing] a bridgehead in Tunisia'. To Ciano, Hitler appeared to be 'neither nervous nor restless' at the unpropitious turn of events, but he did not underestimate the Allied operation and wished 'to meet it with all resources at his disposal'. Göring chimed up to remark 'that the occupation of North Africa represents the first point scored by the Allies since the beginning of the war'.[61]

On 10 November, another forgathering, this time with Laval present, took place. The Frenchman, 'with his white tie and middle-class French peasant attire', stuck out like a sore thumb among all the uniformed Germans and Ciano. Laval tried to engage in disarming small talk, but the Führer treated him 'with frigid courtesy'. Hitler incisively inquired whether France was prepared to provide the Axis, in Tunisia, with 'landing points'. Laval equivocated and attempted to raise the subject of 'concessions from Italy', but Hitler brusquely cut the Frenchman short to state that he did 'not intend to take up at this time a discussion of Italian claims [against France], which are more than modest'. Put on the spot, Laval replied that he personally could not 'take upon himself the responsibility of yielding Tunis and Bizerte to the Axis' and recommended that under the circumstances he be given a peremptory note addressed to the Vichy Government specifying Axis intentions in Tunisia.[62]

However, the Germans' imminent undertaking—the total occupation of France—was not divulged to Laval during the talk, even though the wheels were already in motion. Ribbentrop confidentially informed Ciano that Laval would only be advised of the *fait accompli* the following day at 8 a.m. He was to be told that 'on account of information received during the night', the Führer had deemed it necessary to occupy Vichy France.[63]

Meanwhile, Operation Torch was proceeding according to plan. By 10 November, all three objectives—Casablanca, Oran, and Algiers—had been captured by the Allied invaders. General Franco's forces in Spanish Morocco, not wishing to involve themselves, remained inactive, and within a week the Anglo–Americans had traversed the Algerian border into northwest Tunisia. Churchill declared: 'Now this is not the end. It is not even the beginning of the end. But it is, perhaps, the end of the beginning.'[64] Torch ended on 16 November. The next step for the Allies was to prepare for the invasion of the Italian peninsula—the 'soft underbelly' of Europe, as Churchill dubbed it.

Mussolini later acknowledged that Operation Torch, and the American landing in Algiers in particular, had been a grave development that substantially undermined Italian morale:

> In Italy the moral repercussions of the American landing in Algiers were immediate and profound. Every enemy of Fascism promptly reared his head; the first of the traitors, minor figures even though some were National Councillors, emerged from the shadows. The country began to feel the strain. As long as only the English were in the Mediterranean, Italy, with Germany's help, could hold firm and resist, though at the cost of ever greater sacrifice; but the appearance of America disturbed the weaker spirits and increased by many millions the already numerous band of listeners to enemy radio…

The Duce also admitted that the Anglo–American offensives of early autumn had altered the course of the war: 'The sixteen days from 23rd October to 8th November were of incalculable historical importance…. From that moment [onwards] the strategic initiative passed to the Allies.'[65]

The Germans moved into Vichy France (Operation Anton) on 11 November as planned,* ostensibly to protect the Reich against the danger of a possible Allied incursion into Western Europe. They encountered no resistance. The Vichy Government protested that this was a breach of the Compiègne Armistice, but in a letter to Pétain a fortnight later Hitler accused the Vichy French in North Africa of abetting the Anglo–American invasion. Hitler wrote:

> The landing of American and British troops in French Northwest and North Africa, which, as it now becomes evident, took place in agreement with numerous treacherous generals and officers, had removed the preliminary condition on which the whole treaty was laid down in the preamble of the Armistice and compelled Germany to carry out immediately and in agreement with its allies the necessary security measures.[66]

The Germans also invaded Tunisia, and in three weeks' time 24,000 Axis troops had assembled on Tunisian soil to counter the Anglo–American invasion force advancing swiftly through French Northwest Africa.

On 21 November, a session of the Council of Ministers was held during which Mussolini recapitulated and clarified the current state of affairs. The Italian dictator declared:

> (a) that the food situation is a great deal better than forecasts, which had been very gloomy;

* Also on 11 November, Italian forces occupied Corsica (Operation C2), and the Italian Fourth Army occupied Provence as far as the Rhône River.

> (b) that the military situation in Cyrenaica is such as to lead to stopping the enemy at Agheila Marada, and perhaps to get the upper hand, while the trend of operations in Tunisia is favourable to the Axis;
> (c) that the internal situation is excellent, except for the alarmists;
> (d) that Hitler, acting on a suggestion made by him, has agreed to send one hundred anti-aircraft batteries for the protection of our cities, which are suffering severe punishment every night from the R.A.F.[67]

Although the occupation of Vichy France by the German Seventh Army (under Colonel-General Johannes Blaskowitz) was achieved in the space of a single day, the Germans did not succeed in capturing intact the large French Fleet moored at Toulon. The Vichy Government correctly deduced that the opportunistic Germans intended to seize it for their own use. Therefore, Darlan's successor, Counter-Admiral Gabriel Auphan, issued orders for its destruction; and on 27 November, three battleships, seven cruisers, and several dozen lesser vessels were scuttled by French crews. For German naval commanders, the loss of the powerful French Fleet was a heavy blow, but on the other hand it meant that Charles de Gaulle and his Free French forces would not gain possession of it either. Ciano recognized the obvious benefit gained by Italy thereby: 'For us Italians there is one advantage—that in any eventuality a [rival] naval power in the Mediterranean has been cancelled for many years.'[68]

On 2 December, Mussolini delivered a speech to the Chamber of Fasces and Corporations. He had not done so since 10 June 1941. It was, Mussolini explained, 'a political and military report, more military than political. It will consequently be a speech of data, of figures, of facts: in other words it will be the balance-sheet of the first thirty months of war.' Mussolini repeated Churchill's harsh criticism of his unscrupulous war policy:

> Mussolini [Churchill said] was not able to resist the temptation of stabbing in the back a prostrated France, and what he thought was a hopeless England....
>
> His mad dream of imperial glory, his longing for conquest and booty, the incomparable arrogance of his tyranny led him to that shameful and fatal gesture. In vain I warned him; he would not discuss it. The wise appeal of the American President had no effect on that heart of stone....
>
> His hyena's nature exceeded every limit of decency and good sense....
>
> Today his Empire is gone.

To this harsh condemnation—which was undeniably true—Mussolini defiantly retorted: 'The last word has not yet been spoken.' The Duce also exhorted the Italian population to evacuate urban areas to avoid Allied bombardment: 'We must get the population out of the cities, above all the women and children. And we must organize a total evacuation, or almost total. It is the duty of all those who can find a place to live far from the urban and industrial centres, to do so.'[69]

Ciano diarized his impressions of the Duce's address:

> The reception of the speech by the National Council was very warm, even if in the hall it was easy to recognize people who disagree in private. Physically the Duce appeared quite thin, but nonetheless vigorous and at times as fiery as ever. The speech? It is too early to say what effect it will have. But it is clear that it does not introduce new facts or opinions, nor indeed could it have done so. It will not be difficult for English propaganda to refute it effectively...[70]

Ciano left for Rastenburg in Mussolini's stead on 17 December for a meeting with Hitler. The Duce, still suffering from gastrointestinal complications, did not 'care to interrupt his electrotherapy cure' and make the lengthy trip to East Prussia himself. The previous day Mussolini had instructed Ciano to advise Hitler 'to come to an agreement with Russia, or at least to fix upon a defensive line that can be held by small forces'. This would allow the Axis divisions on the Russian Front to be redeployed to defend against the Anglo–Americans 'in Africa, in the Balkans, and perhaps even in the West'. Why? Because, Mussolini prophesized, 'Nineteen forty-three will be the year of the Anglo–Saxon effort.' Mussolini believed that victory in the East was no longer attainable. Thus he considered it 'extremely advisable' to make peace with Stalin.[71] But Hitler, who was by then pathologically obsessed with capturing the industrial city of Stalingrad at all costs, was categorically opposed to the proposal.

The following snide exchange at the *Wolfsschanze* (Wolf's Lair) between Mario Pansa and Walther Hewel, Italian diplomat and German 'special ambassador' respectively, was documented by Ciano in his *Diary* entry dated 18 December:

> PANSA: Had our [Italian] Army many losses?
>
> HEWEL: No losses at all; they are running.
>
> PANSA: As you [the Germans] did in Moscow last year?
>
> HEWEL: Exactly.[72]

Upon his return to Rome from Führer Headquarters on 22 December, Ciano submitted to Mussolini his report. He also expressed to the Duce his 'unfavourable impressions' of Cavallero and the sycophancy he displayed with the Germans. Displeased at what he was hearing, Mussolini said firmly: 'The usefulness of Cavallero is over. A few years ago he had a keen brain, but that is no longer true.'[73]

On the eighteenth anniversary of his historic speech of 3 January 1925 (in which the reins of dictatorship had passed into his hands), Mussolini addressed the new Party Directorate to synopsize the course of the war up to the present, in particular the recent Allied successes at El Alamein and French North Africa. In order to infuse into his collaborators a sense of optimism for the future, the Duce also postulated that in the year 1943 the Italians would surmount all obstacles. The Duce spoke forcibly and plausibly:

> The first part of our present war shows the following characteristics. It took place in distant countries: in Ethiopia, in Africa, (there were only three days' fighting on the Western Front), in Greece—always on the other side of the sea. The Italian people are accustomed to this war which is not too close, and have acquired the habit of indifference under these circumstances. They will have come to the conclusion that war will always be far off, that it will be fought and settled in areas which are distant from metropolitan territory.
>
> All this changed after 23 October 1942, when the [Italian] Supreme Command discussed the date on which the British would attack. I maintained that the attack would take place at the end of October, partly because the British would wish to benefit by the fact that this would spoil the celebrations of our Twentieth Anniversary.... That in fact is what happened. In August 1942 the Italo–German offensive at El Alamein failed. Not because the soldiers failed to fight as splendidly as always. But we must remember that in war, victory is won or lost at sea rather than on land. We have lost a very large number of tanks laden with petrol and oil, both necessary fuels without which our motorized divisions cannot function.... On 23 October the British took the initiative for the first time and obtained a success which they could never have had in the preceding three years. At the same time the terrorist ('scientific' according to Churchill) bombardment of our Italian cities began. This combination was planned so as to exert moral pressure on the Italian people at the time of the lack of success in the land war.
>
> But the date of 8 November is still more important. On 8 November there happened something which required no prophet but which any ordinary observer of human affairs could have foretold: North Africa was occupied by the North Americans. Only people deliberately wishing to deceive themselves could have expected any effective result from showing political favour to France. France hated us, hates us still and will do so until the end of time,

hence all this policy of 'petting' (as sailors call it) France is absolutely barren of results.... This disembarkation of 8 November had certain psychological effects even upon many Italians.... Events had made these somewhat feeble spirits lose their balance. It was thought impossible that the Anglo–Americans would not reach Ostia in a few days. Then the balance was restored because we responded to the Anglo–Saxon move. We occupied all France, Corsica, and Tunisia. The occupation of France is important because at any rate in Metropolitan France misunderstandings have ceased. France no longer has its metropolitan territory; it has no colonial territory; it has no gold, it has no navy, army, or air force; it has nothing. The French people does not even possess its own soul, and this is perhaps its most serious loss because sometimes this means the final decline of a people.

How did it come about that the battle of El Alamein was decisive? Because the other arm of the pincers was lacking. The German troops should have poured down from the Caucasus. But this was not possible because anyone who has some knowledge of geography knows that the valleys there run parallel to the sea, one after the other, and we needed to get down to Batum. In the absence of this strategic manoeuvre it was clear that the battle was bound to end as it did.

Who is going to win this war? You will say the best armed people. That is not enough. The people with the largest supply of raw materials. Still not enough. The people with the greatest generals: not even this. This war will be won by the armed forces with the deepest political understanding. The days have gone by in which it was said that the soldier must not be a politician; no, that is a mistake. This could be said at the time when there were ten or fifteen parties. You could not allow ten or fifteen different kinds of political propaganda in barracks. But now there is only one party and one regime, consequently the armed forces can never be too political or too strongly Fascist. If they are not political we cannot win. We need Fascist soldiers to fight for Fascism because this is a war of religion and of ideas. Today all territorial objectives take second place. This does not mean that these objectives are not always in our minds, but that they have become of secondary importance. They are always present with us, because they enter into the general European settlement which must recognize our rights to living space.

But today's problem is a problem of ideas.... Now we are facing the year 1943 which will be a year of fundamental importance in Italian history. It will be a year in which the regime must show its strength and the Italian people must pass a very serious test. There is no doubt that the international Aventine will bring its whole forces to bear upon Italy. This too could be foreseen. I have always regarded it as more important to occupy Egypt than to occupy England. If England were occupied, the problem would not be solved; but once the hinge of three continents constituted by Egypt had been occupied, and we had come down to the Indian Ocean, and had made contact with the Japanese, we should have broken the back of British Imperialism. This has not happened because each one holds ideas which derive from his historical situation. Ours has always been a Mediterranean one, the German a continental one.... This has allowed us to take possession of huge areas rich in raw materials which we can use to prolong our resistance, but there is no doubt that at a certain moment we must throw our weight towards the West because the war will be decided in the West, in the Mediterranean.

We are therefore privileged to foreseen that an enemy attack will be directed particularly against Italy. Why? Because it is thought that Italy is the weaker of the two allies, but particularly because the enemy counts on a failure of our morale. For this reason it was thought that under enemy bombardment the people would at a certain moment show a desire for peace, any sort of peace, a separate peace. It is essential that everyone should be convinced, that every Fascist should be convinced, that this would be the most catastrophic solution and would dishonour us for centuries....

I do not believe that they (the Allies) will try to open a land front against us. It is too late; we have already taken our measures. Therefore the enemy must seek a place where conditions are most favourable. I believe that it is probable that the Anglo–Saxon attack will take place in the Balkans.

Hitherto we have seen the following situation: the great power of resistance in Germany. From time to time there have been rumours in Italy about German morale; they always start with a misunderstanding. Because there are no signs of enthusiasm in Germany, it is thought that the German people does not want victory. The German people from the highest to the lowest knows what is at stake because it is clear that the Anglo–Saxons would tomorrow impose on Germany those conditions which were imposed by the Treaty of Versailles; that is, Germany would be paralyzed for generations.... As regards the German anti-aircraft batteries which have been sent to Italy and which have already proved excellent, Fascists must be friendly to these men who have come to live with us. A certain excessive susceptibility is a weakness, a negative feature of the Italian character; Italians are unwilling to be helped by anyone. This is going too far.

The Italian people now has the chance to show what it is made of. The problem is a serious one for us. We must ask ourselves whether twenty years of the Fascist regime have changed things only on the surface, leaving them much the same below. We shall see in the course of 1943.

> If you ask me 'What is your opinion?' it is this: the Italian people will stand firm and astound the world.... By the end of 1943, which will not be the last year of war but will be a decisive year during which we shall see whether the balance will fall, the Italian people will have surmounted every test.
>
> The Party must be the instrument through which our armed forces become steadily more politically minded. Propaganda must fit in with time and place. Then there is propaganda carried on by everyone belonging to the Party: in the family circle, in the local Party Headquarters, in the social organizations, in conversation.... It is not necessary for the Fascists in Italy to number four millions. It is not even a bad thing, because it is impossible to govern a big country if you are shut up in an ivory tower. The important thing is that there should be a few hundred thousand well-informed, decided, ready, united Blackshirts, all absolutely dependable men, ideologically speaking. I believe that the Italian people has the qualities enabling it to resist, to hold firm, and to conquer. At the end of 1943 we shall be able to say proudly that we have in fact realized our aims. At the present moment we have transformed the Italian people if not altogether, at least in part; this was the supreme task of our revolution.... This year will decide whether the Italian people must resign itself to being a land of tourists, a large Switzerland.... I look forward to these months with passionate interest and absolute certainty.... These are the directives which I give on this third of January. In addition, every month a meeting of the entire Directorate, including the inspectors, will be held at Palazzo Venezia, and I will preside. Thus we will work together.[74]

On 8 January 1943, Ciano had luncheon with the intellectual Giuseppe Bottai and the Germanophile Roberto Farinacci, both members of the Fascist Party and Chamber of Corporations. The pair were infuriated about the imminent loss of Libya to the British, about which they could do nothing. Bottai grumbled: 'After all it is another goal that has been reached. In 1911 Mussolini uttered his "away from Libya". After thirty-two years he has kept his word.'[75] Three days earlier, Ciano had seen Mussolini, who too was unhappy about the situation in Libya. The Duce, Ciano wrote, 'realizes that the loss of Tripoli will cut deeply into the morale of the people. He would like a desperate house-to-house defence like that in Stalingrad. [But] he knows that this will not happen. Furthermore, it is impossible. The city can be broken into from all sides, and can be shelled from the sea.' Mussolini let fly with an angry tirade against Cavallero and especially 'that madman Rommel, who thinks of nothing but retreating in Tunisia'.[76]

Mussolini spoke to the Council of Ministers once again on 23 January. Ciano described the occasion: 'After the administrative agenda Mussolini talks of the military situation. The negative side is the Allied initiative on all land fronts, a positive side is the success of the submarine campaign. He puts a great deal of emphasis on this.' To the assembled ministers, Mussolini also forecast that the war would go on for 'another three or four years'. That same day a *communiqué* reported a grim piece of news: Tripoli had fallen to the British Eighth Army.[77]

A secret Allied conference, code-named 'Symbol', was held at Casablanca from 14 to 24 January. At the Casablanca Conference, as it was thereafter known, Roosevelt and Churchill discussed Allied strategy for the future course of the war in Europe. Stalin was not present due to the exigencies of the Battle of Stalingrad, then in its latter stages. The democratic leaders agreed on two major undertakings in the European theatre: an invasion of Sicily and an Anglo–American bombing campaign against Germany. On 24 January, Roosevelt revealed to the press that he and Churchill had decided on a new war policy: unconditional surrender. Peace terms would be inflexible and the ideology of militaristic imperialism common to Germany, Italy, and Japan would be eradicated.

Roosevelt explained: 'The elimination of German, Japanese, and Italian war power means the unconditional surrender by Germany, Italy, and Japan. That means a reasonable assurance of future world peace. It does not mean the destruction of the population of Germany, Italy, or Japan, but it does mean the destruction of the philosophies in those countries which are based on conquest and the subjugation of other people.'[78]

The Italians received news of the Casablanca Conference three days later, on 27 January. Ciano had a sense of foreboding: 'It is too early to judge, but it seems to be a serious thing, very serious indeed.'[79]

In late January, the Italian Army in Russia* came to a grim end at Stalingrad, where the troops of the German Sixth Army and their Italian, Romanian, and Hungarian comrades in arms were surrounded and largely annihilated by Soviet forces. Of the 130,000 Italian fighters encircled by the Red Army, some 20,000 had perished in combat. Over three times that number were taken prisoner. Those who were lucky enough to escape the net eventually made it back to Italy. Many were horrifically disfigured; both the frigid Russian winter and the Soviet foe had been merciless. As in Greece, the Italian war in Russia had been catastrophic.

* The Italian Army in Russia (A.R.M.I.R.), formerly the Italian Expeditionary Force in Russia (C.S.I.R.), was established in July 1942. It consisted of ten divisions: the *Julia*, the *Tridentina*, the *Cuneense*, the *Ravenna*, the *Cosseria*, the *Sforzesca*, the *Celere*, the *Pasubio*, the *Torino*, and the *Vicenza*. The Italian Army in Russia (under General Italo Gariboldi) initially achieved some success against Soviet forces at the Don River.

On 5 February, the majority of Mussolini's cabinet ministers (save two) were dismissed from their posts. The purpose of the unprecedented cabinet reshuffle was to silence those who were not in accord with Mussolini's war policy. The main culprit was the anti-German Ciano, who had been ardently opposed to the Italo–German alliance as early as August 1939, and who had long since made his views known. The others—including Grandi, Bottai, Guidi, and Pavolini—were removed chiefly to make it appear that henceforth the new Italian administration—now purged of its detractors—would demonstrate greater solidarity with the Germans. Ciano was replaced as foreign minister by Mussolini himself, with Giuseppe Bastianini as undersecretary.

Ciano recalled the occasion, which affected him deeply:

> At four-thirty in the afternoon the Duce calls me. The moment I enter the room I perceive that he is very much embarrassed. I grasp what he is prepared to tell me. 'What are you going to do now?' he begins, and then adds in a low voice that he is changing his entire Cabinet. I understand the reasons. I share them, and I do not intend to raise the least objection. Among the various solutions of a personal nature that he offers me I decisively reject the governorship of Albania ... I choose to be Ambassador to the Holy See.[80]

Two days later, a formal announcement of Ciano's new posting to the Holy See was made, and on 8 February Ciano, with a heavy heart, wrote his penultimate *Diary* entry: 'I hand over my office at the Ministry for Foreign Affairs. Then I go to the Palazzo Venezia to see the Duce and take leave of him.' Mussolini tactfully reassured his dispirited son-in-law: 'Now you must consider that you are going to have a period of rest. Then your turn will come again. Your future is in my hands, and therefore you need not worry.' Mussolini added ruefully: 'If they [the Germans] had given us three years' time we might have been able to wage war under different conditions or perhaps it would not have been at all necessary in order to wage it.'

Referring to Ciano's valuable, revealing, and compromising *Diary*, Mussolini inquired of his protégé if he had all his papers in order. Ciano pointedly replied:

> Yes, I have them all in order, and remember, when hard times come—because it is now certain that hard times will come—I can document all the treacheries perpetrated against us by the Germans, one after another, from the preparation for the conflict to the war on Russia, communicated to us when their troops had already crossed the frontier. If you

> have need of them I shall furnish the details, or better still, I shall, within the space of twenty-four hours, prepare that speech which I have had in mind for three years, because I shall burst if I do not deliver it.

Mussolini invited Ciano to visit him on a daily basis, if he so wished, and then the Italian dictator and his young confidant bid one another farewell. Ciano summed it up: 'Our leave-taking was cordial, for which I am very glad, because I like Mussolini, like him very much, and what I shall miss most will be my contact with him.'[81]

The ongoing guerrilla situation in Yugoslavia was one in which the Italians and Germans did not see eye to eye. In short, the Italians were willing to collaborate, or at least tolerate, General Mihailović's Chetniks, but were dead set against the Chetniks' enemy, the Communist partisans led by Tito. The Germans, in turn, wished to eradicate all insurrectionist elements in Yugoslavia regardless of their pro- or anti-Axis stance. And now, with the Tunisian campaign in progress, the danger of an Anglo–American landing in the Balkan sector could not be ignored. Hitler had been preoccupied with this matter for some time, and Ribbentrop accordingly came to Rome bearing a lengthy letter from the Führer dated 16 February. The letter strongly urged Mussolini to take decisive action against Mihailović's Chetniks:

> I [Hitler] regard the situation in the Balkans with the gravest concern....
>
> Should there be a [British] landing at some point in the Balkans, Duce, the Communists, the followers [Chetniks] of General Draža Mihailović, and all the other Komitadji [Balkan rebels] would immediately concur in supporting the enemy newcomers by attacking German and Italian troops....
>
> Apart from present operations against the Communists, I discern a particular danger, Duce, in the developments of the Mihailović movement....
>
> Mihailović is endeavouring to secure the arms and material required for the execution of his plans by pretending to help your troops in the pacification of the country. His formations thus receive all they need in the way of arms, ammunition, supplies, and when they are ready to strike, they will even be in a position to choose the terrain on which to attack us....
>
> In the interests of our common objectives, I feel it is desirable that your Second Army should regard Mihailović and his movement as sworn enemies of the Axis Powers, and I ask you, Duce, to instruct your commander [General Mario Roatta] to this effect.
>
> The liquidation of the Mihailović movement will in any case no longer be an easy task, considering the forces he now has and the large numbers of armed Chetniks....

> Should it not be possible, Duce, to disarm Communists and Chetniks alike and definitely pacify the country, a revolt will break out in the event of a [British] landing, communications lines with the Peloponnese will be cut, and the few German divisions will be engaged in fighting Communists and Chetniks.[82]

Ribbentrop advocated to Mussolini the necessity of exterminating the Chetnik threat. But with this policy the Italian party were not in accord. Army General Roatta posited that Mihailović's Chetniks were, in fact, of some benefit to the Axis; Bastianini, former governor of Dalmatia, did not believe that the various revolutionary bands would unite should an Allied landing take place; and the Duce himself pointed out that they had not yet discovered a way to effectively combat the guerrillas. The upshot was that the Italians agreed to meet the Germans halfway; once the Chetniks had outlasted their usefulness, or if the Anglo–Saxons invaded the Balkan peninsula, the Chetniks would be forcibly disarmed.

In Tunisia, Rommel's forces attacked the advancing Allies on 14 February in an attempt to interdict their progress. On 19 February, Rommel's battle-hardened warriors struck at the Kasserine Pass, defended by green American troops. The latter were routed by the ferocious assault; hundreds perished and scores more were captured. Next day Rommel's forces penetrated through the two-mile-wide pass, but thereafter poor weather and toughening Allied opposition hindered the Italo–German thrust.

Rommel had a strained meeting with his superior, Albert Kesselring (*Wehrmacht* commander-in-chief south), on 22 February. Because advance units of Montgomery's Eighth Army had already arrived at the town of Medenine, Rommel wished to discontinue his drive and pull back to reinforce the Mareth Line. Kesselring disagreed; he wanted Rommel to press on. But by nightfall Kesselring relented, the *Comando Supremo* gave the nod, and on 25 February, Rommel's forces arrived at the Mareth Line.

In a letter dated 9 March, Mussolini communicated to Hitler his views regarding the Tunisian crisis and the Russian conflict. At the urging of General Vittorio Ambrosio, chief of the Italian General Staff (Cavallero's successor), the Duce first stressed that:

(1) Tunisia had to be held 'at all costs';

(2) Axis forces should make their stand at the Mareth Line;

(3) Italo–German troops had to receive adequate supplies of weaponry and fuel; and

(4) for the first three aims to be met, air parity with the Allies in the Sardinia–Sicily–Tunisia triangle had to be achieved.

As for Russia, Mussolini had become skeptical as to whether the increasingly futile war against the Soviet behemoth was truly worthwhile.

The Duce wrote: 'Unless you are absolutely certain of destroying her strength once and for all, I ask myself whether it is not risking too much. It means repeating the struggle against the infinite, elusive, and practically unattainable space of Russia, while the Anglo–Saxon peril grows in the West. Once Russia is eliminated or neutralized, one way or the other, victory will be ours.'[83]

Hitler's irrational obsession with destroying the U.S.S.R. was a cause of great distress for the Italian Supreme Command, for they knew full well that the Eastern campaign was tying down the majority of German forces in what was probably a lost cause, and that consequently southern Italy was left vulnerable to Allied attack and invasion. To the Italians' dismay, the Führer considered Eastern Europe the primary theatre of war, not North Africa.

After some serious deliberation, Mussolini had devised a scheme to remedy the disastrous position in which the Axis Powers now found themselves. It occurred to Mussolini that if the Soviet Union could be removed from the equation—either diplomatically or by stalemate—then the majority of Axis forces in Eastern Europe could be transferred to North Africa and the Allied forces there eliminated or at least held in check. If so, perhaps an Allied request for peace negotiations might ensue. In any event, Mussolini now believed that it was impossible to defeat the U.S.S.R. on account of its immenseness. In a letter dated 25 March, Mussolini shared his contemplations with Hitler:

> In nearly two years of war ... you succeeded in weakening Russia to the extent that, for a long time to come, she will no longer be a threat to the Axis Powers.
>
> Therefore, I may rightly say that the Russian chapter can now be closed—if possible, with a separate peace or else with the establishment of a defensive line—a powerful Eastern wall—which the Russians could not overcome.
>
> I have arrived at this conclusion chiefly because, in my opinion, Russia can never be annihilated. She is defended by her very size—a territory so vast that it can never be conquered or held.
>
> Summer offensives and winter withdrawals cannot continue indefinitely without resulting in a wearing-out of forces which, even if bilateral, will be advantageous in the end to the Anglo–Americans alone. To this I will add that relations between Stalin and the Allies are presently anything but good, and the moment is most favourable.
>
> I am convinced that Russia can never be annihilated, owing to her enormous distances, even if the Japanese were to enter the war (against Russia), an eventuality far from probable. It is therefore necessary to conclude the Russian chapter in one way or another...[84]

The logic was sound, but the Führer would not be receptive to advice of this nature, not even from his Fascist partner. Prince Otto von Bismarck, counsellor at the German Embassy in Rome, accurately predicted that the Duce would make no fuss at the Klessheim conference a fortnight later: 'I do not foresee, on the part of Mussolini, any particular embarrassing request. His fleet does not exist, his army is problematical. His future is even more so. He feels himself to be weak.... I can say, since I have seen the minutes of the talks between Mussolini and Hitler, that the Duce has never taken the initiative and never raised general questions as to the political line to adopt.'[85]

On 7 April, the Axis dictators met for a conference lasting four days at Klessheim Castle, Austria. During the talks, the Duce was unwell. Plagued with stomach disorders, for which he required a special diet of rice, oatmeal, fruit, and non-fat milk, he scarcely spoke, allowing the Führer to prattle on uninterruptedly. A feeble effort by Mussolini to raise the issue of a separate peace with the Russians was stifled by a deluge of words from an agitated Hitler.

Before Mussolini's departure on 10 April, Hitler spoke a few words of assurance to his ailing friend: 'Duce, I guarantee to you that Africa will be defended. The situation is serious, but not desperate. Recently I read the story of the siege of Verdun in the First World War; Verdun resisted successfully the attacks of the best German regiments. I do not see why this should not happen also in Africa. With your support, Duce, my troops will make Tunis the Verdun of the Mediterranean.'[86] This kind of thinking was wishful at best and deluded at worst.

Less than a month later, Hitler related to Goebbels how he had managed to reinvigorate his Italian ally at Klessheim. The propaganda minister wrote in his *Diary*:

> The Führer had told me that the Duce had been really brought back into form during the four days' discussions. The Führer did everything he could, and by putting every ounce of nervous energy into the effort, succeeding in pushing Mussolini back on the rails. In those four days the Duce underwent a complete change at which his entourage was also amazed. When he [Mussolini] got out of the train on his arrival, the Führer thought, he looked like a broken old man; when he left again, he was a man in high fettle, ready for any deed.... The Duce understands clearly that there can be no other salvation for him except to win or die with us.[87]

But Himmler, who had arrived at Klessheim on the afternoon of 9 April for his own discussion with Mussolini, thought differently. He remarked to Colonel Eugen Dollmann, his S.S. representative in Rome: 'We can't count on Mussolini anymore because we can't count on the entire [Fascist] regime. This means that in a short time, at the most within a few months, Italy will drop out [of the war], and in the best case, we will have to hold the Southern Front by ourselves. If the condition of the Duce today is a reflection of the condition of the Italian people and the Fascist regime, then the end is near.'[88]

Meanwhile, the Duce had not yet finished making personnel changes. In mid-April, he discharged Carmen Senise, chief of the Italian Police, and appointed Lorenzo Chierici in his stead. On 19 April, veteran Fascist Carlo Scorza took over the post of party secretary from Aldo Vidussoni, a young man with a virulent anti-Slovene bias.* And a month earlier, on 18 March, General Alberto Pariani had replaced Francesco Jacomoni as Albania's ruler.

On 30 April, Mussolini sent Hitler a terse telegram re-emphasizing the lack of Axis aircraft needed to defend against those of the Allies. The situation was critical, and the Duce warned that without adequate reinforcements Tunisia would be lost:

> Führer—Unless it be possible to solve the air force problem in the Mediterranean—on which I have insisted again and again—and in such a way as to counterbalance the overwhelming air superiority of the enemy, not a warship, not a transport, not an airplane will reach Tunisia. And this means the immediate loss of Tunisia and of all our forces there.
>
> All attempts to ship troops there are doomed to failure. Today three destroyers were lost, two of them carrying German troops, and the other loaded with munitions, following attacks by large enemy formations with 70 to 120 fighter escort.
>
> Führer, the problem is urgent—imperatively so. Our troops in Tunisia are fighting magnificently, as the enemy himself is compelled to admit, but if we cannot supply them they are doomed.

Hitler curtly replied to Mussolini's message two days later. He recapitulated the number of aircraft recently dispatched to Italy—574 in March and 669 in April, excluding 'units transferred into Italy or the transport planes'. Hitler also advised Mussolini that the problem was presently being studied and that Field Marshal Albert Kesselring, commander-in-chief south (Italy), would discuss the matter with him.[90]

* On 5 January 1942, Ciano had recorded the disturbing contents of a conversation with Vidussoni: 'Vidussoni comes to see me. After having spoken about a few casual things, he makes some political allusions and announces savage plans against the Slovenes. He wants to kill them all. I take the liberty of observing that there are a million of them. "That does not matter," he answers firmly; "we must imitate the Ascari … and exterminate them!" I hope he will calm down.'[89]

On 3 May, Mussolini addressed the New Party Directorate at the Palazzo Venezia. In a subsequent report his speech was described as 'a supreme appeal to the whole structure of the nation to strengthen our resistance, and, as such, a sign of the danger which hangs over the country'. The Duce attempted to reinvigorate his demoralized Fascist confederates with a pep talk:

> We must look after the best sections of the people, while the police deal with the lower elements which can weaken the resistance of the entire Italian people. You have certainly noticed that from the moment a new direction was given to the life of the Party, the atmosphere cleared immediately. I am convinced that if we hold to this line of absolute moral and political intransigence we shall obtain concrete results. It is not that the Italian people is estranged. We must remember that the best part of the population is not on metropolitan territory. There are 1,300,000 Fascists fighting in Tunisia, in the Balkans, or in lands which will one day belong to the mother country. All Fascists must be convinced—and they must convince the people—that the destiny of Italy for the next generations is now at stake. And there must be no arbitrary, superficial distinctions between Fascism and Italy, because there is absolute, perfect identity between them.[91]

Mussolini delivered what was destined to be his final speech from the balcony of the Palazzo Venezia on 5 May. It was precisely seven years to the day since conquering Italians had marched into Addis Ababa, and the Duce proclaimed to the spirited Roman Fascists gathered in the square below:

> I feel the tension in your voices of the old and unshakable faith. I feel that you, just as I, are certain that the bloody sacrifices of these hard times will be rewarded with victory if it is true, as it is, that God is just, and Italy is immortal. I know, I feel, that millions and millions of Italians suffer from what is called the 'African illness'. There is only one way to recover from this. To go back and that's what we shall do.

The Duce concluded his brief oration with a reference to 'the draft dodgers' and 'the traitors of all ranks and races'; these treasonous elements would be shot.[92]

On the afternoon of 7 May, the British First Army (under Lieutenant-General Kenneth Anderson) liberated Tunis. Shortly thereafter, the American Second Army Corps (under Major-General Omar Bradley) took Bizerte, 40 miles to the north. On 12 May, General Messe, commander-in-chief of Italian North Africa, dispatched a communication to the *Comando*

Supremo advising that his troops were near the end of their tether: 'The First Army, which has had the privilege of being the last and final defender of our flag on African soil, will continue to fight to the end. The enemy is now closing in from all sides. The enormous disproportion of the forces in the field and the steady drop in supplies and artillery ammunition lead us to conclude that resistance cannot continue for very long.' In the early evening the Duce sent Messe a succinct reply: 'Stop the fighting. You are promoted to Marshal of Italy. Honour goes to you and your brave men.'[93] This was in stark contrast to Hitler's inflexible message to the commander of the doomed Sixth Army at Stalingrad, General von Paulus, whom he had ordered to fight to the death.

Next day, per Mussolini's order, the fighting ceased. Nearly a quarter-million seasoned Italo–German combatants—the remainder of Rommel's redoubtable *Afrika Korps* and Mussolini's warriors—discarded their weapons and capitulated. Allied losses in Tunisia were 76,000 men; on the Axis side, they were 40,000. General Harold Alexander dispatched a triumphant communication to Churchill, then in Washington, D.C. His telegraph read: 'Sir: It is my duty to report that the Tunisian campaign is over. All enemy resistance has ceased. We are masters of the North African shores.'[94] One week after the surrender, a great victory parade was held in Tunis. It was attended by Allied high brass, including Eisenhower. On 3 June, Churchill wrote a brief paragraph in Montgomery's autograph book in his inimitable style: 'The total destruction or capture of all enemy forces in Tunisia, culminating in the surrender of 248,000 men, marks the triumphant end of the great enterprise set on foot at Alamein and by the invasion of N.W. Africa. May the future reap in the utmost fullness the rewards of past achievements and new exertions.'[95]

The defeat in Tunisia shattered forever Mussolini's grandiose dream of a twentieth-century *Impero Romano*. The entire Italian Empire in Africa—Libya, Eritrea, Italian Somaliland, and Ethiopia—now lay firmly in the grip of the British. Rommel, a realist, conceded that the North African sector was irretrievably lost. In November 1943, Rommel was transferred to Normandy and designated 'General Inspector'. He was charged with fortifying the 'Atlantic Wall' to defend coastal France from the expected Anglo–American invasion and was later implicated in the 1944 assassination attempt on Hitler's life.

Karl Dönitz, commander-in-chief of the German Navy, journeyed to Rome at the Führer's behest on 12 May. After initial interviews with Admiral Riccardo and General Ambrosio, the *Grossadmiral* met with Mussolini at half-past eleven on the morning of 13 May. Dönitz noted his personal impression of the Duce, whom he described as 'well, optimistic, composed, very frank, sincere, and amicable'. His cordiality notwithstanding, the Duce rejected the offer—made by Dönitz on Hitler's behalf—of five German divisions to help repel a potential Allied assault on metropolitan Italy; three alone would suffice. 'These three divisions,' Mussolini elaborated, 'should include six armoured battalions with 300 tanks, two of which are slated for Sardinia, three for Sicily, and one for southern Italy.' Mussolini was convinced that of the three locales, it was Sicily that faced 'the greatest danger' of an Allied incursion.[96]

After dinner at 10 p.m., Dönitz also had an interview with Field Marshal Kesselring. In the latter's opinion, 'The fact that the Italian *Comando Supremo* had partially refused the Führer's offer of five divisions ... proves that the Italians want to remain masters in their own house.' As such, Kesselring deemed the rebuff 'an act of political importance'.[97]

Hitler drafted a strongly worded letter to Mussolini on 19 May, which was delivered by Kesselring to the Palazzo Venezia the following day. Hitler expressed his serious concerns regarding an expected Anglo–American invasion in the Balkans and the Italians' inability to repel the Allied incursion without German assistance:

> The observations which we have made from the air leave no doubt that the Allies are planning a large-scale invasion of the Mediterranean basin.... It is also clear from documents which have been found* that they also intend to invade the Peloponnese and will in fact do so. Neither the [Italian] High Command nor the Governor of Montenegro [General Pirzio Biroli] will be in a position to prevent such invasions single-handed. The Italian Second Army [in Croatia] is in no position, either from the point of view of equipment and armament or from that of training, to protect the Peloponnese and Greece in general from similar invasions. If the British attempts are to be prevented, as they must be at all costs, this can only be done by German divisions....
>
> As soon as any real danger of invasion appears within the next few days or weeks, a large number of German divisions must be sent immediately to the Peloponnese.[98]

Kesselring had also been tasked with extending an invitation to Mussolini for a summit meeting with the Führer in connection with the recent Axis loss of French Tunisia. It was to be held at once. The Duce, who was understandably disinclined under the circumstances, gave Kesselring a

* The Germans had been duped by Operation Mincemeat, a clever scheme concocted by the British. Phony invasion plans were planted on the corpse of a hobo dressed in a British naval officer's uniform. The body was deposited into the sea before daybreak on 30 April and was discovered several hours later off the coast of Spain. On 8 May, the Spanish turned over the spurious documents to the Germans, which indicated that the Western Allies intended to invade Greece (rather than Sicily, the Allies' actual target).

tergiversatory response ('There is always a host of problems which deserve handling'), then inquired of the field marshal the likely whereabouts of an Anglo–American incursion:

> MUSSOLINI: What do they say at the Führer's Headquarters on the possibilities of an enemy landing?
>
> KESSELRING: They consider one possible in Sicily, Sardinia, or Corsica.

Mussolini concurred, then alluded to the Soviets' desire for a second major front: 'Stalin insists on the opening of a new front (in the West), but this time a proper one, and not a secondary front.'[99] To Hitler's philippic, Mussolini sent a conciliatory reply, and he concluded his message with the following platitude: 'What really matters in these hard times, Führer, is to keep up the prestige of our armed forces, and concentrate the efforts of the Axis on striking down our common enemies and bring victory to our peoples.'[100]

Hitler at this time harboured grave misgivings concerning the reliability of the Italians, which he confided to his generals at Führer Headquarters on 20 May. Hitler believed there was a genuine possibility that the Fascist regime might crumble or that Mussolini might be deposed. Factors influencing Hitler's attitude included the Italians' plummeting morale and the increasingly anti-German mood of the Italian masses and soldiers. General Roatta, commander of the Italian Sixth Army, had recently advised, pessimistically, that 'he did not have too much confidence in the possibility of a defence of Sicily'. Hitler was particularly concerned that Italian forces lacked the resolve to defend Sicily in the event of aggressive Allied operations, and he declared: 'What does worry me is that they [the Italians] do not want to defend it: we can see this lack of determination. The Duce may have the best intentions, but they will be sabotaged.'[101] Hitler accordingly felt it necessity for contingency plans to be readied, and next day O.K.W. chief Keitel issued several operational plans for various fronts should Italy either conclude an armistice with the Allies or switch sides. The most important of these, Operation Alaric, entailed a speedy German occupation of metropolitan Italy by eleven divisions under Rommel.

On 18 May, the Allies initiated increasingly intensive aerial bombardments of Pantelleria. Situated between Tunisia and Sicily, the island stronghold was defended by 12,000 Italians under Vice-Admiral Gino Pavesi. The air offensive was undertaken to determine whether Pantelleria could be conquered without employing land forces. This proved to be unworkable, an amphibious invasion was carried out on 11

June, and the island was captured by British forces (Operation Corkscrew) without incident. The day prior, Pavesi had requested authorization to capitulate on the specious basis that his garrison lacked an adequate supply of water. Mussolini, who had accepted Pavesi's words at face value, granted the request. On 13 June, the neighbouring islands of Lampedusa and Linosa were also taken. As a result of Corkscrew, the Allies now possessed a foothold from which to launch operations against Sicily, 63 miles distant.

The Council of Ministers' final meeting during the Fascist era was held on 19 June. On this occasion, Ministers Vittorio Cini and Alfredo De Marsico broached with Mussolini Italy's options at this critical juncture of the war. The loss of Pantelleria weighed heavily on them. But to these inconvenient naysayers, Mussolini retorted: 'Any discussion is useless. Italy has only one alternative: to conquer or to fall at the side of Germany.'[102] Shortly thereafter, on 22 June, Cini composed Mussolini an honest letter expressing his grave misgivings concerning 'the gravity of the moment and ... the need for changing those methods which had produced such unfavourable results'.[103] His confidence in the Duce severely shaken, he requested that his resignation be accepted. Mussolini obliged him a month later, on 24 July.

On 24 June, Mussolini again received the Party Directorate at the Palazzo Venezia. The Duce's final speech as Italy's head of government, it was a peculiar, rambling address in which he vowed to those present that an attempted invasion of mainland Italy by the Anglo–Americans would be stopped at the shoreline:

> The enemy must play a card. He has proclaimed high and low that he will invade the Continent. This invasion must be attempted because otherwise the enemy would face defeat even before fighting. It is a card that once played cannot be played again. Caesar was able to invade Britannia a second time, after a storm destroyed his ships during the first attempt. Then again, one must distinguish between 'landing', which is possible, 'penetration', and finally, 'invasion'. Clearly this attempt will fail.... As soon as the enemy attempts to land, he must be frozen at the line the sailors call 'the water's edge', that line in the sand where the water stops and land begins...[104]

A week later, on 1 July, the Duce received Mihai Antonescu, Romania's foreign minister, in Rome. The Romanian statesman made a bold proposal: under an Italian initiative, four nations presently in league with Germany—Italy, Hungary, Romania, and Finland—would defect from the Axis, make peace with the Anglo–Americans, and exit the war. Only the

Duce, Antonescu felt, was capable of defying Hitler in this manner. But although Mussolini recognized the urgent necessity of extricating Italy from the war he was unwilling to act, for he feared the Führer's wrath.

Braving heavy winds and choppy seas, on the early morning of 10 July Anglo–American aerial and naval forces carried out an invasion of Sicily. This gigantic enterprise (Operation Husky) was surpassed in scale only by the D-Day landings at Normandy (Operation Overlord) eleven months later. On the Allied side, the operation involved 160,000 troops, 14,000 vehicles, 600 tanks, and 1,800 guns. The invasion force consisted of two armies: the American Seventh Army (under Lieutenant-General Patton) and the British Eighth Army (under General Montgomery). Confronting them were nine Italian divisions (315,000 men) and four German divisions (90,000 men). Over the course of the next five weeks, the Allies drove the enemy back to a small pocket in northeast Sicily. The stubborn Italo–German defenders took advantage of Sicily's rugged landscape to stage a protracted retreat. Palermo fell on 22 July. From the seaport of Messina, some 100,000 Axis troops (40,000 Germans, 60,000 Italians) successfully evacuated the island across the narrow Strait of Messina, only 2.5 miles wide, to the 'toe' of Italy. The Sicilian campaign lasted a total of thirty-eight days. As a result, the Allies regained significant control of the Mediterranean, and Allied convoys were able to resume their passage along trade routes.

Due to the rapid progress of the Allies in Sicily, Hitler began to perceive that Italian opposition to the enemy was half-hearted at best. He sent an irate letter to Mussolini via General Rintelen on 12 July warning that if Italian forces in Sicily refused to stand their ground, he would discontinue German aid. Instead of replying, Mussolini contacted Alfieri. He instructed the Italian ambassador to have Efisio Marras, the Italian military attaché in Berlin, seek an audience with the Führer at once to ask that German fighter planes be dispatched to Sicily, and to inform the Führer that without these reinforcements Sicily could not be held. But Hitler did not deign to respond; for the past week (as of 5 July) German forces had been engaged in offensive operations (Operation Citadel) on the Russian Front, at Kursk.

General Ambrosio advised Mussolini in a written communication two days later that Italy was finished. Three years of war-making had taken their toll. Despite being wholly unprepared for a general war, Italy had expended her limited resources in foreign arenas. Ambrosio contended that unless the establishment of another Allied front could be prevented, it would be left to the political leadership 'to consider whether it would be expedient to spare the country further sorrow and ruin, and to anticipate the end of the struggle, seeing that the final result will undoubtedly be worse in one or more years'.[105]

Propaganda leaflets containing an earnest joint message from Roosevelt and Churchill were dropped over Rome on 17 July (see Appendix D for the full text):

> At this moment the combined armed forces of the United States and Great Britain ... are carrying the war deep into the territory of your country. This is the direct consequence of the shameful leadership to which you have been subjected by Mussolini and his Fascist regime. Mussolini has carried you into this war as the satellite of a brutal destroyer of peoples and liberties. Mussolini plunged you into a war which he thought Hitler had already won. In spite of Italy's great vulnerability to attack by air and sea, your Fascist leaders sent your sons, your ships, your air forces, to distant battlefields to aid Germany in her attempt to conquer England, Russia, and the world....
>
> The time has now come for you, the Italian people, to consult your own self-respect and your own interests and your own desire for a restoration of national dignity, security, and peace. The time has come for you to decide whether Italians shall die for Mussolini and for Hitler—or live for Italy, and for civilization.[106]

For the harried Italian population, the leaflet's eloquent text could not have been more on the mark. Mussolini had failed to deliver on his promises. The grandeur of ancient Rome—its prestige, its power, its influence—none of this had materialized. Instead, the Italians had to endure countless hardships: the flower of their youth needlessly perishing at the fronts in the Balkans and Africa, their magnificent cities reduced to rubble, the total loss of their hard-won colonial possessions. The Italian masses had more than had their fill. Over a twenty-year period, Fascist propaganda had touted the enormous achievements of the regime: that the twentieth-century Italians had been transformed from an ineffectual and unmartial people into a regimented and dynamic mass. But this was not so; the Fascist regime was permeated with corruption, peculation, and cronyism. The efficiency and vigour attributed to the Fascist State was in actuality a myth. Meanwhile, the Italian homeland was being battered by Allied bombers, hunger was rife, and workers were striking in Turin and Milan.* The end was near, and the Allied invasions of North Africa and Sicily were the crowning blows to a tottering structure.

* On 5 March, Italian workers had gone on strike at the Fiat factory in Turin, and only after most of the workers' demands were met was the labour stoppage ended. Strikes had also occurred in Milan.

6

The Bloodless Coup, 1943

History—above all, modern history—has shown that a regime never falls for internal reasons. Moral questions, economic distress, party struggles never place a regime in jeopardy.... A regime, whatever regime it may be, falls only under the weight of defeat.[1]

Mussolini, from his *Memoirs*

The time had now come for Mussolini to face the consequences of his disastrous war policy. He alone was responsible for the Italian failures in Greece, Soviet Russia, North Africa, and now Sicily. It was none other than he who had forced an unprepared Italy into the war. The fault could not be attributed to the king, the Fascist Party, the Cabinet, or the *Comando Supremo*, and throughout the first half of 1943 the disapprobation of all these entities intensified as the crises both on the homefront and battlefront worsened. In an attempt to comb out the inconvenient naysayers and objectors, the Duce had in February dismissed most of his cabinet ministers. But this measure had changed little.

Two men in particular had both the ear and confidence of King Emmanuel III and his court. These were General Ambrosio, chief of the general staff; and the duke of Acquarone, minister of the royal house. Pietro d'Acquarone was the king's close confederate. For some time now he had served as an agent between the monarch, the anti-Fascists, and certain Fascist councillors whose faith in the Duce had long since eroded. All were plotting behind the scenes—one way or another—to oust Mussolini from power, topple the Fascist regime, and negotiate an armistice with the Western Allies. But the Duce still sat firmly in the saddle despite the fact that his stock worldwide had long since plummeted. No longer was he regarded by his contemporaries as Hitler's equal. Nevertheless, Mussolini had ruled for so long and the Fascist institutions were by this point such an ingrained part of the fabric of Italian society that the conspirators were uncertain of how to proceed against him.

The king, a circumspect man, considered that at the appropriate time Marshal Pietro Badoglio, the ex-chief of staff with whom he had kept in touch for many months, might be a suitable candidate for the premiership. Meanwhile, there were certain veteran Fascists who—in their own interests and those of the Party—sought to use the Grand Council* as the organ with which to legally depose the Duce. Thus there were two parallel conspiracies in the works: one involving the four principals Ambrosio, the duke of Acquarone, Badoglio, and the king; and a second involving certain disaffected Fascist leaders, chiefly Grandi,† Bottai, and Ciano.

The political crisis was now nearing its climax.

In a confidential meeting at the Villa Ada on 15 July, the king informed Badoglio that he was looking to him 'to eventually tak[e] over the administration in Italy'. Badoglio replied that he was 'in no way inclined to take over in any way the succession of Mussolini. He [Badoglio] would be prepared to exercise the powers of government [only] on the orders and full responsibility of the King, and would carry out to the letter his instructions.'[2]

Next day at 8 p.m. Mussolini was confronted by fifteen Fascist leaders at the Palazzo Venezia. These high *gerarchi*—save Grandi and Federzoni, who were in Bologna (and refused to attend), and Ciano, who was at Leghorn—insisted that he convoke a session of the Fascist Grand Council. The last session had been held in December 1939. In his *Memoirs*, Mussolini described the disagreeable encounter:

> Together with the Party Secretary [Carlo Scorza], Farinacci, De Bono, Giuriati, Teruzzi, Bottai, Acerbo, and De Cicco were present. I did not welcome this meeting much, as I did not care for meetings not prepared in advance with a regular agenda.
>
> The following spoke: De Bono, who asked me for details of the course of operations in Sicily; Farinacci, who pressed insistently for a convocation of the Grand Council as almost an absolute necessity to enable everyone to make himself heard; Bottai, who stressed the same subject,

* The Fascist Grand Council was the sole governmental body with the power to recommend to the sovereign that the prime minister be dismissed from office.

† Grandi had met with the king on 4 June. On that occasion, Emmanuel III—who did not wish to undertake any precipitous action without adhering strictly to the letter of the law—had advised him: 'The moment will come. I know that I can count on you. Leave your King to choose the opportune moment and in the meantime help me to obtain the constitutional means.'[3]

> 'not'—he said—'in order to evade our separate responsibilities but to assume them in full'; Giuriati, who made a harangue of a constitutional nature which he amplified in a long letter the next day; Scorza, who stressed the necessity of changing the men in command and replacing them with some of his own candidates (who later on showed a basely treacherous spirit); all of them, or nearly all, insisted on the necessity of convening the Grand Council, if only to enable me to inform the members of the highest assembly in the Regime of certain facts which could not be given to the general public.

At the meeting's conclusion—which, according to the Duce, had 'revealed nothing but a skeptical frame of mind all around'—Mussolini informed his interlocutors that he 'would convene the Grand Council in the second half of the month'.[4]

At a military conference on 17 July, Hitler discussed with his collaborators what needed to be done in order for the Axis 'to hold Italy'. To those present—Dönitz, Jodl, and Mackensen—Hitler spoke of 'the demoralization of the Italian Army'. Not surprisingly, the Führer was in favour of taking draconian steps to remedy the situation and weed out the shirkers and defeatists: 'Only very severe measures, like those applied by Stalin in 1941 or by the French in 1917 will be of any avail. If only individual units were affected, we could appeal to their sense of honour by offering medals etc., but the whole army is in a state of collapse and only barbaric measures can help to save the [Italian] nation.'[5]

On 18 July, after some alterations were made to lessen its severity, the Duce affixed his signature to a letter drafted by General Ambrosio and intended for Hitler. It was a reply to the Führer's accusation that Italian forces had offered inadequate resistance to the Allied invasion of Sicily, now in progress for more than a week. It read in part:

> The rapid success of the enemy landings in some parts of Sicily is not due to lack of courage of the troops defending the coastline but rather to the firepower and equipment the enemy was able to land, supported by large naval forces just a few miles off the coast and the limited capabilities of our own air force and artillery. The coastline defence did all it could with the weapons it had....
>
> With the continued worsening of the war in the Mediterranean, your generous help has been insufficient ... I cannot agree with your comments regarding the conduct of the Italian authorities ... I can assure you, Führer, that Italian forces in Sicily have always acted according to my orders, and continue to do their utmost for the defence of the island....

> My country's sacrifice should not have as its goal to delay the attack aimed at Germany. Germany is militarily and economically stronger than Italy: my country, which entered the war three years ahead of the agreed-upon date and following two other wars, has burned out its resources in Africa, Russia, and the Balkans.
>
> I think, Führer, that the time has come to carefully examine the situation together, to draw the necessary conclusions in the common interest and in the interests of each country.[6]

Unfortunately, this frank letter—which was long overdue—remained on file and was never sent. That same day Mackensen, on behalf the Reich Government, dispatched a communication to the Italians requesting a summit conference to be held in Italy at once. After the successful Allied invasions of Pantelleria and Sicily, Hitler considered it imperative to discuss with Mussolini Axis strategy for the defence of mainland Italy. The Duce agreed, and the German and Italian delegations met on 19 July at the Villa Gaggia, 'a labyrinthine building ... like a crossword puzzle frozen into a house', near the town of Feltre.[7] At the urging of his advisers, Mussolini had agreed to raise the issue of withdrawing Italy—now at the end of her tether—from the war, but once in Hitler's dominating presence failed to do so. Mussolini recalled the occasion:

> After a few moments' rest the talk began; the Führer, myself, Undersecretary Bastianini, the Ambassadors von Mackensen and Alfieri, the Italian Chief of General Staff Ambrosio, Marshal Keitel, General Rintelen, General Warlimont, Colonel Montezemolo and others less important were present.
>
> It was 11 a.m. when the Führer began to speak. He began his speech with a clear and systematic résumé of the raw material situation and the necessity for defending the territories where they were found. He went on to speak of the air force, its employment, and its present and future possibilities. Passing to the battle now being fought in Sicily he promised the dispatch of fresh reinforcements, particularly artillery and troops.
>
> The Führer had been speaking for half an hour when an official [De Cesare] entered the room. He was pale and agitated. He begged pardon for interrupting. He came up to me and said: 'At this moment Rome is undergoing a violent enemy air bombardment.' This news, which I myself conveyed aloud to the Führer and bystanders, made a deep and painful impression. During the rest of the Führer's résumé, news of the attack on Rome continued to come in. Then a talk took place between myself and Hitler in which I stressed the necessity of sending further aid to Italy. This talk continued on the return journey in the car and train. On parting from Hitler I said to him: 'Ours is a common cause, Führer!'[8]

Midway through the Feltre conference, during the pause for luncheon, three members of Mussolini's delegation—Ambrosio, Bastianini, and Alfieri—had approached the Duce to again insist that he inform Hitler of the necessity for Italy to exit the war. Ambrosio was especially emphatic, boldly giving Mussolini an ultimatum 'to get out of the war within fifteen days'. To the trio hounding him, Mussolini wearily replied:

> Perhaps you think that this problem has not been consciously in my mind for a long time.... I admit the hypothesis: to detach ourselves from Germany. It sounds so simple: one day, at a given hour, one sends a radio message to the enemy ... But with what consequences? The enemy rightly will insist on a capitulation. Are we ready to wipe out at one stroke a regime of twenty years and the results of a long bitter effort, to admit our first military and political defeat, to disappear from the world scene? It is so quickly said: detach ourselves from Germany.... What attitude will Hitler take? Perhaps you think that he would give us liberty of action?[9]

After the summit meeting, once the Führer's aircraft had taken flight from Treviso airfield, Mussolini's advisers confronted him once more. Mussolini declared: 'I had no need to make that speech to Hitler because, this time, he has firmly promised to send all the reinforcements which we need.' Shortly thereafter, inside the privacy of their railway car, Ambrosio vented his exasperation to Bastianini: 'Did you hear what he [the Duce] said to Hitler?... He asked him yet again for that war material which they will never send. He still deludes himself, and did not take my words seriously. He is mad, I tell you, mad.'[10]

According to the interpreter Schmidt, this meeting, the fourteenth between the Axis dictators, 'was one of the most depressing in which I have ever taken part. Mussolini himself was so overwrought that on his return to Rome he asked urgently for my report.'[11] So distracted was the Duce by news of the Allied air raid that he had been unable to absorb the substance of Hitler's lengthy exposition, and he needed Schmidt's meticulous notes for reference.

The Allied attack on Rome, the first of the war, had begun at 11:13 a.m. A large wave of American bomber aircraft thoroughly destroyed the San Lorenzo district, killing some 3,000 civilians. Subsequent targets, attacked that afternoon, included the Littorio and Ciampino airports. The Italians had not anticipated that the Allies would resort to bombing Europe's 'Eternal City' owing to its historic significance and innumerable artistic treasures.

In a communication to Pope Pius XII three days prior, Roosevelt had clarified:

> Attacks against Italy are limited, to the extent humanly possible, to military objectives. We have not and will not make warfare on civilians or against non-military objectives. In the event it should be found necessary for Allied planes to operate over Rome, our aviators are thoroughly informed as to the location of the Vatican and have been specifically instructed to prevent bombs from falling on Vatican City.[12]

But the British favoured an aerial attack upon Rome (as retaliation against the Italians for having partaken in the Blitz), and Churchill had approved.

Mussolini's aircraft left Treviso for Rome at 5:30 p.m. As it neared the Italian capital, the crew aboard observed that 'Rome seemed ... to be enveloped in a huge black cloud'. Hundreds of wagons in the Littorio railway station were aflame, the airport was wrecked, and the airfield was 'pitted with bomb craters'. As the airplane flew over Rome, rerouting to the Centocelle airport, 'one received the distinct impression that the attack had been heavy and the damage enormous'.[13]

Mussolini reflected ruefully upon the Allied air attack: 'One more illusion had vanished in smoke, namely, that Rome, the Holy City, would never be raided. That the best anti-aircraft artillery was the Vatican itself, that Myron Taylor had brought the Pope a guarantee to that effect from the American President ... all of that had been wiped out ...'[14]

The bombing of Rome was the very last straw. Coupled with the total loss of the Italian Empire in Africa and the imminent loss of Sicily to the Anglo–Americans, these events—the preliminaries to the Allied conquest of metropolitan Italy—would precipitate the end of the Fascist regime.

Next day Mussolini paid a visit to the Littorio railway station and airport, the University, and the Ciampino airport. The Duce was, according to his own version of events, 'received everywhere with demonstrations of sympathy'. But the fruitless meeting at Feltre continued to weigh heavily on his mind, and that evening Mussolini summoned General Ambrosio to his presence. The Duce advised his chief of staff that he intended to unreservedly inform the Führer in a letter of the necessity to disengage Italy from the war. Ambrosio heatedly replied that this was something the Duce should have done verbally at Feltre when he had the chance. Even if the letter were written, Ambrosio pointed out, it would invariably be discounted by the Germans. Frustrated by the Duce's lack of initiative he offered his resignation on the spot, but Mussolini refused to accept it.

Dino Grandi, Fascist statesman and former ambassador to Britain, had meanwhile returned to Rome from Bologna after deliberating with Luigi Federzoni, his close collaborator, upon which Fascist councillors they could rely. Grandi brought along with him a draft of the motion he planned to present to the Grand Council on 24 July. The resolution called for the restoration of all government entities and for the sovereign to resume command of the Italian Armed Forces (held by Mussolini since Italy's entry into the war in June 1940). Grandi met with Party Secretary Carlo Scorza early on 21 July and, upon the latter's request, provided him a copy. Scorza, however, did not hesitate to bring the document to the Duce's attention. Mussolini recalled in his *Memoirs*:

> On Wednesday at noon, the hour of the usual report, the Party Secretary Scorza presented me with a motion which Grandi and others proposed to present in the Grand Council. I read the document ... and handed it back to Scorza declaring that the document was inadmissible and contemptible. Scorza put it back in his briefcase and did not insist further. It was on that occasion that Scorza made me a rather ambiguous speech in which he spoke of a 'shocker' or rather 'super-shocker' which might be in store, a speech to which I did not attribute great importance.[15]

Mussolini called on the king the following day to relate the particulars of the Feltre conference. According to the Duce, that morning Emmanuel III was 'frowning and nervous'. The king spoke gloomily on the present state of affairs:

> A tense situation. It can't go on much longer. Sicily has gone west now. The Germans will double-cross us. The discipline of the troops has broken down. The airmen at Ciampino fled as far as Velletri [some ten miles away] during the attack. They call it 'dispersing'. I followed the attack the other day from the Villa Ada over which the wave of planes passed. I don't think there were 400 aircraft as they said. There were half that number. The 'Holy City' legend is over. We must tell the Germans our dilemma ...[16]

Mussolini replied that he intended to detach Italy from the Axis by 15 September! But considering the wretched military and political circumstances, this late date, nearly eight weeks away, was wholly unrealistic. Matters would come to a head long before then.

Prior to the council session, Grandi conferred with many leading Fascists, including (but not limited to) Bastianini, Bottai, Ciano, De Bono, De Marsico, De Stefani, De Vecchi, and Federzoni. And to cover all his bases—that is, to avoid the appearance of conspiracy—Grandi also requested an appointment with the Duce. Its purpose was for Grandi to make one final attempt to convince Mussolini to step down of his own volition before calling for a vote of no-confidence against him, for if the Duce resigned it would obviate the need for a special session of the council. A scant fifteen minutes had been allotted for the interview, scheduled for 5 p.m. on 22

July, but it ended up lasting over an hour. During the conversation, Grandi unsparingly informed Mussolini of the contents of his motion. When Grandi finished his spiel, Mussolini—who had permitted his ex-cabinet minister to speak uninterruptedly—calmly answered:

> You will repeat everything you just told me at the meeting of the Grand Council. It could be useful to the country if it is in fact true that the war is lost. I cannot reveal to you some extremely important military secrets; but just be aware that very soon Germany will come out with an extremely powerful secret weapon* that will completely reverse the course of the war. Germany and Italy will win this war. Everything else we shall discuss at the Grand Council.[17]

The interview concluded, Mussolini welcomed his next caller, Field Marshal Kesselring, who had been patiently waiting for his audience with the Duce, which was now overdue. Mussolini apologized to Kesselring for the inconvenience, then commented: 'Do you know Grandi, who has just been with me? We have had a good talk and are in general agreement. He is completely loyal to me.'[18]

Mussolini apparently did not think highly of his Fascist councillors at all. To Lorenzo Chierici, chief of police, he stated in confidence:

> Believe me … these Grand Council members are of low, very low intelligence, wobbly in their convictions, and without much courage. These people live in someone else's shadow; if the source of light should disappear, they too would be cast back into the darkness from whence they came … they just want to believe that I can easily bring back to the stable a Grandi, a Bottai, and even Count Ciano, who I feel is being too obvious in his impatience to replace me.[19]

'At a certain point' during the final days leading up to the deposition of Mussolini, Grandi cunningly proposed deferring the session of the Grand Council—'a clever move to look like an alibi'. But when Scorza inquired of the Duce by telephone whether this was workable, Mussolini stated with firm decision that there could be no delay: 'It was now absolutely essential to reach a general clarification of the position. The date had been fixed. The invitations had been issued. Of all the constitutional organs … the Grand Council was the most suitable for reviewing the problems of war in the light of recent events such as the invasion of national soil.'[20]

* Mussolini was here referring to the German V-2 rockets, of which Hitler had recently informed him. These were long-range supersonic missiles armed with a 2,200-lb warhead.

In Berlin, news of the Italian political crisis had, somewhat belatedly, become known. In his *Diary*, Goebbels noted:

> In the course of the day we received confidential information that a certain change was taking place in Italian domestic politics.... The Old Guard Fascists have requested the Duce to call a meeting of the Fascist Grand Council. At this meeting ... the Duce is to be requested to initiate more energetic policies. He is to be persuaded to get rid of the burden of holding so many offices so that he may regain his initiative and strength for guiding the over-all policies and the war effort of Italy.[21]

The Fascist Grand Council convened what would be their final session at 5 p.m. on 24 July. 'The nervous tension,' Mussolini later wrote, 'became more and more acute. On the afternoon of Saturday, 24 July, Rome turned pale. Cities as well as men have a face, and the emotions of the soul are reflected on that face. Rome felt that something serious was in the air.'[22] Prior to the assemblage 'precautionary measures' had been taken by the authorities. Mussolini's private musketeers, who performed guard duty at the Palazzo Venezia, were relieved of their duties by Umberto Albini, undersecretary of the interior. Albini also ensured that the Palazzo Venezia was staffed with armed policemen to prevent any insurrectionary acts by Blackshirts. Mussolini himself was not unduly concerned about the session's outcome, for since its inception the Fascist Grand Council had been a rubber-stamp entity wholly under his control. Nor was he troubled by any thought of the Sovereign, and prior to the council session the Duce had confided to General Galbiati: 'I have never done anything without his [Emmanuel III's] complete agreement. For over twenty years I have been to see him once or twice a week, and have consulted him on every matter of State and even private questions. He has always been solidly with me.'[23]

Mussolini, with a sheaf of documents before him, began with these introductory words in his own defence:

> The war has reached an extremely critical stage. What seemed impossible (and indeed was thought by some to be an absurd hypothesis) even after the entry of the United States into the Mediterranean, has come to pass—the invasion of our home territory. From this point of view, one may say that the real war began with the loss of Pantelleria. The peripheral war on the African coast was intended to avert or frustrate such an eventuality. In a situation like this, all official or unofficial trends of opinion openly or clandestinely hostile to the Regime make common cause against us, and they have already provoked symptoms of demoralization even among the ranks of Fascism, particularly among the 'vested

> interests', that is, among those who see their own personal positions threatened. At this moment I am certainly the most intensely disliked or, rather, loathed man in Italy, which is only natural on the part of the ignorant, suffering, victimized, under-nourished masses subjected to the terrible physical and moral burden of the 'Liberator' raids and to the suggestions of enemy propaganda. Political and military circles aim their sharpest criticisms at those who bear the responsibility for the military conduct of the war. Let it be said once and for all that I did not in the least desire the delegation of Command of the Armed Forces in the Field given to me by the King on 10 June. That initiative belongs to Marshal Badoglio.[24]

The Duce sought to reassure the assembled councillors, who were clad 'in black Saharan uniform', that he would take matters in hand:

> War is always a party war, a war of the party which desired it; it is always one man's war, the war of the man who declared it; if today this is called Mussolini's war, in 1859 it could have been called Cavour's war. This is the moment to tighten the reins and to assume the necessary responsibility. I shall have no difficulty in replacing men, in turning the screw, in bringing forces to bear not yet engaged, in the name of our country whose territorial integrity is today being violated.[25]

Thereupon Grandi addressed the councillors. He harshly censured 'the activity of the Party', then came to the crux of the matter:

> My motion would tend towards the creation of a 'national home front' which has not existed so far, and which has not existed because the Crown in Italy has held aloof in an attitude of prudent reserve. It is high time for the King to emerge from obscurity and assume his responsibilities. After Caporetto* he took up position and launched an appeal to the nation. Today he is silent. Either he assumes his share of historical responsibility, in which case he has the right to remain Head of the State, or else he does not, in which case he will show how much the dynasty is worth.

Mussolini characterized Grandi's speech as 'a violent philippic: the speech of a man who was at last giving vent to a long-cherished rancour'.[26]

* The Battle of Caporetto. In the autumn of 1917, the Italian Army had sustained a tremendous defeat by German and Austro–Hungarian forces.

Next it was Ciano's turn. The ex-foreign minister summarized Italy's 'diplomatic history' in order to demonstrate that Italy was not responsible for the war and, on the contrary, had done all within her power to avert it. Ciano—his faith in Mussolini severely strained—concluded by stating that he was in accord with Grandi's resolution.

The deliberations continued 'in an exceedingly tense atmosphere'. At midnight, Scorza recommended that the councillors adjourn for the night, but Grandi was vehemently opposed to this suggestion. He arose and shouted: 'No! I am against the proposal. We have started this business and we must finish it this very night!'[27] It was after 2 a.m. when the historic vote affirming Grandi's resolution was finally held. Mussolini bitterly recalled the event: 'The position of each member of the Grand Council could be discerned even before the voting: there was a group of traitors who had already negotiated with the Crown, a group of accomplices, and a group of uninformed who probably did not realize the seriousness of the vote. But they voted just the same!'[28]

Scorza read aloud Grandi's motion. It was fairly brief. First Grandi extolled 'the heroic warriors of every Service who, shoulder to shoulder with the proud people of Sicily ... are renewing the noble traditions of hardy valour and undaunted spirit of self-sacrifice of our glorious Armed Forces'. Next Grandi sought 'the immediate restoration ... of all State functions, allotting to the King, the Grand Council, the Government, Parliament, and the Corporations the tasks and responsibilities laid down by our [pre-Fascist] statutory and constitutional laws'. And finally Grandi requested Mussolini to invite King Emmanuel III 'to assume, together with the effective command of the Armed Forces on land, sea, and in the air, according to Article 5[*] of the Statute of the Realm, that supreme initiative of decision which our institutions attribute to him ...'[29]

Scorza next polled each Fascist councillor[†] individually by name. Nineteen voted 'Yes', seven voted 'No', one abstained (Giacomo Suardo), and one was in favour of an unexpected motion of his own (Roberto Farinacci). Thereupon Mussolini stood and spoke gravely: 'You have provoked a crisis of the Regime. The Session is closed.' But when Scorza, adhering to procedural formalities, attempted to give the 'Salute to the Duce' Mussolini interrupted him with a movement of his hand and said: 'No, you are excused.'[30]

* Article 5 of the *Statuto del Regno* (1848) granted the king, as the supreme head of state, all executive power.

† The Fascist councillors in favour of Grandi's motion were: Giacomo Acerbo, Umberto Albini, Dino Alfieri, Giovanni Balella, Giuseppe Bastianini, Annio Bignardi, Giuseppe Bottai, Tullio Cianetti, Galeazzo Ciano, Emilio De Bono, Alfredo De Marsico, Alberto De Stefani, Cesare Maria De Vecchi, Luigi Federzoni, Luciano Gottardi, Dino Grandi, Giovanni Marinelli, Carluccio Pareschi, Edmondo Rossoni.

The Fascist councillors opposed to Grandi's motion were: Carlo Biggini, Guido Buffarini–Guidi, Ettore Frattari, Enzo Galbiati, Gaetano Polverelli, Carlo Scorza, and Antonino Tringali–Casanova.

With the proceedings concluded, the Fascist councillors took their leave at 2:40 a.m. Many were shaken. Mussolini withdrew to his study where, moments later, he was joined by those councillors who had opposed Grandi's motion. At 3 a.m. Mussolini left the Palazzo Venezia. Party Secretary Scorza, loyal to his chief, accompanied the Duce to his private residence, the Villa Torlonia.

Following his usual routine—from which he had not deviated in over two decades—Mussolini returned to his office at the Palazzo Venezia at 9 a.m. He was unruffled, for although a substantial number of his closest adherents had directly challenged his rule, the Fascist Grand Council was, in the final analysis, an advisory body. Its recommendations were not binding upon him, and Mussolini believed that the king would back him. He was soon to be disabused of this notion.

In spite of the extraordinary rumours swirling about in connection with the ten-hour Council session, the city was quiet. On Mussolini's desk was a desperate letter from Tullio Cianetti, minister of corporations since April. The minister had had second thoughts, and in his apologetic message he conveyed to the Duce his regret for having cast a vote against him. He had not, he claimed, understood at the time the full ramifications of Grandi's motion, and he tendered his resignation. Mussolini did not deign to reply. Meanwhile Grandi, the Fascist 'Judas', had disappeared and could not be located.

Umberto Albini, undersecretary of the interior, arrived at approximately 11 a.m. to bring Mussolini 'the usual morning post containing news of the last twenty-four hours'. Looking over the material, the Duce noticed that 'the most important and regrettable item was the first heavy raid on Bologna'. Once finished with the daily reports, Mussolini turned to Albini:

> MUSSOLINI (incisively): Why did you vote for Grandi's motion last night? You are a guest, not a member of the Grand Council.
>
> ALBINI (flustered): I may have made a mistake, but no one could possibly doubt my absolute devotion to you, a devotion not merely of today but of all time.

And as Albini hastily withdrew from the room, Mussolini observed that 'his livid face revealed him as a self-confessed traitor'.[31] Mussolini then ordered his private secretary to inquire of Major-General Paolo Puntoni, aide-de-camp to the king, when that afternoon the king would see him. Over the telephone Puntoni advised that Emmanuel III would grant the Duce an audience at the Villa Ada at 5 p.m.

Mussolini conducted his political business as usual, and in the early afternoon he received Shinrokuru Hidaka, the Japanese ambassador, to whom he related the substance of his talks with Hitler at Feltre. After the interview, Mussolini, together with General Enzo Galbiati, commander of the Blackshirts, paid a visit to the Tiburtino quarter. The latter had sustained severe damage during the recent Allied bombardment, and upon arrival the Duce was enthusiastically applauded by the locals. He returned to the Villa Torlonia at 3 p.m. His wife Donna Rachele sensed danger, however, and urged him not to call upon the king, whom she considered untrustworthy. But the Duce still believed the king to be his ally.

At precisely five o'clock Mussolini, accompanied by his private secretary (De Cesare), arrived at the royal residence for his scheduled appointment. Mussolini noticed an abundance of *Carabinieri* present but under the circumstances did not deem it unusual. Emmanuel III, clad in military garb, received him at the door. Both men moved into the drawing-room. There ensued the final exchange between the Italian monarch and the Fascist Duce. Mussolini observed that the elderly king was 'in a state of abnormal agitation':

> EMMANUEL III: My dear Duce, it's no longer any good. Italy has gone to bits. Army morale is at rock bottom. The soldiers don't want to fight anymore. The Alpine regiments are singing a song which says they don't want to make war on Mussolini's account any longer.... The Grand Council's vote is terrific—nineteen votes for Grandi's motion and among them four holders of the Order of the Annunciation. You can certainly be under no illusion as to Italy's feelings with regard to yourself. At this moment you are the most hated man in Italy. You can no longer count on more than one friend. You have one friend left you, and I am he. That is why I tell you that you need have no fears for your personal safety, for which I will ensure protection. I have been thinking the man for the job is Marshal Badoglio. He will start by forming a government of experts for purely administrative purposes and for the continuation of the war. In six months' time we shall see. All Rome already knows about the Grand Council's resolution, and they are all expecting a change.
>
> MUSSOLINI: You are taking an extremely grave decision. A crisis at the moment would mean making the people think that peace was in sight, once the man who declared war had been dismissed. The blow to the Army's morale would be serious. If the soldiers—*Alpini* or not—don't want to make war for Mussolini any more, that doesn't matter, so long as they are prepared to do it for you. The crisis would be considered a triumph for the Churchill–Stalin set-up, especially for the latter, who would see the retirement of an antagonist who has fought against him for twenty years. I realize the people's hatred. I had no difficulty in recognizing it last night in the midst of the Grand Council. One can't govern

> for such a long time and impose so many sacrifices without provoking resentments more or less temporary or permanent. In any case, I wish good luck to the man who takes the situation in hand.[32]

The climactic interview had been brief. At precisely 5:20 p.m., Emmanuel III walked Mussolini to the door; the face of the former 'was livid and he looked smaller than ever, almost dwarfish'. The men shook hands a last time and the king withdrew inside. Mussolini walked down the front steps and approached his car. Just then a *Carabinieri* officer, Captain Vigneri, unexpectedly accosted Mussolini. He informed the Duce that the king had tasked him 'with the protection of your person'. But when Mussolini continued on towards his vehicle, the captain indicated an ambulance parked nearby and said, 'No. We must get in there.'[33]

Without further ado, Mussolini and De Cesare climbed into the ambulance, as did the captain, a lieutenant, three *Carabinieri*, and two plainclothes policemen. The ambulance, its door under guard, departed 'at top speed' to a *Carabinieri* barracks at Trastevere. Mussolini was under the impression that these measures were being taken for his safety. In actuality he had been taken into custody and was a prisoner, and it was not long before he perceived the truth.

Afterwards, Mussolini blamed the sovereign for conspiring to depose him, and it is evident that he held a strong grudge: 'The King,' Mussolini wrote spitefully in his *Memoirs*, 'was behind this plot because he had reason to believe that a victory won or snatched from defeat by Fascism would make him more insignificant than ever. For twenty years he had been awaiting a good opportunity. He was waiting until a certain national frame of mind had been reached, a popular and universal emotion which at a given moment would flare up a word.'[34]

Meanwhile, the king had entrusted Badoglio—in spite of the aged marshal's lack of political experience—with the formation of a new non-Fascist government composed of military men and civilian functionaries. At 10:45 p.m. Rome Radio broadcast to the nation the sensational news: Mussolini had 'resigned' as prime minister and the king had appointed Marshal Badoglio his successor! The war, however, would go on. Two proclamations followed, one by Emmanuel III and another by Badoglio. The latter read:

> Italians! By order of His Majesty the King and Emperor, I assume the military government of the country with plenary powers.
>
> The war continues. Although severely stricken in its invaded provinces, in its destroyed cities, Italy remains loyal to its plighted word, in proud defence of its thousand-year-long traditions.

> Let all ranks close around His Majesty the King and Emperor, who is the living image of the fatherland and an example for everyone.
>
> The charge given me is clear and precise. It will be scrupulously executed, and whoever deludes himself into thinking that he can impede its normal development, or attempts to disturb the public order, will be struck down inexorably.
>
> Long live Italy! Long live the King![35]

Soon thereafter all Fascist organizations including the Party, Grand Council, Chamber of Fasces and Corporations, and Special Tribunal for the Defence of the State were dissolved and high Fascist officials removed from office. ‘Fascism fell,’ Badoglio wrote afterwards, ‘like a rotten pear.’[36] On Badoglio’s initiative, Italy signed an armistice with the Allies at Cassibile on 3 September. News of the armistice was publicized five days later in an Allied broadcast. The Germans, who had anticipated Italy’s defection from the Axis, took immediate action and from 8 to 12 September occupied the northern half of metropolitan Italy, including Rome (Operation Axis). A month later, on 13 October, Italy declared war on Germany.

And what of the Duce? Over the course of several weeks, Mussolini was continually relocated by the authorities—from the islands of Ponza and La Maddalena to the Hotel Campo Imperatore in Gran Sasso. He was rescued therefrom on 12 September by German *Fallschirmjäger* (paratroopers) and *Waffen*-S.S. commandos in a daring raid (Operation Oak), installed at Salò on 23 September as the nominal head of a neo-Fascist puppet regime (the Italian Social Republic), and on 28 April 1945 summarily executed by Italian partisans while *en route* to Switzerland with his mistress Clara Petacci and other leading Fascist personages.

APPENDIX A

The Pact of Steel and Secret Additional Protocol, 22 May 1939

The German Reich Chancellor and His Majesty the King of Italy and Albania, Emperor of Ethiopia, consider that the time has come to confirm through a solemn pact the close relation of friendship and affinity which exists between National Socialist Germany and Fascist Italy.

Since a secure bridge for mutual help and assistance has been established through the common boundary between Germany and Italy, fixed for all time, the two Governments acknowledge anew the principles and aims of the policy previously agreed upon by them, and which has shown itself successful in furthering the interests of the two countries as well as in ensuring the peace of Europe.

Firmly bound together through the inner unity of their ideologies and the comprehensive solidarity of their interests, the German and the Italian people are determined also in future to stand side by side and to strive with united effort for the securing of their *Lebensraum* [living space] and the maintenance of peace. In this way, prescribed for them by history, Germany and Italy wish, in a world of unrest and disintegration, to carry out the assignment of making safe the foundations of European culture. In order to establish these principles in treaty form, they have named as plenipotentiaries, the German Reich Chancellor, the Minister of Foreign Affairs, von Ribbentrop, His Majesty the King of Italy and Albania, Emperor of Ethiopia, the Minister of Foreign Affairs, Count Galeazzo Ciano, who, after the exchange of proper credentials, have agreed upon the following terms:

Article I

The Contracting Parties will remain in permanent contact with each other, in order to come to an understanding of all common interests or the European situation as a whole.

Article II

In the event that the common interests of the Contracting Parties be jeopardized through international happenings of any kind, they will immediately enter into consultation regarding the necessary measures to preserve these interests. Should the security or other vital interests of one of the Contracting Parties be threatened from outside, the other Contracting Party will afford the threatened Party its full political and diplomatic support in order to remove this threat.

Article III

If it should happen, against the wishes and hopes of the Contracting Parties, that one of them becomes involved in military complications with another Power or other Powers, the other Contracting Party will immediately step to its side as an ally and will support it with all its military might on land, at sea, and in the air.

Article IV

In order to ensure, in any given case, the rapid implementation of the alliance obligations of Article III, the Governments of the two Contracting Parties will further intensify their cooperation in the military sphere and the sphere of war economy. Similarly the two Governments will keep each other regularly informed of other measures necessary for the practical implementation of this pact. The two Governments will create standing commissions, under the direction of the Foreign Ministers, for the purposes indicated in paragraphs 1 and 2.

Article V

The Contracting Parties already at this point bind themselves, in the event of a jointly waged war, to conclude any armistice or peace only in full agreement with each other.

Article VI

The two Contracting Parties are aware of the importance of their joint relations to the Powers which are friendly to them. They are determined to maintain these relations in future and to promote the adequate development of the common interests which bind them to these Powers.

Article VII

This pact comes into force immediately upon its signing. The two Contracting Parties are agreed upon fixing the first period of its validity at ten years. In good time before the elapse of this period they will come to an agreement regarding the extension of the validity of the pact.

SECRET ADDITIONAL PROTOCOL

On signing the friendship and alliance pact, agreement has been established by both parties on the following points:

1. The two Foreign Ministers will as quickly as possible come to an agreement on the organization, the seat, and the methods of work on the pact of the commissions on military questions and questions of war economy as stipulated in Article IV of the pact.

2. For the execution of Article IV, par. 2, the two Foreign Ministers will as quickly as possible arrange the necessary measures, guaranteeing a constant cooperation, conforming to the spirit and aims of the pact, in matters of the press, the news service and the propaganda. For this purpose in particular, each of the two Foreign Ministers will assign to the embassy of his country in the respective capital one or several especially well-experienced specialists, for constant discussion in direct close cooperation with the responsible Ministry of Foreign Affairs, of the suitable steps to be taken in matters of the press, the news service and the propaganda for the promotion of the policy of the Axis, and as a countermeasure against the policy of the enemy powers.

Berlin, 22 May 1939 in the XVII year of the Fascist Era.[1]

APPENDIX B

The Tripartite Pact, 27 September 1940

The Governments of Germany, Italy, and Japan consider it as a condition precedent of a lasting peace, that each nation of the world be given its own proper place. They have therefore decided to stand together and to cooperate with one another in their efforts in Greater East Asia and in the regions of Europe, wherein it is their prime purpose to establish and maintain a new order of things calculated to promote the prosperity and welfare of the peoples there. Furthermore, it is the desire of the three Governments to extend this cooperation to such nations in other parts of the world as are inclined to give to their endeavours a direction similar to their own, in order that their aspirations towards world peace as the ultimate goal may thus be realized. Accordingly, the Governments of Germany, Italy, and Japan have agreed as follows:

Article 1.

Japan recognizes and respects the leadership of Germany and Italy in the establishment of a new order in Europe.

Article 2.

Germany and Italy recognize and respect the leadership of Japan in the establishment of a new order in Greater East Asia.

Article 3.

Germany, Italy, and Japan agree to cooperate in their efforts on the aforesaid basis. They further undertake to assist one another with all political, economic, and military means, if one of the three Contracting Parties is attacked by a Power at present not involved in the European war or in the Chinese–Japanese conflict.

Article 4.

For the purpose of implementing the present pacts, joint technical commissions, the members of which are to be appointed by the Governments of Germany, Italy, and Japan, will meet without delay.

Article 5.

Germany, Italy, and Japan affirm that the aforesaid terms do not in any way affect the political status which exists at present between each of the three Contracting Parties and Soviet Russia.

Article 6.

The present Pact shall come into force immediately upon signature and shall remain in force for ten years from the date of its coming into force.

At the proper time before expiration of the said term the High Contracting Parties shall, if one of them so requests, enter into negotiations for its renewal.

In faith whereof, the undersigned, duly authorized by their Governments, have signed this pact and have hereunto apposed their seals.

Done in 3 original copies at Berlin, on the 27th day of September 1940, in the XVIIIth year of the Fascist Era, corresponding to the 27th day of the 9th month of the 15th year of the Showa Era.[2]

APPENDIX C

The Italian Ultimatum to Greece, 28 October 1940

The Italian Government has repeatedly noted how, in the course of the present conflict, the Greek Government assumed and maintained an attitude which was contrary not only with that of formal, peaceful, good neighbourly relations between two nations but also with the precise duties which were incumbent on the Greek Government in view of its status as a neutral country.

On various occasions the Italian Government has found it necessary to urge the Greek Government to observe these duties and to protest against the systematic violation, particularly serious since the Greek Government permitted its territorial waters, its coasts and its ports to be used by the British Fleet in the course of its war operations, aided in supplying the British air forces and permitted organization of a military information service in the Greek archipelago to Italy's damage.

The Greek Government was perfectly aware of these facts, which several times formed the basis of diplomatic representations on the part of Italy to which the Greek Government, which should have taken consideration of the grave consequences of its attitude, failed to respond with any measure for the protection of its own neutrality, but, instead, intensified its activities favouring the British Armed Forces and its cooperation with Italy's enemies.

The Italian Government has proof that this cooperation was foreseen by the Greek Government and was regulated by understandings of a military, naval, and aeronautical character. The Italian Government does not refer only to the British guarantee accepted by Greece as a part of the program of action against Italy's security but also to explicit, precise engagements undertaken by the Greek Government to put at the disposal of powers at war with Italy important strategic positions on Greek territory, including air bases in [Thessaly] and Macedonia designed for attack on Albanian territory.

In this connection the Italian Government must remind the Greek Government of the provocative activities carried out against the Albanian nation, together with the terroristic policy it has adopted towards the people of Ciamuria and the persistent efforts to create disorders beyond its frontiers.

For these reasons, also, the Italian Government has accepted the necessity, even though futilely, of calling the attention of the Greek Government to the inevitable consequences of its policy towards Italy. This can no longer be tolerated by Italy.

Greek neutrality has been tending continuously towards a mere shadow. Responsibility for this situation lies primarily on the shoulders of Great Britain and its aim to involve ever more countries in war.

But now it is obvious that the policy of the Greek Government has been and is directed towards transforming Greek territory, or at least permitting Greek territory to be transformed, into a base for war operations against Italy.

This could only lead to armed conflict between Italy and Greece, which the Italian Government has every intention of avoiding.

The Italian Government, therefore, has reached the decision to ask the Greek Government, as a guarantee of Greek neutrality and as a guarantee of Italian security, for permission to occupy with its own armed forces several strategic points in Greek territory for the duration of the present conflict with Great Britain.

The Italian Government asks the Greek Government not to oppose this occupation and not to obstruct the free passage of the troops carrying it out.

These troops do not come as enemies of the Greek people and the Italian Government does not in any way intend that the temporary occupation of several strategic points, dictated by special necessities of a purely defensive character, should compromise Greek sovereignty and independence.

The Italian Government asks that the Greek Government give immediate orders to military authorities that this occupation may take place in a peaceful manner. Wherever the Italian troops may meet resistance this resistance will be broken by armed force, and the Greek Government would have the responsibility for the resulting consequences.[3]

APPENDIX D

Text of a Leaflet Dropped by Allied Aircraft Over Rome, 17 July 1943

This is a message to the Italian people from the President of the United States of America and the Prime Minister of Great Britain.

At this moment the combined armed forces of the United States and Great Britain, under the command of General Eisenhower and his Deputy General Alexander, are carrying the war deep into the territory of your country. This is the direct consequence of the shameful leadership to which you have been subjected by Mussolini and his Fascist regime. Mussolini carried you into this war as the satellite of a brutal destroyer of peoples and liberties. Mussolini plunged you into a war which he thought Hitler had already won. In spite of Italy's great vulnerability to attack by air and sea, your Fascist leaders sent your sons, your ships, your air forces, to distant battlefields to aid Germany in her attempt to conquer England, Russia, and the world. This association with the designs of Nazi-controlled Germany was unworthy of Italy's ancient traditions of freedom and culture—traditions to which the peoples of America and Great Britain owe so much. Your soldiers have fought, not in the interests of Italy, but for Nazi Germany. They have fought courageously, but they have been betrayed and abandoned by the Germans on the Russian Front and on every battlefield in Africa from El Alamein to Cape Bon.

Today Germany's hopes for world conquest have been blasted on all fronts. The skies over Italy are dominated by the vast air armadas of the United States and Great Britain. Italy's sea-coasts are threatened by the greatest accumulation of British and Allied sea-power ever concentrated in the Mediterranean. The forces now opposed to you are pledged to destroy the power of Nazi Germany, which has ruthlessly been used to inflict slavery, destruction, and death on all those who refuse to recognize the Germans as the master race.

The sole hope for Italy's survival lies in honourable capitulation to the overwhelming power of the military forces of the United Nations. If you continue to tolerate the Fascist regime, which serves the evil power of the Nazis, you must suffer the consequences of your own choice. We take no satisfaction in invading Italian soil and bringing the tragic devastation of war home to the Italian people; but we are determined to destroy the false leaders and their doctrines which have brought Italy to her present position. Every moment that you resist the combined forces of the United Nations—every drop of blood that you sacrifice—can serve only one purpose: to give the Fascist and Nazi leaders a little more time to escape from the inevitable consequences of their own crimes. All your interests and all your traditions have been betrayed by Germany and your own false and corrupt leaders; it is only by disavowing both that a reconstituted Italy can hope to occupy a respected place in the family of European nations.

The time has now come for you, the Italian people, to consult your own self-respect and your own interests and your own desire for a restoration of national dignity, security, and peace. The time has come for you to decide whether Italians shall die for Mussolini and Hitler—or live for Italy, and for civilization.

ROOSEVELT
CHURCHILL[4]

APPENDIX E

Excerpt of Hitler's Military Conference, 25 July 1943

HITLER: Do you know about the developments in Italy?

KEITEL: No, I just heard the end of your discussion.

HITLER: The Duce has resigned. It is not confirmed yet. Badoglio has taken over the government....

KEITEL: Voluntarily, my Führer?

HITLER: Probably by request of the King, under pressure of the Court. I told you yesterday about the attitude of the King.

JODL: Badoglio has taken over the government.

HITLER: Badoglio, our most bitter enemy, has taken over the government....

JODL: The decisive thing is: are the Italians going to continue fighting, or not?

HITLER: They say they will fight, but it is certainly treachery. We must realize that this is open treachery. I'm just waiting for information about what the Duce says. What's-his-name wants to speak to the Duce now. I hope he'll get hold of him. I want the Duce to come here right away if he can get hold of him. I want the Duce to come to Germany right away.

JODL: If there is any doubt, there is only one thing to do.

HITLER: I have been thinking about ordering the 3rd Panzergrenadier Division to occupy Rome and to capture the whole government....

JODL: We really ought to wait for exact reports about what is going on.

HITLER: Certainly, but still we have to plan ahead. Undoubtedly, in their treachery, they will proclaim that they will remain loyal to us; but that is treachery. Of course they won't remain loyal.

KEITEL: Has anyone spoken to this fellow Badoglio?

HITLER: In the meantime we've received the following report. Yesterday the Duce was with the Grand Council. At the Grand Council there were Grandi, whom I have always called a swine, Bottai, and above all Ciano. They spoke against Germany at this Council; and specifically that there was no sense in continuing the war and that one must try to extricate Italy in one way or another. A few were opposed. Farinacci *et cetera* were probably also against that, but not so effectively as those who spoke for such a move. This evening the Duce let Mackensen know that he would certainly take up this battle and not capitulate. Then I suddenly heard that Badoglio wanted to speak to Mackensen. Mackensen told him that he had nothing to say to him. Thereupon Badoglio became even more insolent and finally sent a man—

HEWEL: Mackensen sent one of his men to Badoglio.

HITLER: He [Badoglio] said that the King had just charged him with the formation of a government after the Duce had laid down his office.... Now the minister [Ribbentrop] has ordered Mackensen to call at the Foreign Office. He will probably get the official announcement there. I assume that all of this is correct. Secondly, the minister wants to know if I agree that Mackensen should go to see the Duce immediately. I told him that Mackensen should go to see him right away, and try to persuade the Duce to come to Germany. I would assume that he wants to talk to me. If the Duce comes, that is all right. If he won't come, then I don't know. If the Duce will come to Germany and will talk to me, that is a good sign. If he doesn't come, or if he isn't able to get away, or if he resigns because he doesn't feel well, which wouldn't surprise me with such a bunch of traitors—then one doesn't know. Although that so-and-so [Badoglio] declared immediately that the war would be continued, that won't make any difference. They have to say that, but it remains treason. But we'll play the same game while preparing everything to take over the whole crew with one stroke, to capture all that riffraff. Tomorrow I'll send a man down there with orders for the commander of the 3rd Panzergrenadier Division to the effect that he must drive into Rome with a special detail and arrest the whole government, the King and the whole bunch right away. First of all, to arrest the Crown Prince and to take over the whole gang, especially Badoglio and that entire crew. Then watch them cave in, and in two or three days there'll be another *coup*.... How far are they from Rome?

JODL: About 100 kilometres.

HITLER: 100? 60 kilometres. That's all they'll need. If he drives in with motorized troops he'll get in there and arrest the whole works right away.

KEITEL: Two hours.

JODL: 50 to 60 kilometres.

HITLER: That's no distance.

WAIZENEGGER: The division has 42 assault guns.

HITLER: Are they down there with the division?

WAIZENEGGER: Yes, with the division.

HITLER: Jodl, work that out right away.

JODL: Six battalions.

KEITEL: Ready for action. Five only partially ready.

HITLER: Jodl, work out the orders for the 3rd Panzergrenadier Division to be sent down, telling them to drive into Rome with their assault guns without letting anyone know about it, and to arrest the government, the King, and the whole crew.... I want the Crown Prince above all.

KEITEL: He is more important than the old man [Emmanuel III].

BODENSCHATZ: That has to be organized so that they can be packed into a plane and flown away.

HITLER: Right into a plane and off with them.

BODENSCHATZ: Don't let the Bambino get lost at the airfield.

HITLER: In eight days the thing will be reversed again.... The climax will come at the moment when we have mustered enough strength to go in there and disarm the whole gang. The motto of the whole operation must be that the traitorous generals and Ciano—who is hated anyway—are leading a *coup* against Fascism.[5]

APPENDIX F

Thoughts on the Fall of Mussolini by the Prime Minister, 26 July 1943

It seems highly probable that the fall of Mussolini will involve the overthrow of the Fascist regime, and that the new Government of the King and Badoglio will seek to negotiate a separate arrangement with the Allies for an armistice. Should this prove to be the case it will be necessary for us to make up our minds first of all upon what we want, and secondly upon the measures and conditions required to gain it for us.

2. At this moment above all others our thoughts must be concentrated upon the supreme aim, namely, the destruction of Hitler, Hitlerism, and Nazi Germany. Every military advantage arising out of the surrender of Italy, should that occur, must be sought for this purpose.

3. The first of these, in the President's words, 'the use of all Italian territory and transportation against the Germans in the north and against the whole Balkan peninsula, as well as use of airfields of all kinds'. This must include the surrender to our garrisons of Sardinia, the Dodecanese, and Corfu, as well as of all the naval and air bases on the Italian mainland as soon as they can be taken over.

4. Secondly, and of equal importance, the immediate surrender to the Allies of the Italian Fleet, or at least its effective demobilization and paralysis, and the disarmament of the Italian air and ground forces to whatever extent we find needful and useful. The surrender of the Fleet will liberate powerful British naval forces for service in the Indian Ocean against Japan, and will be most agreeable to the United States.

5. Also, of equal consequence, the immediate withdrawal from, or surrender of, all Italian forces in Corsica, the Riviera, including Toulon, and the Balkan peninsula—to wit, in Yugoslavia, Albania, and Greece.

6. Another objective of the highest importance, about which there will be passionate feeling in this country, is the immediate liberation of all British prisoners of war in Italian hands, and the prevention, which can in the first instance only be by the Italians, of their being transported northwards to Germany. I regard it as a matter of honour and humanity to get our own flesh and blood back as soon as possible and spare them the measureless horrors of incarceration in Germany during the final stages of the war.

7. The fate of the German troops in Italy, and particularly of those south of Rome, will probably lead to fighting between the Germans and the Italian Army and population. We should demand their surrender, and that any Italian Government with whom we can reach a settlement shall do their utmost to procure this. It may be however that the German divisions will cut their way northwards in spite of anything that the Italian Armed Forces are capable of doing. We should provoke this conflict as much as possible, and should not hesitate to send troops and air support to assist the Italians in procuring the surrender of the Germans south of Rome.

8. When we see how this process goes we can take a further view about action to be taken north of Rome. We should however try to get possession of points on both the west coast and east coast railways of Italy as far north as we dare. And this is a time to dare.

9. In our struggle with Hitler and the German Army we cannot afford to deny ourselves any assistance that will kill Germans. The fury of the Italian population will now be turned against the German intruders, who have, as they will feel, brought all these miseries upon Italy and then come so scantily and grudgingly to her aid. We should stimulate this process in order that the new, liberated, anti-Fascist Italy shall afford us at the earliest moment a safe and friendly area on which we can base the whole forward air attack upon South and Central Germany.

10. This air attack is a new advantage of the first order, as it brings the whole of the Mediterranean air forces into action from a direction which turns the entire line of air defences in the West, and which furthermore exposes all those centres of war production which have been increasingly developed so as to escape air attack from Great Britain. It will become urgent in the highest degree to get agents, commandos, and supplies by sea across the Adriatic into Greece, Albania, and Yugoslavia. It must be remembered that there are fifteen German divisions in the Balkan peninsula, of which ten are mobile. Nevertheless, once we have control of the Italian peninsula and of the Adriatic, and the Italian armies in the Balkans withdraw or lay down their arms, it is by no means unlikely that the Germans will be forced to withdraw northwards to the line of the Sava and Danube, thus liberating Greece and other tortured countries.

11. We cannot yet measure the effects of Mussolini's fall and of an Italian capitulation upon Bulgaria, Romania, and Hungary. They may be profound. In connection with this situation the collapse of Italy should fix the moment for putting the strongest pressure on Turkey to act in accordance with the spirit of the Alliance, and in this Britain and the United States, acting jointly or severally, should if possible be joined or at least supported by Russia.

12. The surrender of, to quote the President, 'the Head Devil, together with his chief partners in crime', must be considered an eminent object, and one for which we should arrive by all means in our power short of wrecking the immense prospects which have been outlined in earlier paragraphs. It may be however that these criminals will flee into Germany or escape into Switzerland. On the other hand, they may surrender themselves or be surrendered by the Italian Government. Should they fall into our hands, we ought now to decide, in consultation with the United States, and, after agreement with them, with the U.S.S.R., what treatment should be meted out to them. Some may prefer prompt execution without trial except for identification purposes. Others may prefer that they be kept in confinement till the end of the war in Europe and their fate decided together with that of other war criminals. Personally I am fairly indifferent on this matter, provided always that no solid military advantages are sacrificed for the sake of immediate vengeance.[6]

Endnotes

Introduction

1 Hayes, *Fascism*, p. 53.
2 Millett and Murray (eds.), *Military Effectiveness, Volume 2: The Interwar Period*, p. 180.
3 *Ibid.*
4 Carsten, *The Rise of Fascism*, p. 62.
5 Mussolini, *My Autobiography*, pp. 308–9.
6 *Ciano's Hidden Diary, 1937–1938*, p. 201, entry dated 30 November 1938.

Chapter 1

1 Deakin, *The Brutal Friendship*, p. 6.
2 'Basic Principles of Democracy, Communism, Fascism Defined', *The Star Press* (Muncie, Indiana), 16 July 1940, p. 7.
3 Cook, *Readings in Modern and Contemporary History*, p. 336.
4 Knox, *Mussolini Unleashed, 1939–1941*, p. 40.
5 *The Ciano Diaries, 1939–1943*, p. 22, entry dated 4 February 1939.
6 *Ciano's Diplomatic Papers*, p. 260.
7 *Ciano's Hidden Diary, 1937–1938*, p. 200, entry dated 30 November 1938.
8 *Ibid.*, p. 206, entry dated 17 December 1938.
9 *The Ciano Diaries, 1939–1943*, p. 10, entries dated 11 and 12 January 1939.
10 *Documents on German Foreign Policy, 1918–1945*, series D, vol. V, no. 119.
11 *The British War Blue Book*, no. 8.
12 *The Ciano Diaries, 1939–1943*, p. 33, entry dated 25 February 1939.
13 *Ibid.*, p. 34, entry dated 26 February 1939.
14 *Ibid.*, p. 35, entry dated 27 February 1939.
15 *Ibid.*, p. 36, entry dated 3 March 1939.
16 *Ibid.*, p. 42, entry dated 15 March 1939.
17 *Ibid.*, p. 48, entry dated 19 March 1939.
18 *Ibid.*, p. 46, entry dated 17 March 1939.
19 *Ciano's Diplomatic Papers*, pp. 276–7.
20 *Ibid.*, p. 278.
21 *Ibid.*, pp. 278–9.
22 *Ibid.*, pp. 279–80.
23 'Text of Mussolini Speech', *The Boston Globe*, 27 March 1939, p. 9.
24 *Documents on German Foreign Policy, 1918–1945*, series D, vol. VI, no. 100.
25 *The Ciano Diaries, 1939–1943*, p. 54, entry dated 28 March 1939.
26 *The British War Blue Book*, no. 17.

27 *The Ciano Diaries, 1939–1943*, pp. 53–4, entry dated 27 March 1939.
28 *Ibid.*, p. 60, entry dated 5 April 1939.
29 'Invasion of Albania by Italians', *The Advertiser* (Adelaide, S.A.), 8 April 1939, p. 19.
30 Smith, *Mussolini's Roman Empire*, p. 153.
31 Lemkin, *Axis Rule in Occupied Europe*, p. 100.
32 *The Ciano Diaries, 1939–1943*, pp. 66–7, entry dated 16 April 1939.
33 *Ibid.*, p. 85, entry dated 22 May 1939.
34 *Nazi Conspiracy and Aggression*, vol. IV, no. 1874–PS.
35 *The Ciano Diaries, 1939–1943*, p. 67, entry dated 16 April 1939.
36 *Ibid.*, p. 67, entry dated 17 April 1939.
37 *Ibid.*, pp. 67–8, entry dated 18 April 1939.
38 *Ibid.*, p. 68, entry dated 19 April 1939.
39 *Ibid.*, pp. 68–9, entry dated 20 April 1939.
40 Gafencu, *Last Days of Europe: A Diplomatic Journey in 1939*, p. 161.
41 *Ibid.*, pp. 161–5.
42 *Documents on German Foreign Policy, 1918–1945*, series D, vol. VI, no. 341, fn. 10.
43 *Ibid.*, no. 341.
44 *Nazi Conspiracy and Aggression*, vol. II, no. C-120.
45 *Ciano's Diplomatic Papers*, p. 284.
46 *Ibid.*, p. 286.
47 *Ibid.*, p. 283.
48 *Ibid.*, p. 286.
49 *Documents on German Foreign Policy, 1918–1945*, series D, vol. VI, no. 341, fn. 10.
50 'Mussolini's Speech Pleases German Newspapers', *The Corowa Free Press* (N.S.W.), 16 May 1939, p. 3.
51 *The Ciano Diaries, 1939–1943*, p. 84, entry dated 21 May 1939.
52 *Ciano's Diplomatic Papers*, p. 284.
53 *Documents and Readings in the History of Europe Since 1918* (ed. by Langsam and Egan), no. 248.
54 *The Ciano Diaries, 1939–1943*, p. 87, entry dated 25 May 1939.
55 *Documents on German Foreign Policy, 1918–1945*, series D, vol. VI, no. 433.
56 *Nazi Conspiracy and Aggression*, vol. V, no. 2,818–PS.
57 *The Ciano Diaries, 1939–1943*, pp. 93–6, entries dated 5–10 June 1939.
58 *Ciano's Diplomatic Papers*, pp. 289–95.
59 *The Ciano Diaries, 1939–1943*, p. 118, entry dated 10 August 1939.
60 *Ibid.*, p. 582, entry dated 23 December 1943.
61 *Ibid.*, p. 119, entry 11 August 1939.
62 *Ciano's Diplomatic Papers*, pp. 300–1.
63 *The Ciano Diaries, 1939–1943*, p. 119, entry dated 12 August 1939.
64 *Ibid.*, p. 120, entry dated 13 August 1939.
65 *Ciano's Diplomatic Papers*, pp. 303–4.
66 *The Ciano Diaries, 1939–1943*, p. 120, entry dated 13 August 1939.
67 *Ibid.*, p. 125, entry dated 21 August 1939.
68 *Documents on German Foreign Policy, 1918–1945*, series D, vol. VII, no. 192.
69 *Ibid.*, no. 193.
70 *Documents and Readings in the History of Europe Since 1918* (ed. by Langsam and Egan), no. 249.
71 *Nazi–Soviet Relations, 1939–1941* (ed. by Sontag and Beddie), pp. 79–80.
72 *Documents on German Foreign Policy, 1918–1945*, series D, vol. VII, no. 266.
73 *Ibid.*, no. 280.
74 *Ibid.*, no. 271.
75 *The British War Blue Book*, no. 19.
76 *Documents on German Foreign Policy, 1918–1945*, series D, vol. VII, no. 277.
77 *The Ciano Diaries*, p. 129, entry dated 26 August 1939.
78 *Documents on German Foreign Policy, 1918–1945*, series D, vol. VII, no. 301.
79 *Ibid.*, no. 307.
80 *Ibid.*, no. 317.
81 *Ibid.*, no. 341.
82 *Ibid.*, no. 350.
83 *The Ciano Diaries, 1939–1943*, p. 132, entry dated 28 August 1939.
84 *Ibid.*, p. 131, entry dated 27 August 1939.
85 *Ibid.*, p. 132, entry dated 29 August 1939.

86 *Ibid.*, p. 133, entry dated 30 August 1939.
87 *Ibid.*, p. 134, entry dated 31 August 1939.
88 *Ibid.*, p. 134, entry dated 31 August 1939.
89 *Ibid.*, pp. 135–6, entry dated 1 September 1939.
90 *Documents on German Foreign Policy, 1918–1945*, vol. VII, series D, no. 500.
91 *Ibid.*, no. 504.
92 *Ibid.*, no. 535, encl.
93 *The Ciano Diaries, 1939–1943*, pp. 136–7, entry dated 2 September 1939.
94 *Documents on German Foreign Policy, 1918–1945*, series D, vol. VII, no. 554.
95 *The Ciano Diaries, 1939–1943*, p. 137, entry dated 2 September 1939.
96 *The British War Blue Book*, no. 120.
97 *The French Yellow Book*, no. 370.
98 *The Ciano Diaries, 1939–1943*, p. 137, entry dated 3 September 1939.
99 *Documents on German Foreign Policy, 1918–1945*, series D, vol. VII, no. 565.
100 *The Ciano Diaries, 1939–1943*, p. 138, entry dated 4 September 1939.

Chapter 2

1 *The Ciano Diaries, 1939–1943*, p. 197, entry dated 17 January 1940.
2 *Ibid.*, p. 217, entry dated 7 March 1939.
3 Lowe and Marzari, *Italian Foreign Policy, 1870–1940*, p. 366.
4 *The Ciano Diaries, 1939–1943*, p. 139, entry dated 5 September 1939.
5 *Ibid.*, p. 139, entry dated 6 September 1939.
6 *Ibid.*, p. 140, entry dated 8 September 1939.
7 *Ciano's Diplomatic Papers*, p. 306.
8 *The Ciano Diaries, 1939–1943*, pp. 144–5, entry dated 15 September 1939.
9 *Documents on German Foreign Policy, 1918–1945*, series D, vol. VIII, no. 78.
10 *The Ciano Diaries, 1939–1943*, pp. 145–6, entry dated 17 September 1939.
11 *Documents on German Foreign Policy, 1918–1945*, series D, vol. VIII, no. 127.
12 *Vital Speeches of the Day*, vol. VI, p. 15.
13 *The Ciano Diaries, 1939–1943*, p. 153, entry dated 30 September 1939.
14 *Ciano's Diplomatic Papers*, pp. 309–16.
15 *The Ciano Diaries, 1939–1943*, p. 154, entry dated 1 October 1939.
16 Churchill, *The Gathering Storm*, p. 449.
17 *The Ciano Diaries, 1939–1943*, p. 155, entry dated 2 October 1939.
18 *Ibid.*, p. 155, entry dated 3 October 1939.
19 Roussy de Sales, Raoul de (ed.), *My New Order*, pp. 727–56.
20 *The Ciano Diaries, 1939–1943*, p. 156, entry dated 6 October 1939.
21 *Ibid.*, p. 157, entry dated 8 October 1939.
22 *Ibid.*, p. 157, entry dated 9 October 1939.
23 *Foreign Relations of the United States: Diplomatic Papers, 1939*, vol. I, p. 513.
24 *The Ciano Diaries, 1939–1943*, p. 159, entry dated 13 October 1939.
25 'Mussolini Fires Pro-Nazis From His Inner Circle', *Chicago Daily Tribune*, 1 November 1939, p. 2.
26 *The Ciano Diaries, 1939–1943*, p. 167, entry dated 9 November 1939.
27 *Ibid.*, p. 168, entry dated 11 November 1939.
28 *Ibid.*, p. 170, entry dated 20 November 1939.
29 *Documents on German Foreign Policy, 1918–1945*, series D, vol. VIII, no. 384.
30 *The Ciano Diaries, 1939–1943*, p. 174, entry dated 3 December 1939.
31 *Documents on German Foreign Policy, 1918–1945* , series D, vol. VIII, no. 428, fn. 1.
32 *Ibid.*, no. 478, fn. 1.
33 'Blackshirts Hear Talk by Count Ciano', *The Sunday Times* (Perth, Western Australia), 17 December 1939, p. 1.
34 *Documents on German Foreign Policy, 1918–1945*, series D, vol. VIII, no. 478, fn. 2.
35 Kirkpatrick, *Mussolini: A Study in Power*, pp. 439–40.
36 *The Ciano Diaries, 1939–1943*, p. 179, entry dated 16 December 1939.
37 *Documents on German Foreign Policy, 1918–1945*, series D, vol. VIII, no. 478.
38 *Ibid.*, no. 493.
39 *The Ciano Diaries, 1939–1943*, pp. 186–7, entry dated 31 December 1939.
40 *Documents on German Foreign Policy, 1918–1945*, series D, vol. VIII, no. 504.
41 *Ibid.*, no. 505.

42 *The Ciano Diaries, 1939–1943*, p. 197, entry dated 17 January 1940.
43 *Ibid.*, p. 198, entry dated 18 January 1940.
44 Knox, *Mussolini Unleashed, 1939–1941*, p. 54.
45 *The Ciano Diaries, 1939–1943*, p. 200, entry dated 23 January 1940.
46 *Ibid.*, p. 202, entry dated 29 January 1940.
47 *Ibid.*, p. 205, entry dated 7 February 1940.
48 *Foreign Relations of the United States, Diplomatic Papers, 1940,* vol. I, pp. 24–6.
49 *Ibid.*, p. 28.
50 *Ibid.*, p. 29, fn. 37.
51 *Ciano's Diplomatic Papers*, pp. 337–9.
52 *The Ciano Diaries, 1939–1943*, p. 213, entry dated 1 March 1940.
53 *Ibid.*, p. 214, entry dated 2 March 1940.
54 *Ibid.*, p. 216, entry dated 6 March 1940.
55 *Ibid.*, p. 217, entry dated 7 March 1940.
56 *Ibid.*, p. 219, entry dated 10 March 1940.
57 *Ibid.*, p. 219, entry dated 11 March 1940.
58 *Ibid.*, p. 220, entry dated 13 March 1940.
59 *Finland Builds*, p. 24.
60 *Foreign Relations of the United States: Diplomatic Papers, 1940,* vol. I, pp. 96–100.
61 *Ibid.*, p. 100.
62 *Ciano's Diplomatic Papers*, pp. 359–60.
63 *The Ciano Diaries, 1939–1943*, p. 222, entry dated 16 March 1940.
64 *Ibid.*, p. 223, entry dated 18 March 1940.
65 *Ciano's Diplomatic Papers*, pp. 361–5.
66 *The Ciano Diaries, 1939–1943*, p. 223, entry dated 18 March 1940.
67 *Ibid.*, p. 224, entry dated 19 March 1940.
68 *Hansard*, Progress of the War, 19 March 1940, column 1,843.
69 *The Ciano Diaries, 1939–1943*, p. 224, entry dated 20 March 1940.
70 *Ibid.*, p. 227, entry dated 27 March 1940.
71 *Ibid.*, pp. 225–6, entry dated 23 March 1940.
72 *Ibid.*, p. 229, entry dated 31 March 1940.
73 *Ibid.*, p. 230–1, entry dated 2 April 1940.
74 Lowe and Marzari, *Italian Foreign Policy, 1870–1940*, p. 366.
75 Noppen, *Malta 1940–42*, p. 26.
76 *The Ciano Diaries, 1939–1943*, pp. 233–4, entry dated 9 April 1940.
77 *Ibid.*, p. 235–6, entry dated 11 April 1940.
78 *Documents on German Foreign Policy, 1918–1945*, series D, vol. IX, no. 92.
79 *The Ciano Diaries, 1939–1943*, p. 240, entry dated 28 April 1940.
80 *Ibid.*, p. 237, entry dated 22 April 1940.
81 Reynaud, *In the Thick of the Fight, 1930–1945*, pp. 402–3.
82 *The Ciano Diaries, 1939–1943*, pp. 238–9, entry dated 24 April 1940.
83 *Ibid.*, p. 239, entry dated 25 April 1940.
84 *Ibid.*, p. 239, entry dated 26 April 1940.
85 Reynaud, *In the Thick of the Fight, 1930–1945*, p. 403.
86 *Foreign Relations of the United States: Diplomatic Papers, 1940*, vol. II, p. 692.
87 *The Ciano Diaries, 1939–1943*, p. 242, entry dated 1 May 1940.
88 *Foreign Relations of the United States: Diplomatic Papers, 1940*, vol. II, p. 698.
89 *The Ciano Diaries, 1939–1943*, pp. 244–5, entry dated 8 May 1940.
90 *Documents on German Foreign Policy, 1918–1945*, series D, vol. IX, no. 212.
91 *Ibid.*, no. 232.
92 *The Ciano Diaries, 1939–1943*, p. 249, entry dated 13 May 1940.
93 Churchill, *Their Finest Hour*, pp. 25–6.
94 *Foreign Relations of the United States: Diplomatic Papers, 1940*, vol. II, pp. 704–5.
95 *Ibid.*, p. 706.
96 Eade (ed.), *The War Speeches of the Rt. Hon. Winston S. Churchill*, vol. 1, pp. 323–4.
97 *Ibid.*, p. 324.
98 *Documents on German Foreign Policy, 1918–1945*, series D, vol. IX, no. 276.
99 Badoglio, *Italy in the Second World War*, pp. 14–5.
100 *The Ciano Diaries, 1939–1943*, p. 256, entry dated 30 May 1940.
101 *Documents on German Foreign Policy, 1918–1945*, series D, vol. IX, no. 356.

102 *Ibid.*, no. 373.
103 Churchill, *Their Finest Hour*, p. 118.
104 *Ibid.*, p. 115.
105 Snyder, *The War: A Concise History, 1939–1945*, p. 138.
106 *The Ciano Diaries, 1939–1943*, p. 263, entry dated 10 June 1940.
107 *Documents and Readings in the History of Europe Since 1918* (ed. by Langsam and Egan), no. 259.
108 'Address by the President at Charlottesville, Virginia', *The Department of State Bulletin*, vol. II, no. 51, publication 1476, 15 June 1940, p. 637.
109 *The Ciano Diaries, 1939–1943*, p. 264, entry dated 10 June 1940.
110 *Documents on German Foreign Policy, 1918–1945*, series D, vol. IX, no. 410.

Chapter 3

1 Mussolini, *Memoirs, 1942–1943*, p. 74.
2 *Ibid.*, p. 277.
3 *Ibid.*, p. 74.
4 Snyder, *The War: A Concise History, 1939–1945*, p. 142.
5 Miller, *History of World War II*, p. 221.
6 Churchill, *Their Finest Hour*, pp. 225–6.
7 *The Ciano Diaries, 1939–1943*, p. 265, entry dated 17 June 1940.
8 *Documents on German Foreign Policy, 1918–1945*, series D, vol. IX, no. 479.
9 *The Ciano Diaries, 1939–1943*, p. 266, entry dated 18 and 19 June 1940.
10 *Documents on German Foreign Policy, 1918–1945*, series D, vol. IX, no. 488.
11 *Ibid.*, no. 525.
12 *The Ciano Diaries, 1939–1943*, p. 267, entry dated 21 June 1940.
13 Hammerton (ed.), *The Second Great War*, vol. 3, p. 1,019.
14 *Documents on German Foreign Policy, 1918–1945*, series D, vol. X, no. 26.
15 *The Ciano Diaries, 1939–1943*, pp. 270–1, entry dated 29 June 1940.
16 *Ibid.*, p. 271, entry dated 30 June 1940.
17 *Ibid.*, p. 272, entry dated 2 July 1940.
18 *Ibid.*, p. 273, entry dated 4 July 1940.
19 *Ibid.*, entry dated 5 July 1940.
20 *Ciano's Diplomatic Papers*, pp. 375–9.
21 *The Ciano Diaries, 1939–1943*, p. 274, entry dated 7 July 1940.
22 *Ibid.*, p. 275, entry dated 11 July 1940.
23 *Documents on German Foreign Policy, 1918–1945*, series D, vol. X, no. 166.
24 *Ibid.*, no. 177.
25 *Nazi Conspiracy and Aggression*, Supplement A, no. 1,776–PS.
26 *The Ciano Diaries, 1939–1943*, p. 277, entry dated 19 July 1940.
27 Roussy de Sales, Raoul de (ed.), *My New Order*, p. 837.
28 *The Ciano Diaries, 1939–1943*, p. 277, entry dated 19 July 1940.
29 *Ibid.*, pp. 277–8, entry dated 22 July 1940.
30 Churchill, *Their Finest Hour*, p. 261.
31 'Hitler's Peace Terms Rejected', *The Barrier Miner* (Broken Hill, N.S.W.), 23 July 1940, p. 1.
32 *Ciano's Diplomatic Papers*, pp. 381–2.
33 *The Ciano Diaries, 1939–1943*, p. 277, entry dated 20 July 1940.
34 *Il Popolo d'Italia*, 22 July 1940.
35 *Ciano's Diplomatic Papers*, pp. 382–4.
36 Shirer, *The Rise and Fall of the Third Reich*, p. 1,005.
37 *Ibid.*, p. 1,026.
38 *Führer Conferences on Naval Affairs, 1940*, p. 101.
39 'Mussolini's Speech', *The West Australian* (Perth, W.A.), 20 November 1940, p. 9.
40 *The Ciano Diaries, 1939–1943*, p. 280, entry dated 4 August 1940.
41 Snyder, *The War: A Concise History, 1939–1945*, pp. 190–2.
42 *The Ciano Diaries, 1939–1943*, p. 281, entry dated 6 August 1940.
43 *Ibid.*, p. 283, entry dated 10 August 1940.
44 *Ibid.*, p. 283, entry dated 11 August 1940.
45 *Ibid.*, pp. 283–4, entry dated 12 August 1940.
46 *Ibid.*, p. 285, entry dated 17 August 1940.
47 *Documents on German Foreign Policy, 1918–1945*, series D, vol. X, no. 353, encl. 1.

48 *The Spanish Government and the Axis*, pp. 6–7.
49 *Ibid.*, p. 8.
50 *Ciano's Diplomatic Papers*, pp. 386–7.
51 *The Ciano Diaries, 1939–1943*, p. 291, entry dated 9 September 1940.
52 *Ibid.*, p. 293, entry dated 17 September 1940.
53 *Ciano's Diplomatic Papers*, pp. 389–93.
54 *The Ciano Diaries, 1939–1943*, p. 295, entry dated 24 September 1940.
55 *Documents and Readings in the History of Europe since 1918* (ed. by Langsam and Egan), no. 276.
56 *The Ciano Diaries, 1939–1943*, p. 296, entry dated 27 September 1940.
57 *Ciano's Diplomatic Papers*, pp. 393–4.
58 *The Ciano Diaries, 1939–1943*, pp. 298–9, entry dated 4 October 1940.
59 *Ibid.*, p. 300, entry dated 12 October 1940.
60 *Ibid.*, p. 301, entry dated 15 October 1940.
61 Mussolini, *Memoirs, 1942–1943*, pp. 269–71.
62 *Documents on German Foreign Policy, 1918–1945*, series D, vol. XI, no. 199.
63 *Ciano's Diplomatic Papers*, p. 402.
64 Delzell, *Mediterranean Fascism, 1919–1945*, p. 219.
65 Mussolini, *Memoirs, 1942–1943*, pp. 277–8.
66 Schmidt, *Hitler's Interpreter*, p. 220.
67 *Ciano's Diplomatic Papers*, pp. 399–404.
68 *Documents on German Foreign Policy 1918–1945*, series D, vol. XI, ed.'s note, pp. 466–7.
69 Schmidt, *Hitler's Interpreter*, p. 200.
70 *The Ciano Diaries, 1939–1943*, p. 310, entry dated 12 November 1940.
71 Churchill, *The Unrelenting Struggle*, pp. 7–8.
72 Cunningham, *A Sailor's Odyssey*, p. 286.
73 *The Ciano Diaries, 1939–1943*, p. 312, entry dated 18 November 1940.
74 *Nazi Conspiracy and Aggression*, vol. III, no. 444–PS.
75 *Documents on German Foreign Policy, 1918–1945*, series D, vol. XI, no. 353.
76 *Ciano's Diplomatic Papers*, p. 410.
77 *The Ciano Diaries, 1939–1943*, p. 312, entry dated 18 November 1940.
78 *Documents on German Foreign Policy, 1918–1945*, series D, vol. XI, no. 366.
79 *The Ciano Diaries, 1939–1943*, p. 313, entry dated 20 November 1940.
80 *Documents on German Foreign Policy, 1918–1945*, series D, vol. XI, no. 369.
81 'Admiration for Duce', *The West Australian* (Perth, W.A.), 20 November 1940, p. 9.
82 *The Ciano Diaries, 1939–1943*, p. 313, diary entry 20 November 1940.
83 *Documents on German Foreign Policy, 1918–1945*, series D, vol. XI, no. 383.
84 *The Ciano Diaries, 1939–1943*, p. 318, entry dated 4 December 1940.
85 *Ibid.*, p. 320, entry dated 6 December 1940.
86 *Documents on German Foreign Policy, 1918–1945*, series D, vol. XI, no. 477.
87 *The Ciano Diaries, 1939–1943*, p. 321, entry dated 10 December 1940.
88 *Ibid.*, p. 322, entry dated 12 December 1940.
89 *Nazi Conspiracy and Aggression*, vol. III, no. 446–PS.
90 *Ciano's Diplomatic Papers*, p. 412.
91 *Documents on German Foreign Policy, 1918–1945*, series D, vol. XI, no. 538.
92 Clark, *Mussolini*, p. 282.
93 *Documents on German Foreign Policy, 1918–1945*, series D, vol. XI, no. 586.

Chapter 4

1 'British See Italy Near Receivership', *The New York Times*, 24 February 1941, p. 3.
2 *The Ciano Diaries*, p. 392, entry dated 15 October 1941.
3 'Mussolini War Statement', *New York Times*, 12 December 1941, p. 4.
4 *Documents on German Foreign Policy, 1918–1945*, series D, vol. XI, no. 610, encl.
5 *Ibid.*
6 *Documents on German Foreign Policy, 1918–1945*, series D, vol. XI, no. 610.
7 *The Ciano Diaries, 1939–1943*, p. 336, entry dated 16 January 1941.
8 *Ibid.*
9 *Ibid.*, pp. 337, entry dated 18 January 1941.
10 *Ibid.*, p. 338, entry dated 19 January 1941.
11 *Ciano's Diplomatic Papers*, pp. 419–20.

12 *Nazi Conspiracy and Aggression*, vol. IV, no. 1,541–PS.
13 *The Ciano Diaries, 1939–1943*, pp. 338–9, entries dated 19, 20, and 21 January 1941.
14 *The Spanish Government and the Axis*, no. 12.
15 Corvaja, *Hitler & Mussolini: The Secret Meetings*, p. 165.
16 *The Ciano Diaries, 1939–1943*, p. 341, entry dated 25 January 1941.
17 *Ciano's Diplomatic Papers*, pp. 421–30.
18 *The Spanish Government and the Axis*, no. 13.
19 *The Ciano Diaries, 1939–1943*, p. 339, entry dated 21 January 1941.
20 *Ibid.*, p. 333, entry dated 7 January 1941.
21 *Ibid.*, p. 339–40, entry dated 22 January 1941.
22 Corvaja, *Hitler & Mussolini: The Secret Meetings*, p. 163.
23 Kirkpatrick, *Mussolini: A Study in Power*, p. 493.
24 Eade (ed.), *The War Speeches of the Rt. Hon. Winston S. Churchill*, vol. I, p. 352.
25 'British See Italy Near Receivership', *The New York Times*, 24 February 1941, p. 3.
26 *Documents on German Foreign Policy, 1918–1945*, series D, vol. XII, no. 117.
27 *Ibid.*, no. 208.
28 *Ibid.*, no. 223.
29 Gilbert, *The Second World War: A Complete History*, p. 199.
30 Roussy de Sales, Raoul de (ed.), *My New Order*, p. 960.
31 *Nazi Conspiracy and Aggression*, vol. III, no. 873–PS.
32 *Ciano's Diplomatic Papers*, pp. 434–6.
33 *Ibid.*, p. 441.
34 *The Ciano Diaries, 1939–1943*, p. 351, entry dated 3 May 1941.
35 Cavallero, *Comando Supremo: Diario 1940–43 del Capo di S.M.G.*, p. 105.
36 *The Ciano Diaries, 1939–1943*, p. 361, entry dated 2 June 1941.
37 *Ciano's Diplomatic Papers*, p. 442.
38 *Ibid.*, pp. 443–4.
39 *Ibid.*, p. 444.
40 *The Ciano Diaries, 1939–1943*, p. 365, entry dated 10 June 1941.
41 *Ibid.*, pp. 364–5, entry dated 10 June 1941.
42 Copeland, Lamm, and McKenna (eds.), *The World's Great Speeches*, pp. 490–2.
43 Churchill, *The Unrelenting Struggle*, p. 162.
44 *The Ciano Diaries, 1939–1943*, p. 583, entry dated 23 December 1943.
45 *Nazi–Soviet Relations, 1939–1941* (ed. by Sontag and Beddie), pp. 349–53.
46 Shirer, *The Rise and Fall of the Third Reich*, p. 1,078.
47 *Radio Address of the Vice-Chairman of the Council of People's Commissars of the U.S.S.R. and the People's Commissar of Foreign Affairs, V. M. Molotov*, pp. 1–3.
48 Churchill, *The Unrelenting Struggle*, pp. 171–3.
49 *Documents on German Foreign Policy, 1918–1945*, series D, vol. XIII, no. 7.
50 *The Ciano Diaries, 1939–1943*, p. 372, entry dated 1 July 1941.
51 Deakin, *The Brutal Friendship*, p. 15–6.
52 *Information Bulletin*, No. 74, p. 2.
53 Corvaja, *Hitler & Mussolini: The Secret Meetings*, p. 182.
54 Kirkpatrick, *Mussolini: A Study in Power*, p. 498.
55 *Ciano's Diplomatic Papers*, pp. 447–51.
56 Alfieri, *Dictators Face to Face*, p. 157.
57 *Ibid.*, p. 159.
58 *The Ciano Diaries, 1939–1943*, p. 383, entry dated 26 September 1941.
59 *Ibid.*, p. 391, entry dated 13 October 1941.
60 *Ciano's Diplomatic Papers*, pp. 455–60.
61 *The Ciano Diaries, 1939–1943*, p. 402, entry dated 6 November 1941.
62 *Ciano's Diplomatic Papers*, p. 460.
63 *The Ciano Diaries, 1939–1943*, p. 411, entry dated 25 November 1941.
64 *Ciano's Diplomatic Papers*, p. 461.
65 *Ibid.*, p. 465.
66 *The Ciano Diaries, 1939–1943*, p. 414, entry dated 3 December 1941.
67 *Ibid.*, p. 416, entry dated 8 December 1941.
68 *Ibid.*, p. 416–7, entry dated 10 December 1941.
69 *Ibid.*, p. 417, entry dated 11 December 1941.
70 Churchill, *The Grand Alliance*, p. 605.

71 'Mussolini War Statement', *The New York Times*, 12 December 1941, p. 4.
72 *The Ciano Diaries, 1939–1943*, p. 417, entry dated 11 December 1941.
73 'Germany and Italy Declare War on U.S.', *The New York Times*, 12 December 1941, p. 4.
74 *The Ciano Diaries, 1939–1943*, p. 420, entry dated 17 December 1941.
75 *Ibid.*, p. 421, entry dated 19 December 1941.
76 *Ibid., 1939–1943*, p. 426, entry dated 29 December 1941.
77 *Ciano's Diplomatic Papers*, pp. 471–3.
78 *The Ciano Diaries, 1939–1943*, p. 419, entry dated 15 December 1941.
79 *Ibid.*, p. 420, entry dated 16 December 1941.
80 *Documents on German Foreign Policy, 1918–1945*, series D, vol. XIII, no. 564.
81 *The Goebbels Diaries, 1942–1943*, pp. 135–6, entry dated 20 March 1942.
82 *The Ciano Diaries, 1939–1943*, p. 423, entry dated 22 December 1941.
83 *Ibid.*, p. 421, entry dated 20 December 1941.
84 *Ibid.*, p. 424, entry dated 25 December 1941.
85 Deakin, *The Brutal Friendship*, pp. 16–7.

Chapter 5

1 Deakin, *The Brutal Friendship*, p. 84.
2 *Ibid.*, p. 331.
3 *The Ciano Diaries, 1939–1943*, p. 435, entry dated 13 January 1942.
4 *Ibid.*, p. 442, entry dated 2 February 1942.
5 *Ciano's Diplomatic Papers*, pp. 477–9.
6 *The Ciano Diaries, 1939–1943*, p. 436, entry dated 15 January.
7 *Ibid.*, pp. 440–1, entries dated 28–29 January 1942.
8 *Ibid.*, p. 442, entry dated 2 February 1942.
9 *Ibid.*, p. 443, entry dated 4 February 1942.
10 *Ibid.*, p. 444, entry dated 7 February 1942.
11 Churchill, *The Hings of Fate*, p. 92.
12 'Churchill Announces Fall of Singapore', *The Telegraph* (Brisbane, Queensland), 15 February 1942, p. 1.
13 *The Ciano Diaries, 1939–1943*, p. 449, entry dated 16 February 1942.
14 *Ibid.*, p. 451, entry dated 22 February 1942.
15 *Ibid.*, p. 451, entry dated 20 February 1942.
16 *Ibid.*, p. 453, entry dated 25 February 1942.
17 *Ibid.*, p. 451, entry dated 22 February 1942.
18 *Ibid.*, p. 455, entry dated 1 March 1942.
19 *Ibid.*, p. 458, entry dated 7 March 1942.
20 *Ibid.*, entry dated 19 March 1942.
21 *Ciano's Diplomatic Papers*, pp. 481–2.
22 *The Ciano Diaries, 1939–1943*, pp. 477–8, entries dated 29–30 April 1942.
23 *Ibid.*, pp. 478–9, entries dated 30 April–1 May 1942.
24 *Ibid.*, p. 480, entry dated 2 May 1942.
25 *Ibid.*, pp. 499–500, entry dated 20 June 1942.
26 *Ibid.*, p. 501, entry dated 23 June 1942.
27 *Ibid.*, p. 502, entry dated 26 June 1942.
28 *Ibid.*, p. 500, entry dated 21 June 1942.
29 Churchill, *The Hinge of Fate*, p. 383.
30 *Ibid.*, pp. 392–3.
31 *Ibid.*, p. 401.
32 Deakin, *The Brutal Friendship*, p. 19.
33 *Ibid.*, p. 20.
34 *The Ciano Diaries, 1939–1943*, p. 502, entry dated 24 June 1942.
35 *Ibid.*, p. 502, entry dated 25 June 1942.
36 *Ibid.*, p. 503, entry dated 30 June 1942.
37 Badoglio, *Italy in the Second World War*, p. 33.
38 *The Ciano Diaries, 1939–1943*, p. 507, entry dated 21 July 1942.
39 Deakin, *The Brutal Friendship*, p. 20.
40 *Ibid.*, p. 21.
41 *The Ciano Diaries, 1939–1943*, p. 509, entry dated 24 July 1942.

42 *Ibid.*, pp. 510–1, entry dated 4 August 1942.
43 *Ibid.*, p. 518, entry dated 31 August 1942.
44 *Ibid.*, p. 521, entry dated 9 September 1942.
45 *Ibid.*, p. 525, entry dated 27 September 1942.
46 *Ibid.*, p. 528, entry dated 8 October 1942.
47 *Ibid.*, p. 529, entry dated 10 October 1942.
48 *Ibid.*, p. 530, entry dated 11 October 1942.
49 Michaelis, *Mussolini and the Jews: German–Italian Relations and the Jewish Question in Italy*, p. 334.
50 Deakin, *The Brutal Friendship*, pp. 59–61.
51 *The Ciano Diaries, 1939–1943*, p. 534, entry dated 26 October 1942.
52 *Ibid.*, pp. 534–5, entry dated 27 October 1942.
53 Deakin, *The Brutal Friendship*, pp. 38–9.
54 *Ibid.*, p. 40.
55 *The Ciano Diaries, 1939–1943*, p. 535, entry dated 28 October 1942.
56 Montgomery, *The Memoirs of Field Marshal The Viscount Montgomery of Alamein, K.G.*, p. 116.
57 Majdalany, *The Battle of El Alamein: Fortress in the Sand*, p. 125.
58 Snyder, *The War: A Concise History, 1939–1945*, p. 352.
59 Churchill, *The Hinge of Fate*, p. 603.
60 Funk, *Charles de Gaulle: The Crucial Years, 1943–1944*, p. 44.
61 *The Ciano Diaries, 1939–1943*, p. 541, entry dated 9 November 1942.
62 *Ibid.*, p. 542, entry dated 10 November 1942.
63 *Ibid.*, p. 542, entry dated 11 November 1942.
64 Eade (ed.), *The War Speeches of the Rt. Hon. Winston S. Churchill*, vol. 2, p. 343.
65 Mussolini, *Memoirs, 1942–1943*, p. 3.
66 'Hitler's Letter to Marshal Pétain', *The New York Times*, 28 November 1942, p. 4.
67 *The Ciano Diaries, 1939–1943*, p. 546, entry dated 21 November 1942.
68 *Ibid.*, pp. 548–9, entry dated 27 November 1942.
69 Foreign Broadcast Intelligence Service, Federal Communications Commission, 2 December 1942.
70 *The Ciano Diaries, 1942–1943*, p. 550, entry dated 2 December 1942.
71 *Ibid.*, pp. 555–6, entry dated 16 December 1942.
72 *Ibid.*, p. 557, entry dated 18 December 1942.
73 *Ibid.*, p. 558, entry dated 22 December 1942.
74 Deakin, *The Brutal Friendship*, pp. 129–33.
75 *The Ciano Diaries, 1939–1943*, p. 568, entry dated 8 January 1943.
76 *Ibid.*, p. 566, entry dated 5 January 1943.
77 *Ibid.*, p. 574, entry dated 23 January 1943.
78 Rosenman (ed.), *The Public Papers and Addresses of Franklin D. Roosevelt, 1943*, p. 39.
79 *The Ciano Diaries, 1939–1943*, p. 575, entry dated 27 January 1943.
80 *Ibid.*, p. 579, entry dated 5 February 1943.
81 *Ibid.*, p. 580, entry dated 8 February 1943.
82 'Trouble On Balkan Flank', *The Advertiser* (Adelaide, S.A.), 30 November 1945, p. 13.
83 'Duce Urges Cut In Losses In Russia', *The Advertiser* (Adelaide, South Australia), 3 December 1945, p. 9.
84 'Duce Sees Writing On The Wall', *The Advertiser* (Adelaide, South Australia), 5 December 1945, p. 10.
85 Kirkpatrick, *Mussolini: A Study in Power*, p. 526.
86 Deakin, *The Brutal Friendship*, p. 274.
87 *The Goebbels Diaries, 1942–1943*, p. 352, entry dated 7 May 1943.
88 Corvaja, *Hitler & Mussolini: The Secret Meetings*, p. 223.
89 *The Ciano Diaries, 1939–1943*, p. 432, entry dated 5 January 1942.
90 'Duce Sees Writing On The Wall', *The Advertiser* (Adelaide, S.A.), 5 December 1945, p. 10.
91 Deakin, *The Brutal Friendship*, pp. 321–2.
92 Corvaja, *Hitler & Mussolini: The Secret Meetings*, p. 225.
93 *Ibid.*, pp. 226–7.
94 Le Vien and Lord, *Winston Churchill: The Valiant Years*, p. 177.
95 Montgomery, *The Memoirs of Field Marshal The Viscount Montgomery of Alamein, K.G.*, p. 149.
96 *Führer Conferences on Matters Dealing with the German Navy, 1943*, p. 59, annex 3.
97 *Ibid.*, p. 61, annex 5.
98 Deakin, *The Brutal Friendship*, pp. 353–4.
99 *Ibid.*, p. 355.

100 *Ibid.*, p. 356.
101 *Ibid.*, p. 358.
102 *Ibid.*, p. 331.
103 *Ibid.*, p. 331.
104 Corvaja, *Hitler & Mussolini: The Secret Meetings*, p. 230.
105 Kirkpatrick, *Mussolini: A Study in Power*, pp. 533–4.
106 Churchill, *Closing the Ring*, pp. 53–4.

Chapter 6

1 Mussolini, *Memoirs, 1942–1943*, p. 47.
2 Deakin, *The Brutal Friendship*, p. 397.
3 Kirkpatrick, *Mussolini: A Study in Power*, p. 532.
4 Mussolini, *Memoirs, 1942–1943*, p. 49.
5 Deakin, *The Brutal Friendship*, p. 381.
6 Corvaja, *Hitler & Mussolini: The Secret Meetings*, pp. 232–3.
7 Mussolini, *Memoirs, 1942–1943*, pp. 50–1.
8 *Ibid.*, p. 51.
9 Deakin, *The Brutal Friendship*, pp. 407–8.
10 *Ibid.*, pp. 411–2.
11 Schmidt, *Hitler's Interpreter*, p. 263.
12 *Foreign Relations of the United States: Diplomatic Papers, 1943*, vol. II, p. 920.
13 Mussolini, *Memoirs, 1942–1943*, pp. 51–2.
14 *Ibid.*, p. 52.
15 *Ibid.*, p. 53.
16 *Ibid.*, pp. 52–3.
17 Corvaja, *Hitler & Mussolini: The Secret Meetings*, pp. 249–50.
18 Kirkpatrick, *Mussolini: A Study in Power*, p. 549.
19 Corvaja, *Hitler & Mussolini: The Secret Meetings*, pp. 250–1.
20 Mussolini, *Memoirs, 1942–1943*, p. 54.
21 *The Goebbels Diaries, 1942–1943*, p. 403, entry dated 25 July 1943.
22 Mussolini, *Memoirs, 1942–1943*, p. 54.
23 Deakin, *The Brutal Friendship*, p. 465.
24 Mussolini, *Memoirs, 1942–1943*, pp. 55–6.
25 *Ibid.*, p. 60.
26 *Ibid.*, pp. 61–2.
27 *Ibid.*, p. 62.
28 *Ibid.*, pp. 63–4.
29 *Ibid.*, p. 65.
30 *Ibid.*, p. 64.
31 *Ibid.*, p. 79.
32 *Ibid.*, p. 81.
33 *Ibid.*, p. 82.
34 *Ibid.*, p. 47.
35 Delzell, *Mediterranean Fascism, 1919–1945*, p. 223.
36 Badoglio, *Italy in the Second World War*, p. 46.

Appendices

1 *Documents and Readings in the History of Europe Since 1918* (ed. by Langsam and Egan), no. 248.
2 *Ibid.*, no. 276.
3 Delzell, *Mediterranean Fascism, 1919–1945*, pp. 217–9.
4 Churchill, *Closing the Ring*, pp. 53–4.
5 Gilbert, *Hitler Directs His War*, pp. 47–51.
6 Churchill, *Closing the Ring*, pp. 61–3.

Bibliography

General Works

Alfieri, D., *Dictators Face to Face*, trans. by David Moore (London: Elek Books Ltd, 1954)
Badoglio, P., *Italy in the Second World War: Memories and Documents*, trans. by Muriel Currey (London: Geoffrey Cumberlege, 1948)
Carsten, F. L., *The Rise of Fascism* (Berkeley: University of California Press, 1982)
Cavallero, U., *Comando Supremo: Diario 1940–43 del Capo di S.M.G.* (Bologna: Cappelli, 1948)
Churchill, W. S., *Closing the Ring* (London: The Reprint Society, 1961); *The Gathering Storm* (Boston: The Houghton Mifflin Company, 1948); *The Grand Alliance* (Boston: Houghton Mifflin Company, 1950); *The Hinge of Fate* (Boston: Houghton Mifflin Company, 1950); *The Unrelenting Struggle* (Boston: Little, Brown and Company, 1942); *Their Finest Hour* (Boston: Houghton Mifflin Company, 1949)
Ciano, G., *The Ciano Diaries, 1939–1943*, ed. by Hugh Gibson (Safety Harbor: Simon Publications, 2001); *Ciano's Diplomatic Papers*, ed. by Malcolm Muggeridge (London: Odhams Press Limited, 1948); *Ciano's Hidden Diary, 1937–1938* , ed. by Andreas Major (New York: E. P. Dutton & Co., Inc., 1953)
Clark, M., *Mussolini* (London: Routledge, 2014)
Cook, A. N., *Readings in Modern and Contemporary History* (New York: Appleton-Century-Crofts, Inc., 1937)
Copeland, L., Lamm, L. W., and McKenna, S. J., (eds). *The World's Great Speeches* (Mineola: Dover Publications, Inc., 1999)
Corvaja, S., *Hitler & Mussolini: The Secret Meetings*, trans. by Robert L. Miller (New York: Enigma Books, 2008)
Cunningham, A., *A Sailor's Odyssey* (London: Hutchinson & Co., 1953)
Deakin, F. W., *The Brutal Friendship* (New York: Harper & Row, Publishers, 1962)
Delzell, C. F., *Mediterranean Fascism, 1919–1945* (New York: Macmillan Press Ltd, 1971)
Eade, C., (ed.), *The War Speeches of the Rt. Hon. Winston S. Churchill*, vols. 1 and 2 (Bombay: Cassell & Company Ltd, 1951–2)
Gafencu, G., *Last Days of Europe: A Diplomatic Journey in 1939*, trans. by E. Fletcher-Allan (New Haven: Yale University Press, 1948)
Gilbert, F., (trans. and ed.), *Hitler Directs His War* (New York: Oxford University Press, Inc., 1950)
Gilbert, M., *The Second World War: A Complete History*, rev. ed. (New York: Henry Holt and Co., 1991)
Goebbels, J., *The Goebbels Diaries, 1942–1943*, ed. and trans. by Louis P. Lochner (New York: Doubleday and Company, Inc. 1948)
Funk, A. L., *Charles de Gaulle: The Crucial Years, 1943–1944* (Norman: University of Oklahoma Press, 1959)
Hammerton, J., (ed.), *The Second Great War*, vol. 3 (London: The Waverley Book Company Ltd, 1947)
Hayes, P., *Fascism* (London: Allen & Unwin, 1973)
Kirkpatrick, I., *Mussolini: A Study in Power* (New York: Hawthorn Books, Inc., 1964)
Knox, M., *Mussolini Unleashed, 1939–1941: Politics and Strategy in Fascist Italy's Last War* (Cambridge: Cambridge University Press, 1999)
Le Vien, J., and Lord, J., *Winston Churchill: The Valiant Years* (New York: Bernard Geis Associates, 1962)
Lemkin, R., *Axis Rule in Occupied Europe* (Washington: Carnegie Endowment for International Peace, 1944)
Lowe, C. J., and Marzari, F., *Italian Foreign Policy, 1870–1940* (London: Routledge, 2002)

Majdalany, F., *The Battle of El Alamein: Fortress in the Sand* (Philadelphia: University of Pennsylvania Press, 2003)
Michaelis, M., *Mussolini and the Jews: German–Italian Relations and the Jewish Question in Italy, 1922–1945* (Oxford: Oxford University Press, 1978)
Miller, F. T., *History of World War II* (Philadelphia: Universal Book and Bible House, 1945)
Millett, A. R., and Williamson, M., (eds.), *Military Effectiveness, Volume 2: The Interwar Period* (New York: Cambridge University Press, 2010)
Montgomery, B., *The Memoirs of Field Marshal The Viscount Montgomery of Alamein, K.G.* (New York: The World Publishing Company, 1958)
Mussolini, B., *Memoirs, 1942–1943*, ed. by Raymond Klibansky (London: George Weidenfeld & Nicolson, Ltd, 1949); *My Autobiography* (New York: Charles Scribner's Sons, 1928)
Noppen, R. K., *Malta 1940–1942: The Axis' Air Battle for Mediterranean Supremacy* (Oxford: Osprey Publishing Ltd, 2018)
Roussy de Sales, R. de, (ed.), *My New Order* (New York: Reynal & Hitchcock, 1941)
Reynaud, P., *In the Thick of the Fight, 1930–1945*, trans. by James D. Lambert (New York: Simon and Schuster, 1955)
Rosenman, S. I., (ed.), *The Public Papers and Addresses of Franklin D. Roosevelt, 1943* (New York: Harper & Brothers, 1950)
Schmidt, P., *Hitler's Interpreter* (New York: The Macmillan Company, 1951)
Shirer, W. L., *The Rise and Fall of the Third Reich* (New York: Fawcett Crest, 1992)
Smith, D. M., *Mussolini's Roman Empire* (London: Longman, 1976)
Snyder, L. L., *The War: A Concise History, 1939–1945* (New York: Dell Publishing Co., Inc., 1964)

Documentary Sources

Address by the President at Charlottesville, Virginia (United States, Department of State, vol. II, no. 51, pub. 1476, 1940)
The British War Blue Book: Documents Concerning German–Polish Relations and the Outbreak of Hostilities Between Great Britain and Germany on September 3, 1939 (New York: Farrar & Rinehart, 1939)
Documents and Readings in the History of Europe Since 1918, ed. by W. C. Langsam and J. M. Egan (New York: J. B. Lippincott Company, 1951)
Documents on German Foreign Policy, 1918–1945, series D, vols. V–XIII (Washington: United States Government Printing Office, 1949)
Finland Builds (New York: The Finnish New York World's Fair Commission, 1940)
Foreign Broadcast Intelligence Service (Federal Communications Commission, 1942)
Foreign Relations of the United States: Diplomatic Papers, 1939, vol. I (Washington: United States Government Printing Office, 1956)
Foreign Relations of the United States: Diplomatic Papers, 1940, vol. I (Washington: United States Government Printing Office, 1959)
Foreign Relations of the United States: Diplomatic Papers, 1940, vol. II (Washington: United States Government Printing Office, 1957)
Foreign Relations of the United States: Diplomatic Papers, 1943, vol. II (Washington: United States Government Printing Office, 1964)
The French Yellow Book: Diplomatic Documents, 1938–1939 (London: Hutchinson & Co. Ltd., 1939)
Führer Conferences on Matters Dealng with the German Navy, 1943 (Washington, D.C.: United States Navy Department, 1947)
Führer Conferences on Naval Affairs, 1940 (London: British Admiralty, 1947)
Hansard, Progress of the War (1940)
Information Bulletin, No. 74 (Washington: Embassy of the Union of Soviet Socialist Republics, 1942)
Nazi Conspiracy and Aggression, vols. II–V and Supplement A (Washington: United States Government Printing Office, 1946–8)
Nazi–Soviet Relations, 1939–1941, ed. by Raymond James Sontag and James Stuart Beddie (Washington: Department of State, 1948)
Radio Address of the Vice-Chairman of the Council of People's Commissars of the U.S.S.R. and the People's Commissar of Foreign Affairs, V. M. Molotov (Moscow: Foreign Languages Publishing House, 1941)
The Spanish Government and the Axis (Washington: U.S. Government Printing Office, 1946)
Vital Speeches of the Day, vol. VI (New York: The City News Pub. Co., 1940)

Newspaper Sources

The Advertiser (Australia), *The Argus* (Australia), *The Barrier Miner* (Australia), *The Boston Globe* (United States), *Chicago Daily Tribune* (United States), *The Corowa Free Press* (Australia), *Il Popolo d'Italia* (Italy), *The New York Times*, (United States), *The Star Press* (United States), *The Sunday Times* (Australia), *The Telegraph* (Australia), *The West Australian* (Australia)

Index